THE BEST OF **Woodworker's Journal**

Cabinets & Storage Solutions

Furniture to Organize Your Home

THE BEST OF WOODWORKER'S JOURNAL

Cabinets & Storage Solutions

Furniture to Organize Your Home

from the editors of *Woodworker's Journal*

Fox Chapel Publishing

1970 Broad Street • East Petersburg, PA 17520
www.FoxChapelPublishing.com

Compilation Copyright © 2007 by Fox Chapel Publishing Company, Inc.

Text and Illustration Copyright © 2007 by *Woodworker's Journal. Woodworker's Journal* is a publication of Rockler Press.

Cabinets & Storage Solutions: Furniture to Organize Your Home is a compilation first published in 2007 by Fox Chapel Publishing Company, Inc. The patterns contained herein are copyrighted by *Woodworker's Journal*.

Our friends at Rockler Woodworking and Hardware supplied us with most of the hardware used in this book. Visit *rockler.com*. For subscription information to *Woodworker's Journal* magazine, call toll-free 1-800-765-4119 or visit *www.woodworkersjournal.com*.

Fox Chapel Publishing Company, Inc.

President: Alan Giagnocavo
Publisher: J. McCrary
Acquisition Editor: Peg Couch
Editor: Gretchen Bacon
Associate Editor: Patty Sinnott
Series Editor: John Kelsey
Creative Direction: Troy Thorne
Cover Design: Lindsay Hess

Woodworker's Journal

Publisher: Ann Rockler Jackson
Editor-in-Chief: Larry N. Stoiaken
Editor: Rob Johnstone
Art Director: Jeff Jacobson
Senior Editor: Joanna Werch Takes
Field Editor: Chris Marshall
Illustrators: Jeff Jacobson, John Kelliher

ISBN 978-1-56523-344-7

Publisher's Cataloging-in-Publication Data

Cabinets & storage solutions : furniture to organize your home / from the editors of Woodworker's journal. -- East Petersburg, PA : Fox Chapel Publishing, c2007.

  p. ; cm.
  (The best of Woodworker's journal)
  ISBN: 978-1-56523-344-7

  1. Cabinetwork. 2. Storage cabinets. 3. Furniture making.
 4. Storage in the home. 5. Woodwork--Patterns. I. Cabinets and storage solutions. II. Woodworker's journal.

TT197 .C33 2007
684.104--dc22   0710

To learn more about the other great books from Fox Chapel Publishing, or to find a retailer near you, call toll-free 1-800-457-9112 or visit us at *www.FoxChapelPublishing.com*.

Printed in China
10 9 8 7 6 5 4 3 2 1

Note to Authors: We are always looking for talented authors to write new books in our area of woodworking, design, and related crafts. Please send a brief letter describing your idea to Peg Couch, Acquisition Editor, Fox Chapel Publishing, 1970 Broad Street, East Petersburg, PA 17520.

Introduction

Cabinets and storage furniture have been benchmark projects since our forefathers first applied steel to wood. Why? For one, they're an excellent blend of form and function. The basic box—just six parts, a few hinges, and a handful of nails—effectively moved nearly everything our ancestors had from one continent to another. Cabinets are also versatile: Whether fixed or portable, built for security or designed for show, storage boxes adapt readily to the purpose.

Of course, it's certainly a plus that cabinets are also just plain fun to build. A simple box and doors can welcome you into woodworking, while more sophisticated designs laced with intricate joinery can keep you challenged long after that first project fades from memory.

Cabinet and storage projects continue to appeal to *Woodworker's Journal* readers, and they always will. We've had the good fortune to work with some of the best cabinetmakers in the country—Rick White, Mike McGlynn, Bruce Kieffer, and Bill Hylton, to name just a few. This new book highlights 16 of their finest projects for you to build.

If you're just getting comfortable with woodworking tools, start with David Larson's barbecue cart, Mike McGlynn's toy box, or Rick White's blanket chest, so you can ensure your success and end up with a charming project when the dust clears.

Maybe you'd like to dabble in traditional hand-tool techniques or build an authentic reproduction piece. Several projects here will satisfy that goal. Set your sights on the early American dresser, the jelly cupboard, the Arts and Crafts hutch, the collector's cabinet, or one of Mike McGlynn's masterpieces—the Greene and Greene–inspired dresser or the Ruhlmann cabinet. They'll present a sporting challenge, to say the least, with heirloom results.

If it's storage you're after, you'll find some gems. Rick White shares several, including a steamer trunk, an angler's cabinet, and a Scandinavian-style sideboard. You can also make a discreet home for your new flat-screen TV, or you can challenge your routing savvy with Bill Hylton's Eastern Shore chest.

So, grab hold of woodworking's collective torch and embark on some fine cabinetry projects. You're in excellent hands.

Larry N. Stoiaken, Editor-in-Chief

Acknowledgments

Woodworker's Journal recently celebrated its 30th anniversary—a benchmark few magazines ever reach. I would like to acknowledge both the 300,000 woodworkers who make up our readership and Rockler Woodworking and Hardware (*rockler.com*), which provided most of the hardware, wood, and other products used to build the projects in this book. Our publishing partner, Fox Chapel, did a terrific job re-presenting our material, and I am especially grateful to Alan Giagnocavo, Gretchen Bacon, John Kelsey, and Troy Thorne for their commitment to our content.

Larry N. Stoiaken, Editor-in-Chief

CONTENTS

Heirloom Collector's Cabinet 1
by Dean Holzman
Set aside a weekend and some clear maple lumber for building this old-fashioned piece. The mullioned door and batten back add authenticity.

Blanket Chest 9
by Rick White
This charming cherry chest bypasses mortise-and-tenon joints in favor of rabbets and laps, making it easy to build without compromising strength or capacity.

Your Own Steamer Trunk 17
by Rick White
You'll probably never use this sturdy, handsome trunk for an ocean voyage, but it's the perfect accent piece at the foot of the bed for storing winter blankets.

Eastern Shore Chest 27
by Bill Hylton
Here's the perfect project for expanding your routing skills. It combines cope-and-stick joints with sliding dovetails and raised panels.

Jelly Cupboard Reproduction 39
by Tim Johnson
To learn furniture design, reproduce an antique. The original of this piece was built entirely with hand tools, so for a real trip back in time, try doing the same.

Angler's Cabinet 47
by Rick White
If you love to fish, you're sure to have a closet full of fishing gear to contend with. This handsome pine angler's cabinet provides plenty of storage for rods, tackle boxes, and waders.

Early American Dresser 57
by Stuart Barron
Walk a mile in the shoes of a colonial cabinetmaker, and you'll learn a lot about how an heirloom is made. This piece even has a not-so-secret drawer.

Scandinavian-Style Sideboard 67
by Rick White
A short base and a broad, low cabinet define a sideboard. This one has flush-fit drawers and doors and a beveled top for that Scandinavian flavor.

Bowfront Bureau 77
by Rick White
Bending wood can be challenging, but these graceful curves can be managed with simple jigs and bendable plywood.

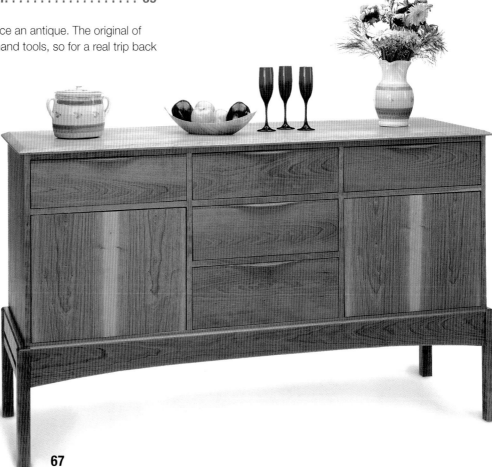

77

Greene and Greene–Inspired Dresser 117
by Mike McGlynn
This chest of drawers has an extraordinary number of parts, and putting them together requires logic and care—but the results will be well worth the trouble.

Weekend Toy Box 127
by Mike McGlynn
Safe and sturdy, stylish and practical, this weekend project is easy to build, and it will remain useful as a keepsake chest or a bench long after the kids have left home.

Flat-Screen TV Cabinet 135
by Mike McGlynn
Here's a modern cabinet with a tricky motorized lift for your flat-screen TV set. It's a slick way to make that dead-black box go away when you aren't watching it.

Ruhlmann Cabinet 141
by Mike McGlynn
This entertainment center is likely to be the trickiest project you'll ever tackle, but it's also likely to be one of the most rewarding.

Backyard Barbecue Cart 89
by David Larson
You can wheel this sturdy, Corian-topped cart around on the deck or patio, and it's roomy enough to store all your outdoor cooking utensils plus a couple of bags of charcoal.

Arts and Crafts Hutch. 97
by Bruce Kieffer
Building an exquisite piece like this is a labor of love. This hutch is not a reproduction, but a totally new design based on traditional mission-era furniture.

Cherry China Cabinet 107
by Rick White
This china cabinet features classic clean lines, gentle arches, and hidden hardware. It's amply sized to store all your table finery, with glass upper doors for displaying your treasures.

127

Heirloom Collector's Cabinet

Set aside a weekend and a few feet of clear maple lumber for building this old-fashioned collector's cabinet. The mullioned door and batten-style back lend an aged authenticity to the project. Follow up with an amber-toned, faux shellac finish.

by Dean Holzman

Most of my woodworking is for the theater—things such as stage sets, chairs made at unusual angles, and cabinets painted in outlandish colors. But every once in a while, I get to build a project that will last a lot longer than the run of the latest play in town.

The woman who had me build this small cabinet needed a place for displaying her collection of figurines, although it could be used for many other purposes, as well. If you like the country look, you'll appreciate the mullioned door and the traditional choice of maple for the cabinet's construction. Maple was often used in American country furniture, and glass-paned doors were a common feature.

Getting Started

To begin, select maple stock for the cabinet sides, top, and bottom (pieces 1 and 2), and rip it to width (see the Material List on page 2). Then, crosscut the pieces to length by stacking each pair and cutting them at the same time (see Figure 1). This is a practice that helps to guarantee square assemblies.

Next, using a combination square and a pencil, lay out the dowel locations on the sides, as indicated in the exploded view drawing on page 2. To drill the dowel holes, I recommend using a drilling jig and drill press. The Dowl-it jig is particularly effective because it's accurate and simple to use. Before drilling holes in your actual project pieces, however, drill

Figure 1: *Stack any pieces that need to match, and crosscut them to length at the same time. This will ensure a square cabinet assembly.*

Figure 2: *Lay out the dowel locations on the cabinet sides, and then position your jig. Slipping a stop collar onto the drill bit will limit the depth of the holes.*

Accurate Holes without a Drill Press

Don't have a drill press? The Dowl-it jig can be an inexpensive substitute (*www.dowl-it.com*, 800-451-6872). Spread the plates of the jig far apart to create a wide, stable base, and chuck a bit in your drill. Slip the bit into the appropriate hole in the jig, and position the setup precisely over your drilling location. Now you can bore an accurate, straight hole that's perfectly square to the surface of the panel.

some ⅜" holes in scrap wood to make sure the dowels (pieces 3) fit properly. You may have to try several bits before you get a good fit. Once you settle on a bit, drill the four holes in the ends of each side piece with the help of the jig, as shown in Figure 2.

Transferring the hole locations from the sides to the top and bottom is extremely easy with the help of steel dowel centers (see Figure 3 on page 4). To help position the sides, clamp a fence 1½" from each end of the top and bottom, slide the sides next to the outside edge of each fence, and press down on the sides to form imprints with the dowel centers. Now, use your drill press and the ⅜" bit to bore the holes. If you don't have a drill press, try the Dowl-it jig technique described in Accurate Holes without a Drill Press at left. After completing this step, chamfer the rim of each hole with a countersink bit.

Before assembling the box, there are four small steps to complete. First, drill the ¼" holes in each side for the shelf supports (pieces 4), as shown in the carcass elevation drawing on page 6. Second, lay out the mortises for the hinges (pieces 5), and use a chisel to clean out the waste (see Chopping Hinge Mortises by Hand on page 5). Third, drill the hole in the bottom for the bullet catch (piece 6). And fourth, rout the ends and front edge of the top and bottom with a ½" roundover bit.

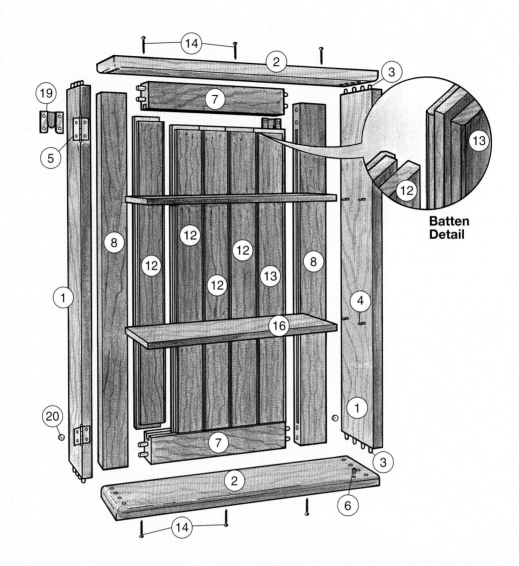

Batten Detail

Material List

		T x W x L			T x W x L
1	Sides (2)	¾" x 5¼" x 24"	**12**	Battens (4)	⁷⁄₁₆" x 2½" x 20½"
2	Top and Bottom (2)	¾" x 6¾" x 18"	**13**	Batten (1)	⁷⁄₁₆" x 2¾" x 20½"
3	Dowels (32)	⅜" x 1½"	**14**	Screws (6)	#8-1½" (Brass)
4	Shelf Supports (8)	¼" Pegs (Brass)	**15**	Mullions (4)	⁷⁄₁₆" x ¾" x 22"
5	Hinges (2)	1½" x 1½" (Brass)	**16**	Shelves (2)	½" x 4¼" x 14⅞"
6	Bullet Catch (1)	¼" Dia. (Brass)	**17**	Retaining Strips (4)	¼" x ⁵⁄₁₆" x 22"
7	Back Rails (2)	¾" x 2" x 11"	**18**	Brads (16)	#17 Wire Gauge
8	Back Stiles (2)	¾" x 2" x 24"	**19**	Flush-Mount Hinges (2)	1½" x 1⅞" (Steel)
9	Door Rails (2)	¾" x 2" x 12½"	**20**	Bumpers (2)	½" Dia. x ⅛" Thick
10	Door Stiles (2)	¾" x 2" x 23⅞"	**21**	Knob (1)	¾" x 1¼" Oval (Brass)
11	Glass (1)	⅛" x 13⅛" x 20½"			

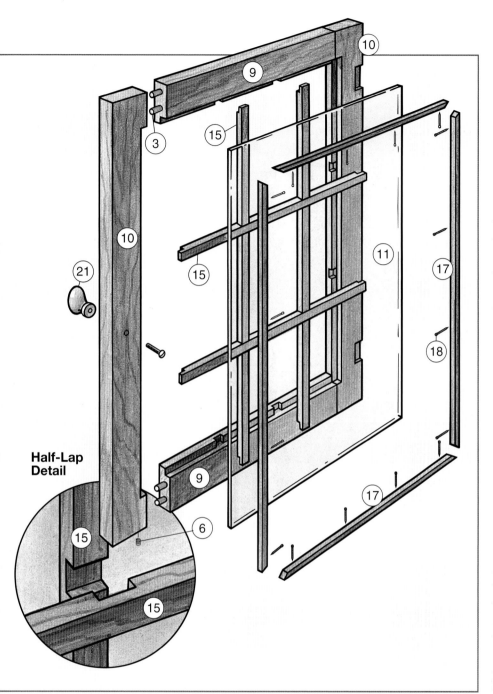

Half-Lap Detail

rabbeting bit, rout 5/16" x 5/16" rabbets on the back of the door frame for holding the glass (piece 11). Square the corners of the rabbets with a chisel, and then take the frames apart.

Next, chuck a 1/4" straight bit in your router table, and prepare to rout grooves in the back frame pieces for holding the battens (pieces 12 and 13). Draw starting and stopping locations on the router fence for routing the stiles, and then plow all the grooves.

The stock for the battens and mullions is 7/16" thick. If you have a planer, you can easily mill some 3/4" material to the right thickness; if you don't have access to a planer, you can accomplish the same results by resawing thicker stock on a band saw or table saw, as shown in Figure 4 on page 4. Once the pieces are properly sized, install a 1/4" dado blade in your table saw, and form the 1/4" x 1/4" tongues on one edge and both ends of four of the battens, as shown in the back assembly detail drawing on page 7. One batten (piece 13) is slightly wider than the others and features a tongue on both edges. After forming the tongues, reset your blade height and fence, and plow a groove in the second edge of the appropriate battens.

For decoration, chamfer the edge shoulders of each batten, as shown in the batten detail drawing on page 2. Cut the chamfers with a standard table saw blade tilted 45° and set low enough to avoid nipping the tongues. When the back frame is assembled, the chamfers will form V-grooves—a feature seen on many old cabinets.

Now, join the top and bottom to the sides with glue and dowels. It's a good idea with dowel joints to tap the dowels into place and then close the joints slowly with clamps. Clamping too quickly, or hitting the dowels sharply with a hammer, could cause the wood to split or the dowel pins to crush as pressure builds up in the holes. Check the box for squareness several times before letting the glue dry overnight.

Making the Back and Doors

While the carcass sits in the clamps, rip some 3/4"-thick maple for the back and door frames (pieces 7 through 10). Cut the stock to length, once again stacking the pieces so you end up with identically sized parts. Next, lay out and drill the dowel holes, as shown in the back and door elevation drawings on pages 6–7. Dry fit the frames to check the fit of the joints, and with your router and a

Figure 3: *To transfer the dowel hole locations, insert steel dowel centers in the sides, and press them into position on the top and bottom pieces.*

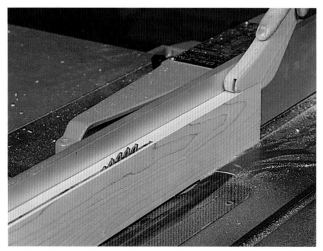

Figure 4: *To resaw ¾" stock, use a push stick to make a number of ½"-deep passes until the blade breaks through the top edge of the stock.*

Figure 5: *After cutting the mullions to length for your door, cut exactly halfway through your stock with a 5⁄16" dado blade to form the tenons.*

Now, glue the back frame around the battens, leaving the battens unglued to allow for wood expansion. While you're at it, glue up the door frame, as well. After the glue has dried, trim the back frame to fit into the cabinet, drill three countersunk pilot holes through the top and bottom into the frame, and drive brass screws (pieces 14) into the pilot holes.

Making the Mullion Frame

Use the rest of your 7⁄16"-thick material for the mullions (pieces 15). Rip the stock a little wider than the Material List calls for, and then hand plane the edges down to the ¾" dimension. Check your planing progress often to make sure the edges remain square.

Since your door is bound to be a little different from mine, be sure to measure the door opening before cutting your mullions to length. After crosscutting the strips, install a ¾" dado blade, raise it 7⁄32", and cut the half-lap joints (see the half-lap detail drawing on page 3). Make test cuts in scrap stock, and adjust the blade height until the joint is right on the money. Then, lay out and cut the half laps in your mullion stock, as shown in the door elevation drawings on page 7. Next, use a 5⁄16" dado blade, the table saw's miter gauge, and a setup block clamped to the fence to cut the tenons on the half laps (see Figure 5).

Assemble the mullion frame, and use it to mark the mortise locations in the door. Trace around each tenon with a utility knife, and clean out the mortises with a chisel, just as you did earlier when you formed the hinge mortises.

Test the fit of the mullion frame in the door, make any corrections, and then glue the frames together. A drop of glue in each mortise and half-lap joint is all it takes.

Carrying Out the Final Fitting

Fitting an overlay door is much easier than fitting an inset door, which is one reason this project is so cabinetmaker friendly. Plane the edges of the door flush with the sides of the cabinet, and trim the door's ends using the table saw to get 1⁄16" gaps. Using the table saw works only if the doors and cabinet are square; if your project is out of square, you'll have to hand plane all four door edges to fit.

Now, use a square and knife to transfer the hinge mortise locations directly from the cabinet to the door. Remove the waste using the technique described in Chopping Hinge Mortises by Hand. Then, mark and drill the pilot holes for the hinge screws. Mount the door in the cabinet to check its swing and fit, and then remove it for installing the glass.

Cut shelves (pieces 16) for your cabinet, and rip retaining strips (pieces 17) for holding the glass in the door. Miter the retaining strips to length, and drill pilot holes for the brads (pieces 18). Don't fool yourself into thinking the pilot holes are unnecessary—without them, you're bound to split the strips or bend the nails.

Sand the cabinet to 150 grit, and then select your stain and topcoat. To make the cabinet look old, I colored the wood with medium-amber-maple aniline dye stain. Mix the water-based stain full strength, and apply it with a sponge. After allowing it to soak in for several minutes, wipe off the excess. If the color isn't dark enough for you, apply more stain; if the color is too dark, wipe the cabinet with a damp rag to remove some of the stain. Wiping on four coats of an oil finish after staining will create a pleasant sheen and a fitting topcoat for this cabinet.

Completing the Final Details

Secure the back assembly in the carcass, and install the flush-mount fasteners (pieces 19), as shown in the back elevation drawings. To keep the cabinet hanging plumb after installing the flush-mount fasteners, stick small adhesive bumpers (pieces 20) to the bottom back corners. Next, drill a pilot hole in the door for the knob (piece 21), and install the glass with the retaining strips and brads. Hinge the door to the cabinet, and tap the bullet catch into its hole. Drill a corresponding hole in the bottom edge of the door, and install the strike plate for the catch.

As you can see, this is a simple cabinet, but to really do it justice, you must still take care with the building process. Learning a few tricks of the trade on projects like this will make it easy to step up to more complicated designs later on.

Chopping Hinge Mortises by Hand

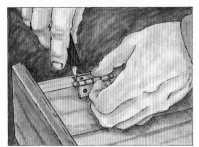

Step 1: *Make several passes around the hinge with a knife to cut deep lines.*

Step 2: *Chamfer the mortise outline to relieve the edges and define the depth.*

A sharp chisel and a steady hand can make short work of chopping out a mortise for a hinge, and it's more efficient than setting up a router and jig if you only have a few mortises to do. Begin by holding the hinge in position and outlining the mortise with a utility knife (Step 1). Next, use a chisel to make chamfering cuts

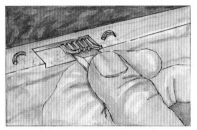

Step 3: *Chop the mortise with a mallet and chisel, and then pare off the waste.*

around the outline that define the depth of the mortise (Step 2). Wrap up the procedure by making a number of vertical chopping cuts to loosen the waste and cleaning out the mortise to the depth of the chamfers (Step 3).

QuickTip

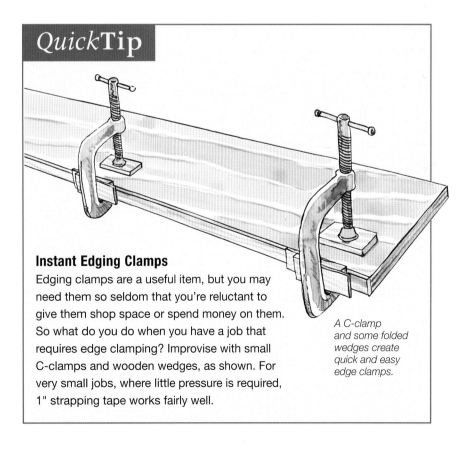

Instant Edging Clamps

Edging clamps are a useful item, but you may need them so seldom that you're reluctant to give them shop space or spend money on them. So what do you do when you have a job that requires edge clamping? Improvise with small C-clamps and wooden wedges, as shown. For very small jobs, where little pressure is required, 1" strapping tape works fairly well.

A C-clamp and some folded wedges create quick and easy edge clamps.

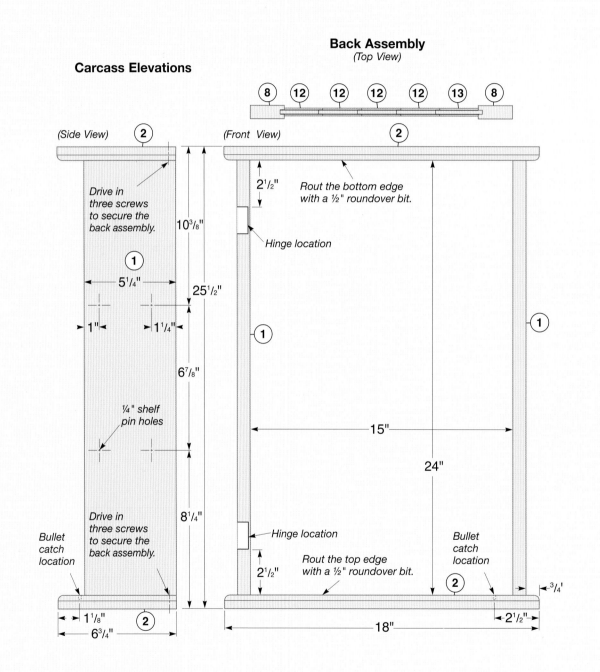

Carcass Elevations

Back Assembly
(Top View)

⑧ ⑫ ⑫ ⑫ ⑫ ⑬ ⑧

(Side View) ②

(Front View) ②

Drive in
three screws
to secure the
back assembly.

2½"

Rout the bottom edge
with a ½" roundover bit.

Hinge location

10³/₈"

①

5¼"

25½"

1" 1¼"

①

6⁷/₈"

¼" shelf
pin holes

15"

①

24"

8¼"

Drive in
three screws
to secure the
back assembly.

Hinge location

Bullet
catch
location

2½"

Rout the top edge
with a ½" roundover bit.

Bullet
catch
location

②

³/₄"

1⅛" ②

6³/₄"

18"

2½"

Door Elevations

Door Frame

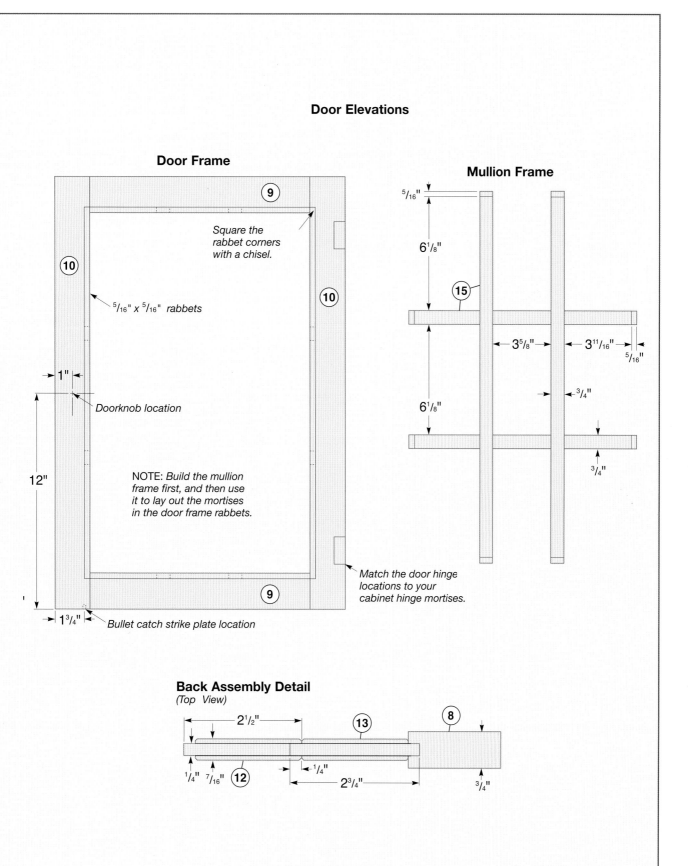

(9)

(10)

(10)

Square the
rabbet corners
with a chisel.

$^5/_{16}$" x $^5/_{16}$" rabbets

1"

Doorknob location

12"

NOTE: *Build the mullion
frame first, and then use
it to lay out the mortises
in the door frame rabbets.*

(9)

1$^3/_4$"

Bullet catch strike plate location

Mullion Frame

$^5/_{16}$"

6$^1/_8$"

(15)

3$^5/_8$"   3$^{11}/_{16}$"

$^5/_{16}$"

$^3/_4$"

6$^1/_8$"

$^3/_4$"

Match the door hinge
locations to your
cabinet hinge mortises.

Back Assembly Detail
(Top View)

2$^1/_2$"

(13)

(8)

$^1/_4$" $^7/_{16}$"   (12)

$^1/_4$"

2$^3/_4$"

$^3/_4$"

Blanket Chest

You'd never know by looking at it, but this charming cherry chest bypasses traditional mortise-and-tenon joints in favor of a unique combination of rabbet and lap joints, making the chest easier to build without compromising its strength. A finishing scheme of both paint and clear finish also lends a handsome effect to this piece, which is sure to become a family heirloom.

by Rick White

Winters can be just a bit chilly up here in Minnesota. Thankfully, modern housing keeps us warm and cozy, but our ancestors weren't so lucky. When the first hoarfrost settled on the cottonwoods, those hardy folks reached into Grandma's old blanket chest for another layer of warmth.

This chest follows in that same tradition, providing attractive and functional year-round storage for winter blankets. It combines the warmth of natural cherry with a historically authenticated Windsor green water-based enamel paint. Where it surpasses the original is in its hardware, which includes a pair of inexpensive but effective lid supports that are designed to protect children's fingers from pinches.

Making a Flat Panel

To create this family heirloom, the first step is to choose some top-quality stock for the lid (piece 1). The appearance of the solid cherry lid is one of the most critical features of this chest. If you're not used to creating wide panels, here are some pointers to help you over the hurdles.

Several narrow boards, rather than a few wide ones, make for the most stable panel, and some woodworkers will even rip and reglue wider boards to achieve this. The key is to have an uneven number of boards (or an even number of boards of varying widths) so the panel doesn't have an eye-catching joint running right down the middle. Some would also alternate the grain patterns by looking at the ends of the boards and making sure that every other crown points down. Biscuits or dowels are helpful to keep everything in line when clamping large panels like this. A center clamp will exert pressure on the center of a panel to keep it flat while clamping (see Figure 1).

If you own a planer, you can make two small panels first, plane them, glue them up, and then belt sand the last joint. But for a professional look, I recommend gluing up 4/4 stock and having a local cabinet shop run it through their wide belt sander.

The bottom of the chest (piece 2) is also a glued-up panel. Make this from poplar rather than cherry; it will be painted anyway, and poplar is less expensive. Making the lid and bottom together will save time on setups. While you're at it, go ahead and glue up some of your nicer cherry stock for the eight decorative panels.

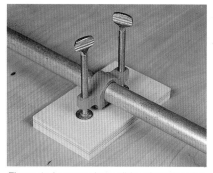

Figure 1: *A center clamp slides along the pipe of a standard clamp and applies pressure to the center of larger glued-up panels.*

The skeleton of my blanket chest is poplar, an old favorite of cabinetmakers and furniture builders. It's a fast-growing hardwood with fine, closed grain, so it's commonly used as a base for veneers or as hidden or painted structural members.

Each side of the blanket chest carcass can be treated as a subassembly—a frame that contains panels. The front and back frames are identical, as are the two side frames.

The first step in building these frames is to cut the parts to size, referring to the Material List on page 10. All the cuts are square except for the short taper on the lower ends of the stiles (pieces 3 and 4). This taper can be laid out using the dimensions given in the stile detail drawing on page 10 and then cut to size on your band saw.

Chest Exploded View

Corner Detail
(Top View)

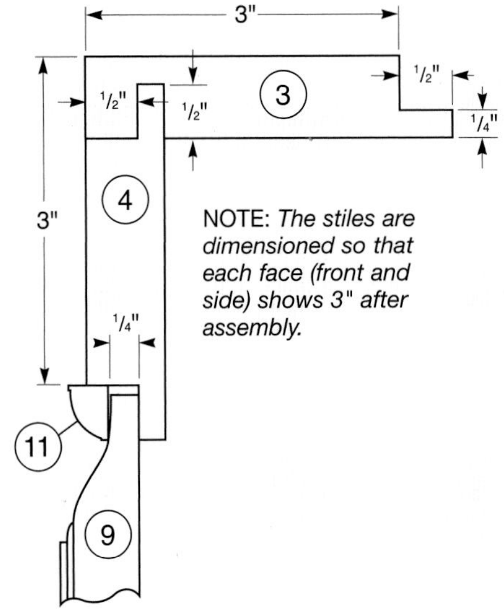

3"
1/2"
1/2"
3
1/2"
1/4"
3"
4
NOTE: *The stiles are dimensioned so that each face (front and side) shows 3" after assembly.*
1/4"
11
9

Stile Detail
(Inside View)

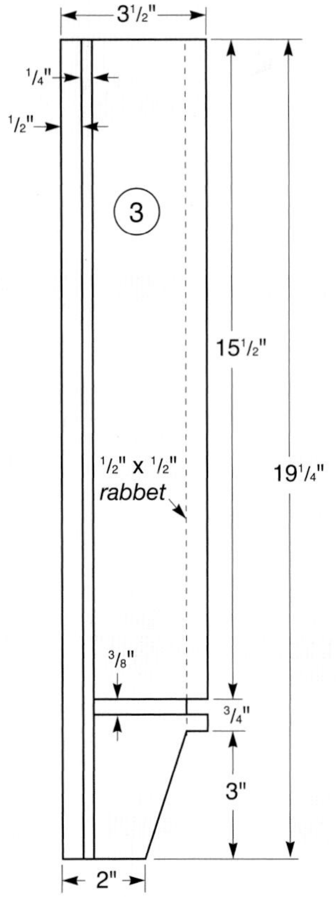

3 1/2"
1/4"
1/2"
3
15 1/2"
19 1/4"
1/2" x 1/2" rabbet
3/8"
3/4"
3"
2"

Material List

		T x W x L
1	Lid (1)	¾" x 17¼" x 38"
2	Bottom (1)	¾" x 15¼" x 35"
3	Front and Back Stiles (4)	¾" x 3½" x 19¼"
4	Side Stiles (4)	¾" x 3¼" x 19¼"
5	Front and Back Rails (4)	¾" x 3½" x 30"
6	Side Rails (4)	¾" x 3½" x 10¼"
7	Interior Stiles (4)	¾" x 3½" x 10¼"
8	Front and Back Panels (6)	¾" x 7⅞" x 10⅛"
9	Side Panels (2)	¾" x 10⅛" x 10⅛"
10	Front and Back Horizontal Moldings (12)	⅜" x ½" x 8"
11	All Vertical and Side Horizontal Moldings (20)	⅜" x ½" x 10¼"
12	Solid-Brass Hinges (3)	1½" x 2"
13	Lid Supports (2)	
14	Windsor Green Enamel Paint (1 Quart)	

Raising Panels on the Router Table

Vertical-style panel-raising bits are the only way to go these days. They are safer than big horizontal cutters, are easy to use, and provide the home woodworker with plenty of profile options. The key to using these bits is to always support your workpiece vertically with an appropriately sized auxiliary fence.

For best results, your router should have at least a 1½ horsepower motor. The load exerted on these long cutters is substantial, especially in denser hardwood stock. That is why vertical panel-raising bits are generally not available with ¼" shanks.

Routers featuring variable-speed controls are recommended by the bit manufacturers. Variations in both the speed of the router's motor and the rate of feed can have a strong impact on the quality of the cut. Wood that is cut too quickly across the grain will have torn fibers, and an overly slow cut can leave you with burn marks. You can improve the quality of your work and reduce strain on the router bit by taking six or seven passes on each edge of a panel, moving your fence after each pass. To minimize tearout, rout the end grain first and then the sides. Chatter and chipping are two good indicators that your cut is too deep and that you should adjust your fence.

The keys to using vertical panel-raising bits are to support them with an auxiliary fence on your router table and to take multiple light passes.

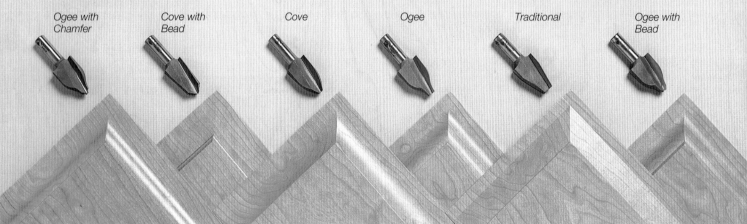

Ogee with Chamfer Cove with Bead Cove Ogee Traditional Ogee with Bead

I used lap joints on the front, back, and side frames, and rabbet and dado joints on the corners, as shown in the corner detail drawing on page 10. There are two reasons for using lap joinery: It does a great job of securing the stiles to the rails, and at the same time, it creates recesses for the cherry panels. Since I'm using molding to hold the panels in place, a traditional mortise is not necessary.

To make the lap joints, insert a dado head in your table saw, and set the blade height and the fence for a ½" x ½" cut. Mill rabbets on both edges of the side stiles and on the tapered edges of the front and back stiles, as shown in the detail drawing.

This same rabbet is milled on one edge of the front, back, and side rails (pieces 5 and 6) and on both edges of the interior stiles (pieces 7). The second half of the lap joint is a ½"-wide tongue that is milled on the ends of the rails and interior stiles. To make this tongue, decrease the blade height to create a ¼"-deep cut, and use your miter gauge to maintain squareness.

With the dado head set up, you can now create the tongue, which runs around the edge of the bottom panel. Set the depth of cut to ⅜", and form the ¼"-wide tongue. There's one more operation you can perform with the dado set installed: forming the grooves in the front and back stiles to

accommodate the tongues you just milled on the side stiles. The grooves will require an adjustment in the kerf width, so remove the dado head and reset it to ¼". Now, set the height to ½", align your fence ½" away, and create the grooves (see the stile detail drawing on page 10).

Assembling the Frames

With all the initial machining done, it's time to assemble the four frames. Gluing the lap joints can be tricky because the joint tends to buckle as the clamp applies pressure. One way to avoid this problem is by using C-clamps to hold a short length (about 8") of scrap on either side of the joint. Set the C-clamps so they're finger tight only; that way, you can still close the joint under pressure from the pipe clamps. Slip a piece of wax paper between the scrap and frame so excess glue won't secure the scrap to your workpiece. When the pipe clamps are snug, tighten the C-clamps fully to hold the two cheeks of the lap joint together while the glue cures. As you assemble the frames, check for squareness by measuring diagonally across the faces, and adjust your clamps accordingly.

With all four frames glued up, you can now run the grooves that hold the bottom panel. This task is best done with a router rather than a table saw because two of the four grooves are stopped before they emerge from the end of the frame.

To make the two stopped dadoes, equip your router table with a ⅜"

straight bit, and set the depth of cut to 5⁄16". Stick some masking tape to your router table fence, and mark the location of the router bit on it. You'll have two marks ⅜" apart showing the points where the bit enters and exits the workpiece (see Figure 2).

The top rail of each frame will run along the fence, which should be set 15½" from the bit. Using the marks on the masking tape as a guide, slowly push the piece down on the bit so the leading edge is ½" beyond the left-hand mark. Feed the piece from right to left, stopping when the right edge is just ½" to the right of the two marks. Square up the stopped dadoes with a sharp chisel.

Figure 2: *Align marks on your router table fence and the stiles to locate the two stopped dadoes that will hold the bottom panel.*

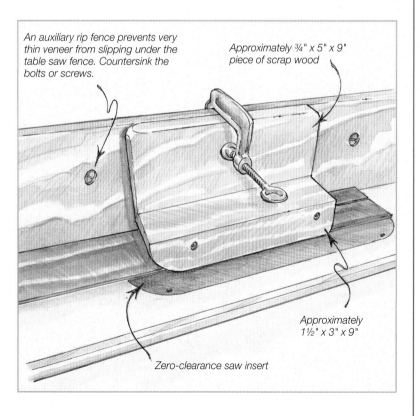

Assembling the Carcass

Now, it's time to start bringing the chest together. Begin by laying the back frame flat on your workbench with the outside face down. Rotate the frame until the ends extend beyond the edges of your worktop (so you can clamp it later), and then drop the bottom panel into its groove. Don't glue the panel in.

The two side frames do get glued in, and they're inserted next, followed by the front frame. Then, clamp everything together. If you are a relatively new woodworker, you should be aware that many people tend to overtighten clamps, squeezing too much of the glue out of the joints. Try to resist those last two turns on the crank; simply make the joint snug while the glue cures. Be sure to check and recheck your diagonals now, adjusting as necessary to keep everything square.

Installing the Panels

With the carcass assembled and waiting for its cherry panels (pieces 8 and 9), this is an excellent time to apply paint to all the poplar areas. Doing so now eliminates the need to apply masking tape to the panels later. While you have the paint out, you should also coat the embossed moldings (pieces 10 and 11).

Your panel stock should be ready by now, so go ahead and trim the eight panels to size, lightly marking the best ones for the front and sides. The raised panel is created using a vertical panel-raising bit in the router table (see Raising Panels on the Router Table on page 12). Make a number of passes, moving your fence $\frac{1}{16}$" farther back each time, until you have $\frac{1}{4}$" of stock left on the lip. Rout the end grain first, and then the long grain, to help minimize short-grain tearout.

Finishing Up

The eight panels and the lid should be sanded and finished prior to installation. An excellent finish for cherry is several coats of natural Danish oil, which quickly develops the rich patina of the wood.

To miter the ends of the moldings, you should build a small jig, as described in A Mitering Jig for Small Moldings on page 15. The groove in the jig holds the thin, flexible stock steady while you run it across the table saw. Use a fine-toothed plywood blade to make these cuts.

Securing the panels in place may prove to be a little tricky. The embossed molding is relatively thin, and the $\frac{1}{2}$" rabbet has to accommodate both the panel and the molding. Set the chest on its back so you can work on a flat surface as you install the panels. Once all the moldings are mitered to

*Quick*Tips

Speedier Joint Setups Take Planning

When you're designing the joints in a piece of furniture or casework, think not only how they will look and work but also how they will be machined. For example, if you install a $\frac{3}{8}$" dado head in the table saw and set the height at $\frac{3}{8}$", you can cut both parts of a rabbet and dado joint without ever changing your setup. If you place $\frac{3}{8}$" dowel joints and $\frac{3}{8}$" shelf supports in the same relative locations in a cabinet, you can use a single drill press setup for both tasks. And if you make stiles, rails, and trim pieces the same width, you can rip and joint them all at the same time.

Switch to Plywood When Making Spline Joints

Spline joints are a great way to join two long edges. But while most woodworkers have no problem routing the grooves for the spline, they often let the ball drop when it comes to making the actual spline. A ripped piece of hardwood won't work, as it will split along the grain—right where you need the most strength. Plywood is the perfect answer: Its alternating plies prevent splitting, and it comes in thicknesses that are perfectly suited to the router bits you use to make the grooves.

the correct length, glue and tack them in place with brad nails, trapping the panels in their frames. Set and fill the nail heads, and then touch up the paint.

Mark the locations for the hinge mortises on both the lid and the carcass, and use a router equipped with a straight bit to remove most of the waste. Finish up with a sharp chisel. Drill pilot holes for the screws, and install the hinges (pieces 12).

The lid supports (pieces 13) come in left and right configurations and are relatively easy to install. You'll find complete instructions printed on the bag. Simply measure for the screw locations, and then surface mount each support.

Other Handy Uses for This Chest

Storing blankets may not be the only use for this chest; with a little imagination, you can adapt it to suit a number of different uses. For example, cleats installed a few inches from the top could support a drop-in tray for linens or place mats. It's also just about the perfect size for a toy chest, although in that case, you may want to build the whole piece out of poplar and paint it in brighter colors. Either way, when you complete this chest you're bound to end up with an heirloom that will get passed down through future generations.

Mitering small moldings can be dicier than it looks, especially on a table saw. This easy-to-make cradle attaches to your saw's miter gauge and holds the workpiece safely during the cut.

The jig is made by plowing a ½" groove in a piece of 1" x 3" scrap. The wood left under the groove should be only ⅛" thick to prevent small cutoffs from falling back into the blade.

Set your miter gauge at 45° to the right, attach the piece of scrap to it, and run the assembly through the blade. Now, reset the fence at 45° to the left, switch miter slots, and repeat the process. When cutting miters on the small moldings, line up your mark with the edge of the jig for a perfect cut every time.

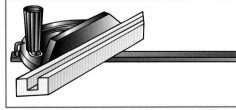

Your Own Steamer Trunk

Before the days of Samsonite, big voyages required big steamer trunks. While travel has changed quite a bit over time, the allure of a solid steamer trunk hasn't passed away with the jet age. You'll probably never use this sturdy, handsome trunk for a trip, but it's the perfect accent piece at the foot of the bed for storing winter blankets and sweaters.

by Rick White

Remember the wonderful old road movies with Bob Hope and Bing Crosby? Those two zany characters traveled from one exotic locale to another, creating chaos wherever they went. Aside from their antics, one of the recurring images from those movies was that whenever Bob and Bing disembarked from their ship, they were surrounded by steamer trunks plastered with stickers from their many ports of call. Those classic camelback trunks captured all the excitement and wonder of faraway places and unusual cultures.

This steamer trunk will probably never see the baggage hold of a steamship, but I still wanted it to have an air of authenticity. That's why I settled on the camelback top, the extensive use of brass hardware, and the walnut "strap" design. The curved top makes for a slightly more challenging project, but don't be scared off by this feature. The curved pieces are shown in detail on the accompanying drawings.

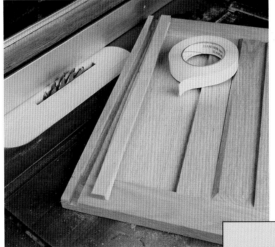

Figure 1: *For balance, tape a ¼"-thick strip to the side panels when making the bottom groove dado cuts.*

¼"-thick strip

Starting with the Corners

The framework provides the real strength in this project's construction, while the thin panels merely serve to enclose the box. Since the corner posts (pieces 1) link the four frames together, this is the best place to start. Referring to the Material List on page 18, rip these pieces ¹⁄₁₆" oversize, and joint their edges square and to the correct width. Then, cut the pieces to length.

Sort your eight corner pieces into four pairs, watching for color and grain similarities, and mark the top of each pair with its position in the trunk construction.

Trunk Exploded View

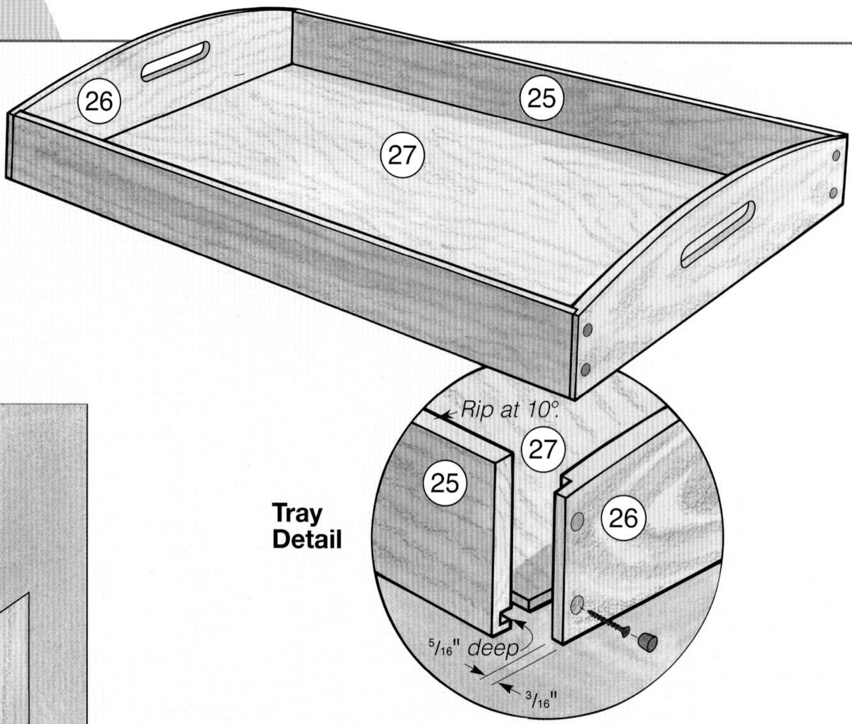

26
25
27
Rip at 10°.
27
25
26
5/16" deep
3/16"

Tray Detail

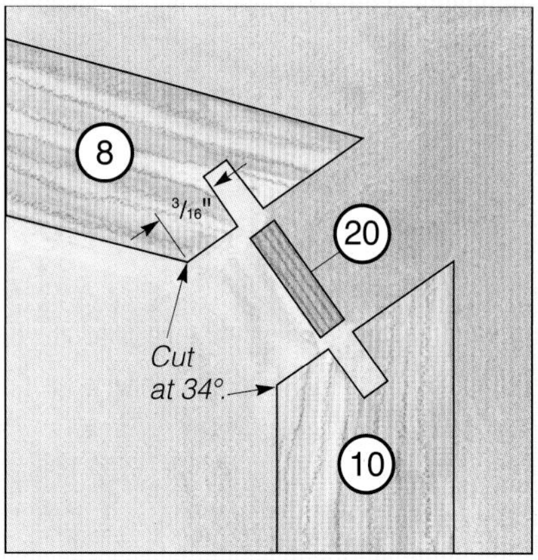

8
3/16"
20
Cut at 34°.
10

Lid Corner Detail

Lid Assembly Detail
(End View)

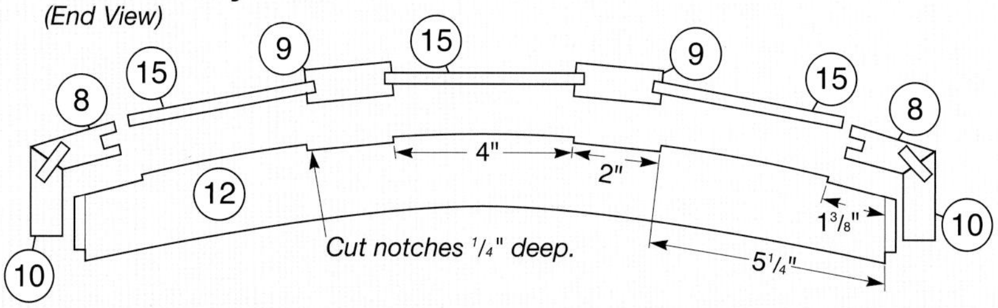

15
9
15
9
15
8
8
4"
2"
12
1 3/8"
10
10
Cut notches 1/4" deep.
5 1/4"

Material List

	T x W x L		T x W x L
1 Corner Posts (8)	¾" x 2" x 14"	**15** Lid Panels (3)	¼" x 4⅝" x 34½" (Plywood)
2 Upper Front and Back Rails (2)	¾" x 2" x 32¾"	**16** Upper Side Panels (2)	¾" x 4⅝" x 16⅝"
3 Upper Side Rails (2)	¾" x 2" x 16¾"	**17** Tray Support Ledgers (2)	¾" x ⅞" x 16"
4 Middle Front and Back Rails (2)	¾" x 2" x 32¾"	**18** Bottom (1)	½" x 19" x 35" (Plywood)
5 Middle Side Rails (2)	¾" x 2" x 16¾"	**19** Splines (4)	⅛" x ¾" x 14" (Plywood)
6 Lower Front and Back Rails (2)	¾" x 2" x 32¾"	**20** Splines (2)	⅛" x ¾" x 34½" (Plywood)
7 Lower Side Rails (2)	¾" x 2" x 16¾"	**21** Screws (30)	#8-1½"
8 Lid Front and Back Rails (2)	¾" x 2" x 34½"	**22** Plugs (30)	⅜" Dia. (Walnut)
9 Lid Middle Rails (2)	¾" x 2" x 34½"	**23** Bandings (2)	5/16" x 2" x 36" (Walnut)
10 Lid Front and Back (2)	¾" x 2" x 34½"	**24** Shim (1)	¼" x 4¼" x 2⅞" (Walnut)
11 Lid Sides (2)	¾" x 3⅜" x 20"	**25** Tray Front and Back (2)	½" x 3¾" x 32¾"
12 Lid Supports (5)	¾" x 3" x 19"	**26** Tray Sides (2)	½" x 4¾" x 17¾"
13 Front and Back Panels (4)	¼" x 4⅝" x 32⅝" (Plywood)	**27** Tray Bottom (1)	¼" x 17⅛" x 32¾"
14 Lower Side Panels (2)	¼" x 4⅝" x 16⅝" (Plywood)	**28** Feet (4)	½" x 2" x 2"

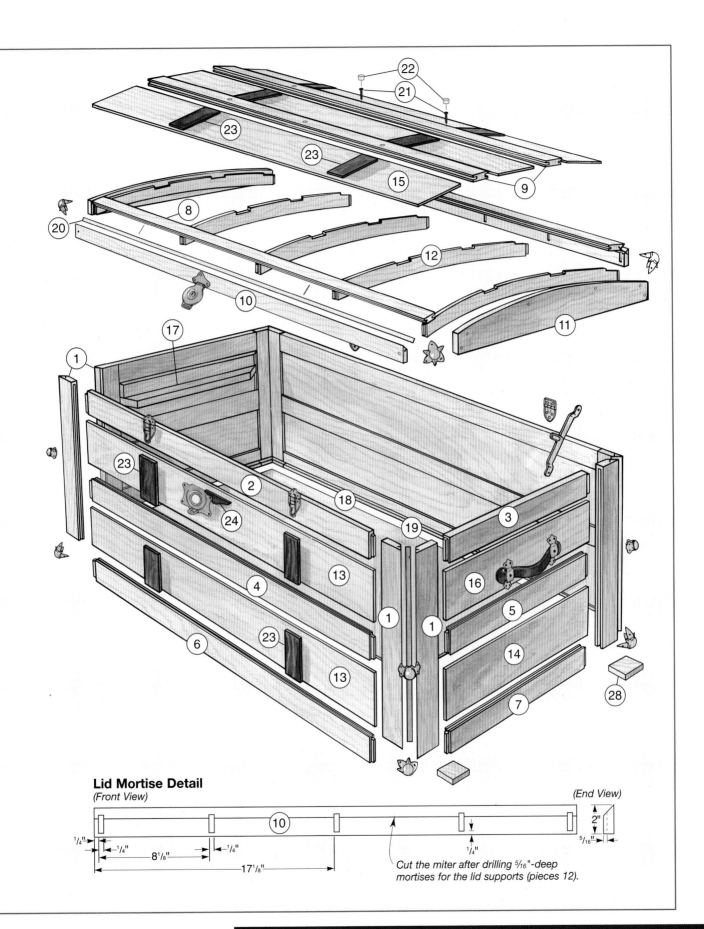

Lid Mortise Detail

(Front View)

(End View)

⑩

$1/4"$ $1/4"$ $1/4"$

$8^1/8"$

$17^1/8"$

$1/4"$

$2"$

$5/16"$

Cut the miter after drilling $5/16"$-deep
mortises for the lid supports (pieces 12).

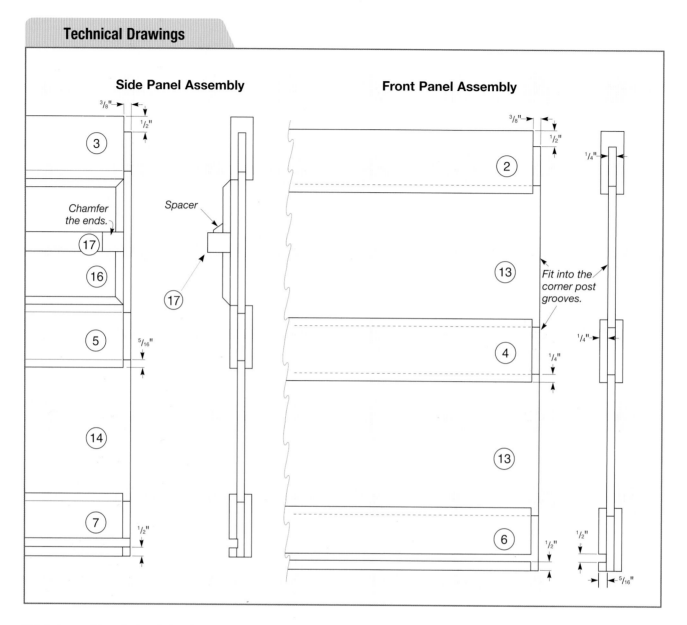

Side Panel Assembly

³/₈"
¹/₂"
③
Chamfer the ends.
⑰
⑯
Spacer
⑰
⑤   ⁵/₁₆"
⑭
⑦   ¹/₂"

Front Panel Assembly

³/₈"
¹/₂"
②   ¹/₄"
⑬
Fit into the corner post grooves.
④   ¹/₄"
⑬
⑥   ¹/₂"   ¹/₂"   ⁵/₁₆"

This helps avoid confusion during the building process. To cut the groove in one edge of each piece, chuck a ³/₁₆" straight bit in your router table, and lay out the stopping point for each groove, as shown in the corner detail drawing on page 21. Stopping the groove short of the top leaves a little meat above the rail tenon when the trunk is assembled, resulting in a stronger load-bearing joint for lifting the completed project. (Note: Use a ³/₁₆" bit since ¼" plywood usually isn't a full ¼" thick. With this bit, first make a pass to form the mortise, and then take a second pass to shave the mortise about ¹/₃₂" wider. Once you get

a snug fit for the plywood, cut the rail tenons to fit the mortises.)

Now, use a piece of scrap wood that's the same thickness as your corner pieces to test your router table setup. You want to be sure that the bit is exactly centered when you rout the ³/₈"-deep grooves. Don't miter the other edge of the corners until after the panels are fully assembled.

Forming the Rails
With the corner grooves completed, you can build the rest of the framework for the trunk. Following the dimensions provided in the Material List, cut your

stock to size for all the rails (pieces 2 through 9), and label each piece with its position in the assembly. Take the rails over to your router table to cut the mortises in all the appropriate edges—that is, wherever a panel will be inserted (see the side and front panel assembly drawings, above).

After routing grooves in the rails, step back to your table saw to cut material for the lid front, back, sides, and supports (pieces 10 through 12). The sides and supports feature curved top edges, but for now, just cut the material to the overall dimensions provided in the Material List.

All the rails for the box portion of the project join the corner pieces with tenons. In addition, the lid supports join the lid front and back with short tenons. To cut these tenons, set up a ⅜" dado blade in your table saw, and clamp a protective wood face to the saw's fence. Raise the blade a hair over ¼", and adjust the fence so it grazes the blade. Now, use your miter gauge to pass a test piece over the blade, and then test the tenon's fit with the grooves in the corner pieces. Once the tenon on your test piece fits well, cut the tenons for the rest of the rails and supports.

Don't forget that the tenons on the upper rails (pieces 2 and 3) need a ½" shoulder at their tops so they'll sit flush with the corners (see the side and front panel assembly drawings).

Cutting the Panels

All but two of the panels in the trunk are cut from ¼"-thick rift-sawn red-oak plywood (pieces 13 through 15). The two upper side panels (pieces 16) are made of ¾" solid stock for extra strength, since these pieces secure the handles and carry the load of the trunk when it's lifted off the ground, in addition to supporting the tray inside the trunk. Cut the plywood panels to the sizes specified in the Material List, and find some matching ¾" stock for the upper side panels.

The plywood panels will fit right into the grooves you made earlier, but the ¾" upper side panels will require a little extra machining. Start with a ⅜" dado blade to rabbet the back of each panel (see the corner detail and side panel assembly drawings). The tongues remaining after the rabbets are cut must fit comfortably in the rail grooves. Switch to a ¾" dado blade to cut the grooves for the tray support ledgers (pieces 17), and then chamfer the edges.

Assembling the Box

For the most part, the pieces for the box portion of the trunk are completed, so now you can begin assembling each wall of the project. First, do a dry run without any glue to check the fit of all the parts. While you're at it, make sure the upper and lower rails are flush with the ends of the corners and that the middle rails are exactly centered. Mark each of these joints so reassembly will be easier.

Take apart each wall, and put glue on the tenons and in the grooves where the tenons will be inserted. Reassemble the parts, and draw each wall tight with bar clamps. Don't forget to measure diagonals to ensure squareness.

Clean up any glue squeeze-out, and sand the joints flush. The bottom (piece 18) will be held in grooves (see the side panel assembly drawing) in the front, back, and side walls. These grooves are easily cut on your table saw with a ½" dado blade, but you'll need to balance the end walls on a couple of ¼" strips during the cut to compensate for the extra thickness of the upper panels. After cutting the ⁵⁄₁₆"-deep grooves in the front and back walls, use double-sided tape to secure the strips to the end walls, and then raise the blade another ¼" to make the cuts, as shown in Figure 1 on page 17.

The four walls are now ready to be joined together with splined miters. Cutting these joints follows much the same procedure you just completed when cutting the grooves for the bottom panel. To cut the miters, tilt your blade exactly 45° (test cut some scrap wood to get this perfect), and clamp a wood face to your fence. Without the wood face, the tip of your first mitered edge might slip under the fence during the second cut. I used a right-tilting table saw. If you have a left-tilting saw, you'll

Corner Detail

The corner joints provide structural strength for the steamer trunk, and the ½" bit of wood at the top of each mortise helps alleviate stress on the glue joints when lifting the trunk.

The miters and spline grooves are cut after the panels are assembled.

Cut the grooves for the bottom after the panels are assembled.

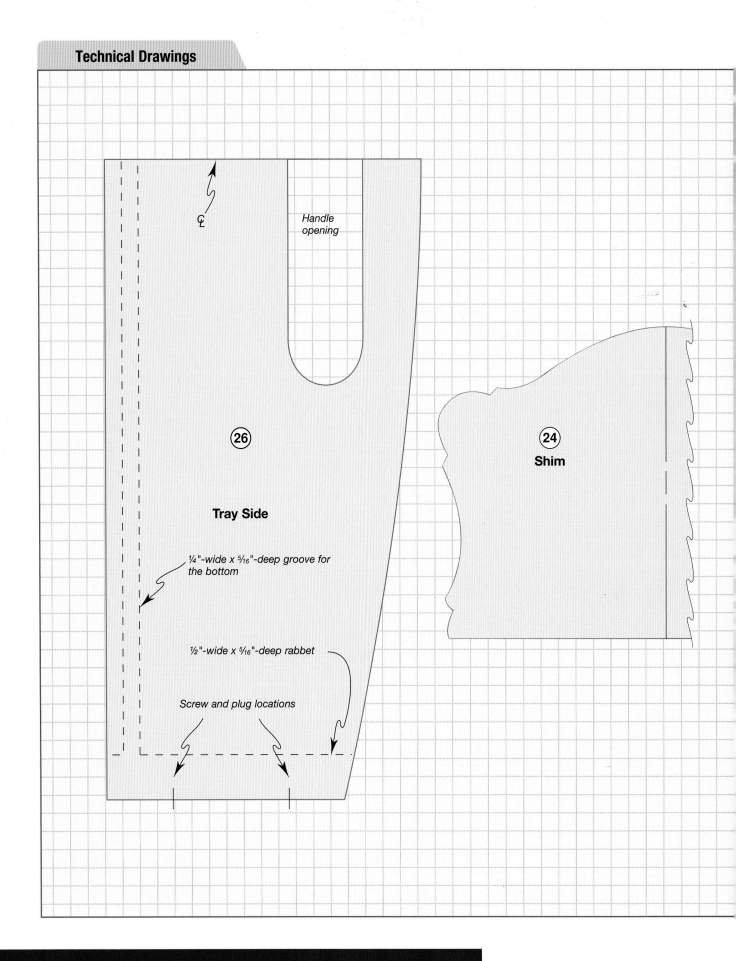

Handle
opening

₵

㉖

Tray Side

¼"-wide x ⁵/₁₆"-deep groove for
the bottom

½"-wide x ⁵/₁₆"-deep rabbet

Screw and plug locations

㉔

Shim

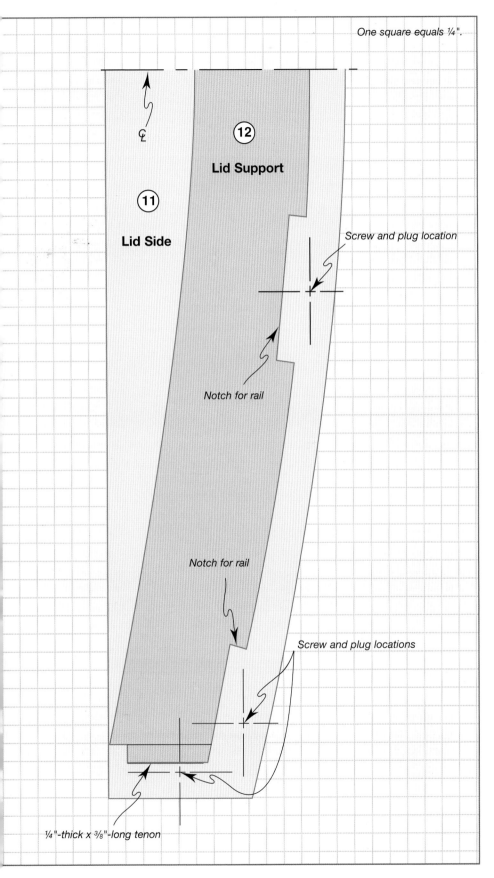

⑫

Lid Support

⑪

Lid Side

Screw and plug location

Notch for rail

Notch for rail

Screw and plug locations

¼"-thick x ⅜"-long tenon

have to cut the miters with the inside surface of the walls riding on the saw table. Since the upper side panels stick out ¼", you'll have to use the ¼"-strip method on the end walls to keep these pieces balanced during the cuts.

Once the miters have been completed, set up your saw for the spline cuts (see Figure 2 on page 24). Since all these cuts must be made with the inside surface riding on the saw table, you'll have to continue using the ¼" strips on the end walls. Keep the blade tilted 45°, and adjust the blade height and fence position to make the cuts. First, make the spline groove cuts in the front and back walls, and then readjust the fence and raise the blade to make the end wall cuts.

Using ⅛" plywood, rip four ¾"-wide splines (pieces 19) for the corner joints. Dry assemble the four walls with the splines and the bottom panel in place to make sure everything fits, and then glue the box together. You'll notice during the dry assembly that the bottom panel prevents the splines from going all the way to the bottom of the joint. Just butt the spline into the bottom panel, and let the excess run out the top for now. Don't worry about the exposed spline groove showing at the bottom—it will be covered by the brass corner hardware later on.

Making the Lid
You cut tenons on the lid supports (pieces 12) earlier, but you still need to cut the mortises in the lid front and back (pieces 10). Lay out these mortises (see the lid mortise detail drawing on page 19), chuck a ¼" brad-point bit in your drill press, and drill out the waste in each mortise to a depth of ⁵⁄₁₆". Don't bother cleaning up with your chisel yet, because in the next step, your miter cut will remove the tops of the mortises. They'll be a lot easier to clean up at that stage.

Figure 2: *When cutting the spline grooves, once again use ¼" strips to balance the side panels.*

As noted, the front and back of the lid (pieces 10) meet the front and back rails (pieces 8) with another spline-mitered joint. However, due to the curve of the lid, the miters aren't exactly 45°. Tilt your saw blade 34°, and rip the top edge of the front and back pieces and one edge of each rail. Once the pieces are ripped, lower the blade, keeping it at the same angle, and adjust the fence to cut a spline groove in each edge.

Rip two ⅛"-thick splines (pieces 20), and glue each set of mitered pieces together. I recommend using band clamps to hold the narrow lumber at this odd angle.

The lid supports are curved and have a series of notches along the top edge to accommodate the rails in the lid. Photocopy and cut out the patterns for the lid support and side on page 23,

and then trace the shapes onto your stock. Band saw the supports and sides to shape, checking the fit of your rails in each of the support notches before proceeding. The width of the rails should fit snugly into the notches, and the lower wall of the rail mortises should be flush with the top of the support. Before you glue and assemble the lid, be sure to test the fit of the front and back subassemblies you just glued together. They should fit nicely into the end notches on the supports, as shown in the lid assembly detail drawing on page 18.

When all the lid pieces clearly fit together, drill counterbored pilot holes to secure the front and back subassemblies to the lid supports, and spread a little glue in each mortise in the front and back pieces. Slip the lid support tenons into the mortises, and clamp the subassemblies to the five support pieces.

Fitting the rest of the lid is just a matter of popping everything into place. Loosely assemble the three lid panels (pieces 15) and two middle rails (pieces 9), and then flex this assembly to get the outside panel edges to start sliding into the front and back rails. Once the

edges are all aligned, press down on the arched center of the assembly to force the panels into the grooves. You may need to adjust the rails a little to slip them into the support notches. When all the pieces fit well and are firmly seated on the supports, drill six counterbored pilot holes to secure the rails to the supports (see the exploded view on page 19), and cover the screws (pieces 21) with walnut face-grain plugs (pieces 22). Now, simply add the sides. Counterbore pilot holes where each rail meets a side piece, drive in screws, and fill the holes with walnut plugs.

Walnut Strapping and a Few Details
The top of this chest arches just a little bit, but it's not necessary to steam bend the walnut banding (pieces 23) to get a good fit. Instead, start with ⁵⁄₁₆"-thick pieces, cut to fit between each rail, and sand one face of each slightly with a drum sander until it matches the curve of the lid panel. After fitting all the curved sections of banding, spread glue on the walnut and press the banding into place. You can sand the tops after the glue dries so they conform to the arch. Apply the straight pieces to the box when you're done with the lid, and

Hardware and Banding Locations

Mount the hinges on the rear of the trunk in the same locations as the hasps are shown on the front of the trunk.

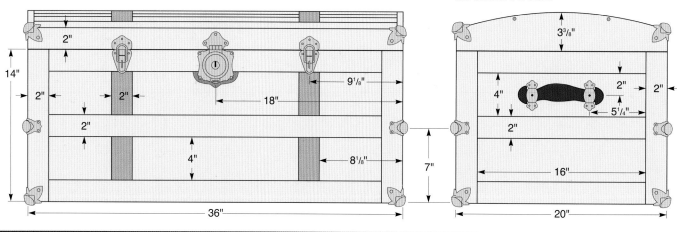

plane them flush with the rails. Be sure to line up the walnut strapping on the box with the walnut on the lid.

Earlier, you cut a groove in each upper panel in the side walls for mounting the ledger strips (pieces 17). These strips will support the tray when it's completed in the next phase of the project. But for now, cut the ledger strips to length, chamfer their ends, and glue them into place.

Mounting the main latch for the trunk hardware requires a shim (piece 24) so that it sits level with the upper rail on the front wall. Using the shim pattern on page 22, trace the lock shim shape onto some ¼"-thick walnut, and cut it with a band saw. Sand the edges smooth, center the piece on the upper front panel, and glue it into position.

One final detail to take care of is to glue the small feet (pieces 28) to the bottom corners of the trunk. These feet provide solid backing for screwing the bottom corner hardware into place.

At this point, sand the whole project to 220 grit, and wipe it down with mineral spirits to find any glue spots that need to be removed.

Building the Tray

The tray is a simple structure that fully uses the space in the arched lid (see Figure 3). Begin by cutting the front, back, and sides (pieces 25 and 26) to the sizes in the Material List. Don't cut the sides to shape until after the joints are formed. Install a ¼" dado blade in your table saw, and cut 5/16"-deep grooves along the entire length of the front, back, and sides to accommodate the bottom piece (see the tray detail drawing on page 18). As long as the dado blade is installed, go ahead and rabbet the ends of the side pieces.

Next, photocopy and cut out the pattern of the tray side on page 22, trace it onto your stock, and band saw the sides to shape. To form each handle, drill an access hole first, and then cut the opening with a jigsaw. To get the front and back pieces to conform to the shape of the sides, rip the top edge of both pieces to final size with the blade set at a 10° angle.

Cut the bottom (piece 27), and dry fit the tray parts to check their fit. When they all go together well, put glue in the bottom grooves, and drill the counterbored pilot holes in the corner joints for the screws. Drive the screws in, fill the holes with walnut plugs, and sand the tray to 220 grit.

Adding Trunk Hardware

Steamer trunk hardware has a unique look about it. It's somewhat oversize and durable, perhaps still reflective of a time when its primary purpose was to protect the trunk from burly baggage handlers. Start installing your hardware by mounting the hinges (be sure the strapping stays lined up!), and then move to the lock mechanism, the handles, the lid supports (see Figure 4), and finally, the corner pieces (all 12 of them). It's pretty straightforward, except for the top corners, which have to be slightly stretched outward to accommodate the curved top.

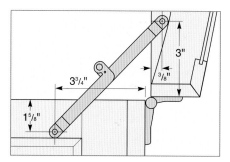

Figure 4: *Due to the construction of the steamer lid, the lid supports must be installed differently from the instructions provided with the hardware.*

Finishing Up

I recommend using a durable finish such as varnish or polyurethane to protect this project. First, apply a coat of sanding sealer, and then sand it smooth. Follow with two more coats of finish, sanding between coats to remove any dust nibs or rough spots. After the last coat of finish dries, reinstall all the hardware. Now, you can get busy planning your next big trip. You'll certainly be traveling in style—with or without an exotic port of call.

Figure 3: *The structure of the camelback lid makes it as interesting to look at as the outside of the steamer trunk, and the curved top of the tray takes full advantage of the extra space.*

Eastern Shore Chest

Here's the perfect project for expanding your skill base with a router. This chest combines cope-and-stick joints, sliding dovetails, panel raising, and a few flutes just for fun. It has the appearance and quality of an heirloom keepsake, so it's an excellent candidate for investing in premium lumber and taking your time to get things just right.

by Bill Hylton

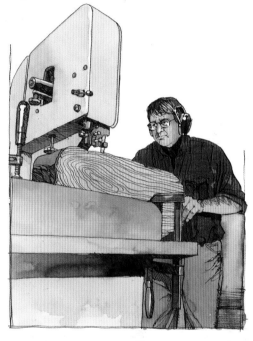

This lidded chest was a dream project for me for about 6 or 7 years before working on this story. For inspiration, I modeled it after a similar chest I saw in the Museum of Early Southern Decorative Arts in Winston-Salem, North Carolina.

A few years later, I created the final design while writing a book about furniture construction, called *Illustrated Cabinetmaking*. It served as the basis for a drawing showing how a frame-and-panel chest should be made.

I got my overall dimensions from the museum. Using a photo, I then worked out the dimensions and made educated guesses as to the joinery and construction of the base, the chest bottom, and the back. With the help of a CAD program, the chest took its final form for this project.

I call it the Eastern Shore Chest because the archetype was built around 1760 in the part of Virginia that's on the eastern shore of the Chesapeake Bay. It's in no way a reproduction or a duplicate of the museum piece. For example, I used cope-and-stick joints, unknown in the 1700s, to construct the frame-and-panel assemblies. I also opted to use some eye-popping walnut rather than choose a painted finish, as found on the original.

Planning and Shopping

This is an ideal project for contemporary, router-cut cope-and-stick joinery. So, you won't find the front, back, and end assemblies constructed with mortise-and-tenon joints. If you happen to have *Illustrated Cabinetmaking*, you can compare the drawings for the "Frame-and-Panel Chest" project with the drawings published here. I changed the construction of the base frame, the style of the breadboard ends on the lid, and the molding profiles.

The most obvious departure from the original chest is the wood and the finish. What better way to highlight the panels than to use highly figured stock and a clear finish? I chose walnut, as it's a native species that might have been used in the 1700s to make a chest like this.

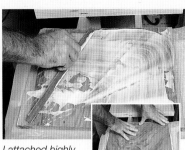

I attached highly figured, shop-made veneer to plain-sawn walnut panels. Apply glue to the panel only. Note that the panel is sitting on a plywood caul protected by wax paper.

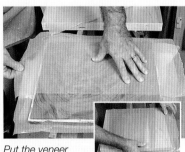

Put the veneer onto the glued panel, and prepare to clamp it up between a sandwich of plywood cauls protected from the excess glue by layers of wax paper.

Use plenty of clamps to ensure that sufficient pressure is applied across the clamping cauls. Allow plenty of time for the glue to cure—at a minimum, overnight.

I opted to use a less costly secondary wood—poplar—for parts of the chest that don't show. This was a common practice in the 1700s, and it still is today. The back assembly, chest floor, back frame member, and feet are all made of poplar.

For hardware, I used a pair of hand-forged fishtail hinges from Dave Fisher of Fisher Forge (610-562-5425, *www.fisherforge.com*), and I bought cut nails—3d and 4d fine finish nails—from Tremont Nail Company (800-842-0560, *www.tremontnail.com*).

Taking Care of the Prep Work

My first job was to redraw the plans, incorporating the changes I wanted to make. Then, I prepared a cutting list, and from that, I estimated the amount of stock I'd need. It's good practice to start a project by roughing out all the parts. This means laying out the parts on your stock and then crosscutting, jointing, and planing the stock to rough dimensions. Mill your parts about 1" longer, ⅛" or ¼" wider, and about ⅛" thicker than their finished sizes. It's also wise to stack up the parts with stickers between them and allow them to acclimate to your shop. There usually is enough of a margin for reflattening a board that develops a modest bow, cup, or twist. Mild twisting did occur with one of my lid boards.

When my wood was ready, I started with the frame-and-panel assemblies, moved on to the base, and then assembled the chest body and mounted it on the base. The lid and moldings were made and installed last.

Before dressing out the working stock, you may want to prepare some poplar and make test cuts with your cope-and-stick bits and with the panel raiser. It will help to establish the settings you'll need for the appearance that suits you.

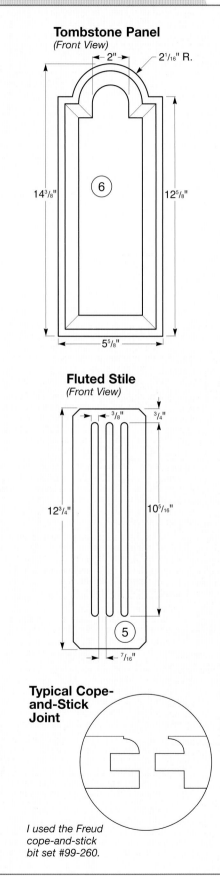

Cabinet Exploded View

Tombstone Panel
(Front View)

2"
2¹/₁₆" R.
14³/₈"
6
12⁵/₈"
5⁵/₈"

Fluted Stile
(Front View)

³/₈"
³/₄"
12³/₄"
10⁵/₁₆"
5
⁷/₁₆"

Typical Cope-and-Stick Joint

I used the Freud cope-and-stick bit set #99-260.

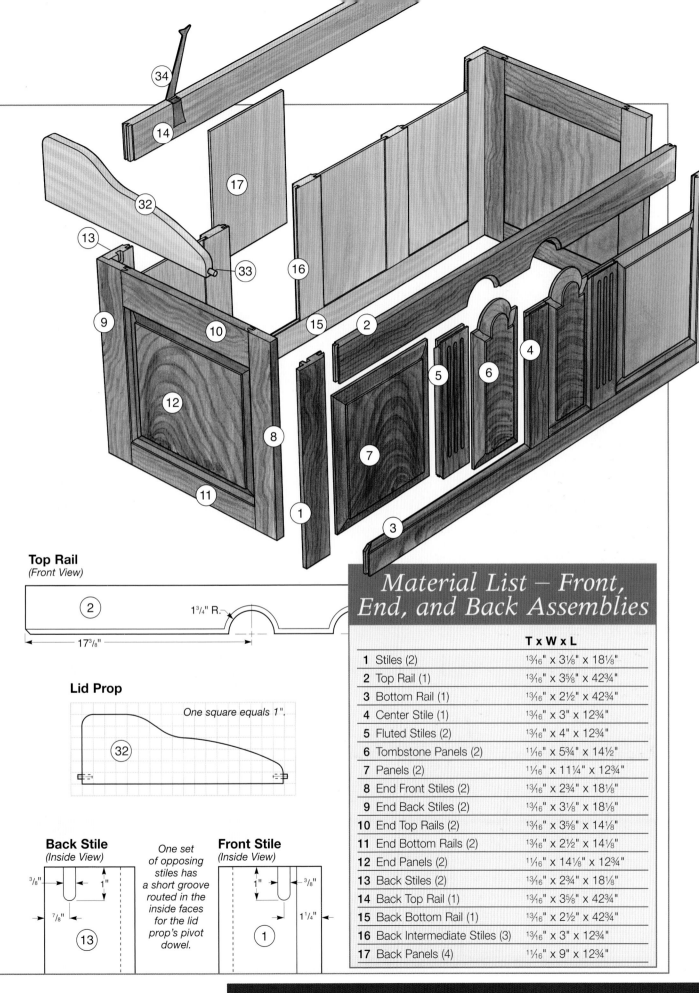

Top Rail
(Front View)

2

$1^3/_4$" R.

$17^3/_8$"

Lid Prop

One square equals 1".

32

Back Stile
(Inside View)

$3/_8$"

1"

$7/_8$"

13

One set of opposing stiles has a short groove routed in the inside faces for the lid prop's pivot dowel.

Front Stile
(Inside View)

1"

$3/_8$"

$1^1/_4$"

1

Material List – Front, End, and Back Assemblies

		T x W x L
1	Stiles (2)	$^{13}/_{16}$" x $3^1/_8$" x $18^1/_8$"
2	Top Rail (1)	$^{13}/_{16}$" x $3^5/_8$" x $42^3/_4$"
3	Bottom Rail (1)	$^{13}/_{16}$" x $2^1/_2$" x $42^3/_4$"
4	Center Stile (1)	$^{13}/_{16}$" x 3" x $12^3/_4$"
5	Fluted Stiles (2)	$^{13}/_{16}$" x 4" x $12^3/_4$"
6	Tombstone Panels (2)	$^{11}/_{16}$" x $5^3/_4$" x $14^1/_2$"
7	Panels (2)	$^{11}/_{16}$" x $11^1/_4$" x $12^3/_4$"
8	End Front Stiles (2)	$^{13}/_{16}$" x $2^3/_4$" x $18^1/_8$"
9	End Back Stiles (2)	$^{13}/_{16}$" x $3^1/_8$" x $18^1/_8$"
10	End Top Rails (2)	$^{13}/_{16}$" x $3^5/_8$" x $14^1/_8$"
11	End Bottom Rails (2)	$^{13}/_{16}$" x $2^1/_2$" x $14^1/_8$"
12	End Panels (2)	$^{11}/_{16}$" x $14^1/_8$" x $12^3/_4$"
13	Back Stiles (2)	$^{13}/_{16}$" x $2^3/_4$" x $18^1/_8$"
14	Back Top Rail (1)	$^{13}/_{16}$" x $3^5/_8$" x $42^3/_4$"
15	Back Bottom Rail (1)	$^{13}/_{16}$" x $2^1/_2$" x $42^3/_4$"
16	Back Intermediate Stiles (3)	$^{13}/_{16}$" x 3" x $12^3/_4$"
17	Back Panels (4)	$^{11}/_{16}$" x 9" x $12^3/_4$"

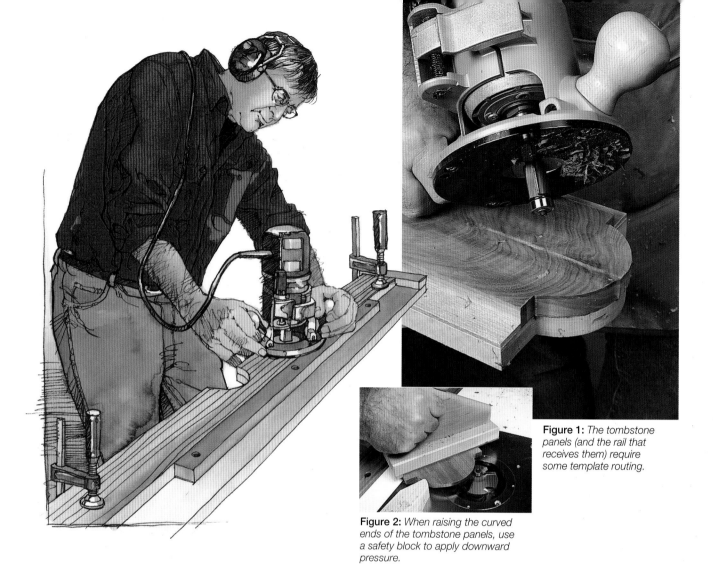

Figure 1: *The tombstone panels (and the rail that receives them) require some template routing.*

Figure 2: *When raising the curved ends of the tombstone panels, use a safety block to apply downward pressure.*

As it turned out, to get the panel profile I wanted, I had to cheat the system. The geometry of panel-raising bits is inflexible. The width of bevel I was after was ¾", not the standard 1". From Freud (*www.freudtools.com*), I bought bit #99-511 to produce the width of bevel I wanted, but the 25° to 26° bevel angle was steeper than desirable. My test cuts showed that to get the correct fillet around the raised field, I'd have to add ⅛6" to the thickness of all my stock. Of course, that meant cutting the sticking profile a little deeper, too. Consequently, the rails and stiles are ¹³⁄₁₆" thick, and the panels are ¹¹⁄₁₆" thick (see the Material List on page 29).

If you experiment similarly with your bits, label the final set of test samples, and save them for use in setting the bits for the actual working cuts.

The next step was to prepare the frame stock and panels. The latter was easy, a matter of dressing the parts to ¹³⁄₁₆", ripping them to width, and crosscutting them to length. The panel blanks were a slightly different matter.

Building the Chest Body

Construction of the chest body is largely a straightforward frame-and-panel affair. In brief, you cut the parts to width and length, rout the copes and then the sticking, raise the panels, and assemble. There are a few departures in this chest, and at least one in the way that I generally prefer to do things.

One of my idiosyncrasies with this type of project is that I like to allow the stiles (just the full-length ones) to run long. It's one less alignment to make during assembly, when things can seem

a little frantic. Instead, I allow some excess to project past the rails. After the glue dries and the clamps come off, I trim off the excess and at the same time square the assembly.

In this chest, you have some intermediate stiles, which must be coped, and a front top rail that must be contoured for the tombstone panels. The two small cutouts can be roughed out with a jigsaw and then routed to match a template. Do this before routing the copes and the sticking. In addition, you have the flutes to cut into the two stiles that flank the tombstone panels.

The panels represent the biggest departures from the norm. What I wanted in the panels was highly figured grain. I also wanted to book-match the pairs of panels, especially on the chest front. What I chose to do, with some help from a friend who had the right tools for the job (specifically, a 20" band saw and a drum sander), was to resaw a block of expensive stock into veneers. I milled stock for the panels from straight-grained walnut and then glued a leaf of veneer to each.

I won't detail here how to resaw on the band saw. Suffice it to say that if your resaw capacity isn't 12" to 13", you can resaw a 6"- to 7"-wide block and book-match the leaves to form wider veneers for the panels.

Once you have the veneers cut, they must be surfaced. Planing veneers can be perilous, even when they are straight grained. Surfacing curly, burl, or crotch-grained veneers is best done on a wide belt sander or drum sander. I was able to smooth the face and back of each leaf at the same time and reduce them to a thickness of just under $\frac{1}{8}$" on a wide drum sander.

The conventional wisdom is that you must veneer both the face and the back to balance the panel. (If you don't, the panel is likely to warp.) Here, the panels are completely trapped in their frames, so it isn't absolutely necessary to veneer the panel backs. I didn't.

Veneering panels for the chest requires a dozen or so clamps, including some deep-throated ones; a couple of pieces of $\frac{3}{4}$" plywood, MDF (medium-density fiberboard), or melamine; and some wax paper. Apply yellow glue to the panel, not the veneer, and then place the veneer on the glue. Spread wax paper on one plywood clamping board, set the panel on it, cover it with more wax paper, and add the second clamping board. (Wax paper prevents squeeze-out from gluing the panel to the plywood.) Then, apply your clamps. (See Veneering Basics on page 28 for more tips.)

Be mindful of how raising the panels will parse their thickness. You

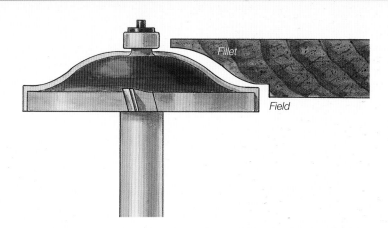

Old-World Panel Geometry Requires Careful Stock Selection

Fillet

Field

When you look at a raised-panel cabinet, the size of the field (the flat center plane) as it relates to the bevel's width (or fillet) helps create the look of the piece. And, of course, the fillet also has to be balanced against the widths of the stiles and rails. Getting the right look can be tricky business!

Most standard panel-raising bits form a 1" fillet. The original cabinet on which this project is based has $\frac{3}{4}$" fillets, made with a hand plane. To achieve a $\frac{3}{4}$"-wide bevel on your cabinet's raised panels, use a Freud #99-511 bit. To create the exact fillet using that specific bit, you'll have to size your stock to these exact thicknesses: $\frac{13}{16}$" for the stiles and rails and $\frac{11}{16}$" for the raised panels.

need a $\frac{1}{4}$"-thick tongue, and you also need the raised field to be the thickness of the veneer. The seam between the substrate and the veneer will show if it falls on the bevel. I raised the panels before working them to final thickness, sneaking up on the "disappearance" of the seam from the bevel. Then, I thickness sanded the panels to get the proper tongue dimension and to reduce the thickness of the raised field.

Raising a Tombstone Panel
The two tombstone panels on the chest front require some extra work—some of it handwork—to shape and raise them. To begin, make a template to shape the two panels (after they've been veneered). I made mine from $\frac{3}{4}$" MDF, and I mounted $\frac{1}{4}$"-thick fences to

locate the panel. After cutting the rough contour on the top of a panel, set it on your template, clamp it securely, and then use a router and flush-trimming bit to rout it to match the template (see Figure 1). Of course, the tight inside corners will have to be pared square with a chisel.

Raise the panel on the router table next. Because of the arch, you can't use the fence to raise the top edge, but you can—and should—use it when raising the side and bottom edges. To reduce tearout, do the top edge first (see Figure 2), and then do one side, the bottom, and the second side. Now comes the handwork. (Relax … the panels are small, and there are only two of them.)

Lay out the inside corners on the raised field and at the shoulders of the

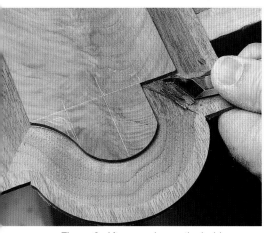

Figure 3: *After squaring up the inside corners of the field with your bench chisels, switch to skew chisels—first right and then left—to finish the fillet.*

tongue that borders the bevel. Draw a line across the outside corners of the raised field, and then drop perpendicular lines from the arch to this shoulder line. The line at the tongue can be sketched freehand.

With your bench chisels, cut away the inside corners of the raised field. You want square, straight shoulders. That done, use a small rule and a utility knife to slice a line from the inside corner of the field to the inside corner at the edge of the panel. This is the juncture

between the planes of the bevel. You must pare the bevels to this line, sloping them to match the rest of the bevel. For this work, you'll need a pair of skewed chisels—one angled left, the other angled right (see Figure 3).

Assemble the units one at a time. The end units are easy, since each is composed of only two rails, two stiles, and a panel. The front and back units are more involved, so a dry run is essential. Make sure that the parts go together easily, that your alignment marks are in place, and that all of your clamps are at hand. Here's the assembly sequence:

1. Apply glue with a small brush to the stub tenon on the center stile, and push the tenon into the top rail. Use a center mark on the stile, and align it with a mark on the rail. Apply a clamp to seat the stile.

2. Fit the panels in place—no glue, of course, to allow for wood movement.

3. Apply glue to the flanking intermediate stiles, and fit them to the rail. Apply clamps to seat and hold them.

4. Install the remaining panels.

5. Remove the clamps, and tip the assembly up so glue can be applied to the stub tenons on the three stiles.

6. Fit the bottom rail onto the assembly. Use center marks to align the rail without having to slide it (to keep glue out of the groove so it won't stick to the panel).

7. Apply glue to the rail ends. and fit the full-length stiles.

8. Extend long clamps across the assembly at each rail, and then reapply clamps across the assembly at each stile.

That's it. Once the units all are assembled, trimmed, and sanded, cut the rabbets that join them. You also need to cut a stopped dado in the front and back for the lid prop. That done, assemble the four units to form the chest body.

Building the Base

The base frame, upon which the chest body rests, is a flat frame formed from three pieces of 5/4 walnut (the front and two end members) and one piece of 5/4 poplar (the back member). The back joins the ends with mortise-and-loose-tenon joints. The ends and front are joined with splined miters. Mill the stock, and cut the parts (see the Material List on page 35). Then, cut the joints, and glue your frame together.

Making the feet is more involved. Each is an assembly, consisting of two shaped faces joined end-to-end in a miter joint and reinforced with a triangular glue block. The assembled feet are simply glued to the underside of the base frame at the corners.

Begin constructing the feet by making a cardboard pattern, using the drawings at right. Note that the faces for the ends of the chest are ½" narrower than those on the front. The back faces are simple poplar blocks.

Cut the blanks to size next. First, mill the stock to ⅞" thick and rip it to width. Then, cut a 45° bevel on one end of each piece. While you can trace the contour of the bracket on the blank, cut to the line on the band saw, and smooth the edges, I took a different tack. First, I laid out the centerpoints of the concave arcs on each blank, measuring from the bottom and the beveled edges. At the drill press, I used Forstner bits to bore holes at these spots (see Figure 4). This ensured

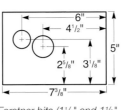

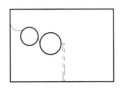

Figure 4: *Lay out the centerpoints of the concave arcs on each blank, measuring from the bottom and the beveled edges. Then, use appropriately sized Forstner bits (1⅛" and 1½", respectively) to bore holes at these spots.*

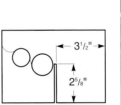

Figure 5: *Next, trace the pattern onto each face, using the holes to orient the pattern. Remember that there are left and right, as well as end and front, pieces.*

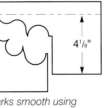

Figure 6: *Cut the vertical shoulder on the table saw. That way, you'll get a straight cut of a consistent height on each blank. White pencil or chalk is easier to see on walnut than a regular pencil line is.*

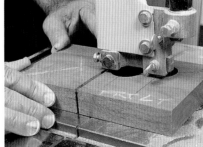

Figure 7: *Use the band saw to cut the convex arcs, freeing the waste (which is the perfect size to use as glue blocks later, when attaching the feet). Sand the saw marks smooth using a drum sander on your drill press.*

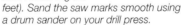

that the arcs would be consistently sized and placed. After tracing the pattern onto each face (see Figure 5), I cut the vertical shoulder on the table saw, which ensured a straight cut of a consistent height on each blank (see Figure 6). On the band saw, I cut the convex arcs, freeing the waste (see Figure 7). Use the waste as glue blocks later, when attaching the feet.

After sanding the contoured edges (use a drum sander chucked in your drill press), rip the excess from each face. Glue the feet together in two stages, assembling the miters first and then adding the glue blocks (see Figure 8 on page 34). As you do this, be sure to create the assemblies you need (that is, glue a right front face to a left side face). Glue the feet to the frame.

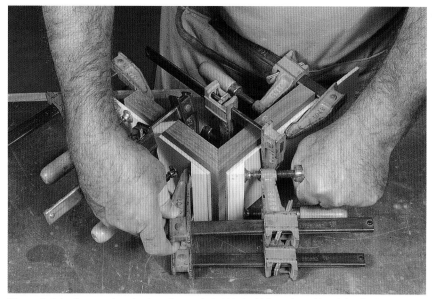

Figure 8: *I made some handy clamping cauls to help hold the mitered foot joint firmly. The triangular blocks are glued to ¼" plywood. The plywood is then clamped to the foot blank, and pressure is applied to the triangular blocks—easy and effective.*

Mounting the Body on the Base

Once the chest body and the base assembly are glued up, you can join them. Set the chest body bottom on the bench or assembly table. Apply a bead of glue to the edges, and align the base on it. Mark the center of the body and the base, and line up the two marks, making sure the back edge of the base is flush with the plane of the chest back. Apply a couple of clamps to hold things in place. Then, drill pilot holes, and drive twelve 4d cut nails through the base into the edges of the chest body.

Make and install the chest floor next. Use random-width strips of poplar, thicknessed to ¾", for this. Cut shiplaps on the edges, and fit the strips one by one to the chest, as shown in the drawings on page 35. Install the strips with 3d cut nails.

While you're working on the chest, make and fit the lid prop. A till was a common feature on chests like this, and the till lid doubled as a prop for the chest lid. You'd open the chest lid, lift the till lid just past perpendicular, and then lower the chest lid against its corner. I didn't include the till, but I did adapt the till lid as a lid prop.

Cut the prop, and trim it to just fit between the front and back of the chest. Bore a hole into each end for a pivot dowel, and drive a dowel into each hole, trimming as necessary so they'll drop more easily into the dadoes cut for the purpose. Shape the prop however you like, but leave it about 6" wide at the back end so it can support the lid. That corner can be trimmed after the lid is hinged to the chest.

For the base molding, use a cove-and-bead profile, which you can make on the router table with a ⅜"-radius roundover bit and a ½"-diameter roundnose bit. Form the profile on both edges of a long strip of walnut, and then rip them from the blank. Crosscut the parts to rough length, and then miter cut the ends and glue them to the chest and base.

Making the Breadboard Lid

The lid is a broad panel with breadboard ends—mitered at the front and square at the back. The molding along the front edge and across the ends has a quarter-round profile, with a Roman ogee below it forming the lip. The lid is hinged to the chest with hand-forged fishtail hinges.

Breadboard ends help prevent the broad panel from cupping and also make it easier to attach the lid molding across the ends, since you end up with a long-grain-to-long-grain glue joint. The joints present the challenge. The breadboard end is cross-grain, so gluing it securely to the end of the lid virtually guarantees the panel will buckle in humid conditions and split in dry ones. I decided to use an unglued sliding dovetail to mount the ends to the panel. Since the ends are joined to the lid at the front with miters, glue them there.

Here's how to make the lid: Start with 5/4 stock, face jointing and planing it to ⅞" thick (see the Material List on page 36). Cut the two breadboard ends, and set them aside. Next, edge glue boards to form a panel 19⅞" wide and 50" long. Rip the panel to exactly 17⅛". The 2⅝" strip that you end up with (⅛" is lost to the cut) will be mitered and become the front edge that joins the breadboard ends. Finally, cut equal amounts from both ends of the panel, reducing its length to 44¾".

Cutting Sliding Dovetail Joints

Rout a centered dovetail groove in one edge of each breadboard end. Use a ½", 7° or 8° dovetail bit and make the groove exactly ¾" deep. It's beneficial to use a 5⁄16" straight bit to rout

Figure 9: *After plowing a 5⁄16" groove centered on the edge of the breadboard ends (to remove most of the waste), form a ¾"-deep dovetail groove.*

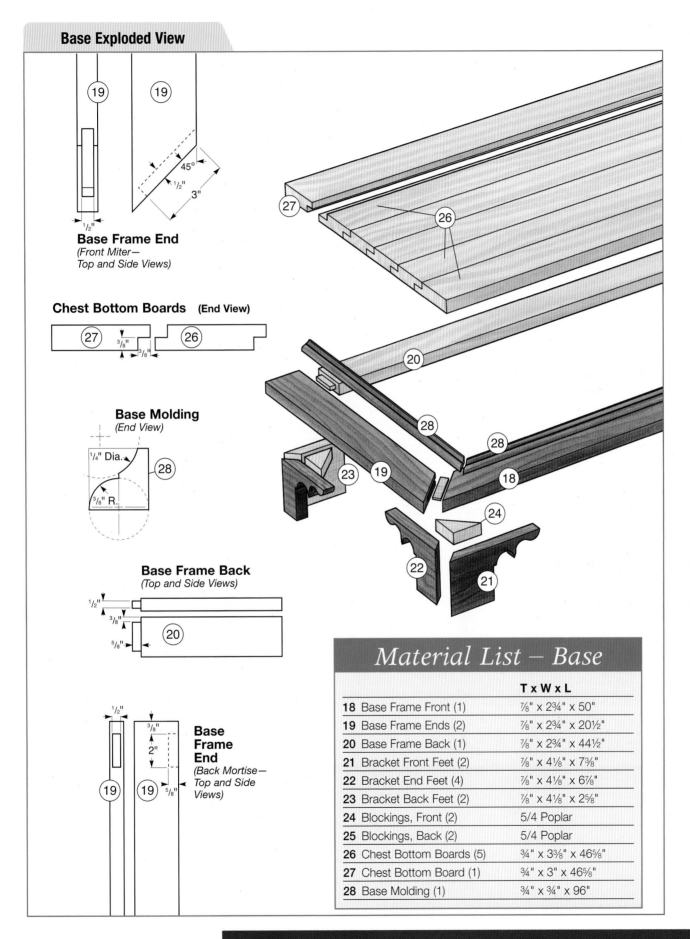

Base Exploded View

Base Frame End
*(Front Miter—
Top and Side Views)*

45°
1/2"
3"
1/2"

Chest Bottom Boards   **(End View)**

27   3/8"   3/8"   26

Base Molding
(End View)

1/4" Dia.
3/8" R.
28

Base Frame Back
(Top and Side Views)

1/2"
3/8"
5/8"
20

**Base
Frame
End**
*(Back Mortise—
Top and Side
Views)*

1/2"
3/8"
2"
5/8"
19   19

Material List – Base		
		T x W x L
18 Base Frame Front (1)		⅞" x 2¾" x 50"
19 Base Frame Ends (2)		⅞" x 2¾" x 20½"
20 Base Frame Back (1)		⅞" x 2¾" x 44½"
21 Bracket Front Feet (2)		⅞" x 4⅛" x 7⅜"
22 Bracket End Feet (4)		⅞" x 4⅛" x 6⅞"
23 Bracket Back Feet (2)		⅞" x 4⅛" x 2⅝"
24 Blockings, Front (2)		5/4 Poplar
25 Blockings, Back (2)		5/4 Poplar
26 Chest Bottom Boards (5)		¾" x 3⅜" x 46⅝"
27 Chest Bottom Board (1)		¾" x 3" x 46⅝"
28 Base Molding (1)		¾" x ¾" x 96"

Lid Exploded View

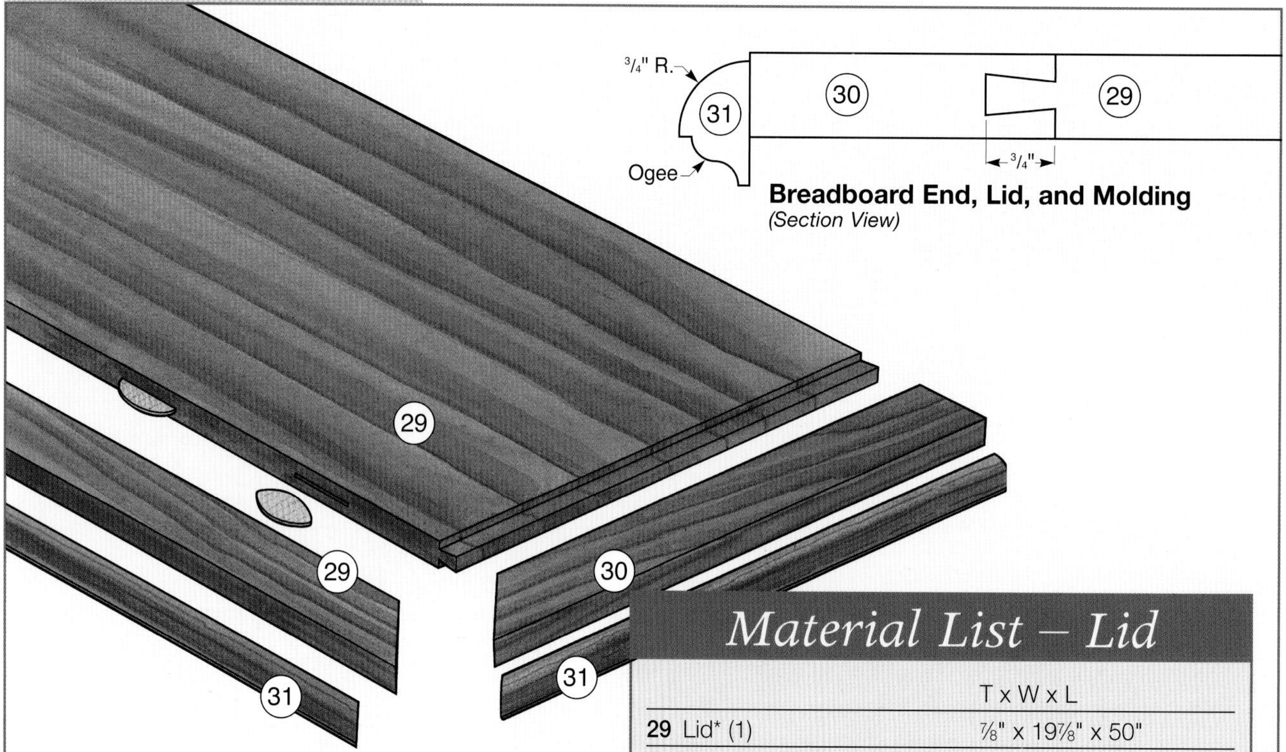

Material List – Lid

	T x W x L
29 Lid* (1)	7/8" x 19 7/8" x 50"
30 Breadboard Ends (2)	7/8" x 2 5/8" x 19 3/4"
31 Molding (1)	3/4" x 1 1/4" x 90"
32 Lid Prop (1)	3/4" x 6" x 17 7/8"
33 Pivots (2)	3/8" Dia. x 1 1/4" Dowel
34 Strap Hinges (2)	Wrought Iron

** Overall size; after ripping the front edge off, the length is trimmed to 44 3/4".*

a centered groove first. This eliminates as much waste as possible before switching to the dovetail bit and forming the dovetail groove (see Figure 9 on page 34).

When you cut the grooves, also cut the same groove in a gauge made of the same stock as the breadboard ends. (Use the scrap crosscut from the panel, for example.) The gauge should be about 4" long.

The next process is to cut a mating dovetail on both ends of the panel (see Figure 10). Don't touch the bit as you change over the table setup. You need to use the same height setting for the tail that you did for the slots. Just shift the fence to house all but an edge of the bit. Make setup cuts on your scraps of the lid stock, sneaking up on the width of dovetail that fits the grooves you've already cut. When the fence setting is perfect, cut a dovetail across each end.

Now, miter the breadboard ends and the strip ripped from the panel. The ends are easy, but the panel strip must fit just right. The miter-to-miter distance must exactly match the shoulder-to-shoulder length of the lid. Miter one end of the strip, and then clamp it to the panel to mark the opposite end.

To help align the mitered element with the lid when regluing it to the lid, use biscuits. After mitering the ends, clamp the strip in place, mark the biscuit locations, and then cut the slots.

Assemble the lid. First, drive the breadboard ends onto the dovetails—no glue, remember. It helps to clamp the front strip to the panel—again, no glue—while you do this. Then, remove the strip, spread glue along its edge and on the miters, and remount it. Install clamping forms for flat miters to the lid as you do this, so you can apply a clamp perpendicular to each miter.

Adding the Lid Molding

The lid molding consists of two profiles routed on the same piece of wood. Because it's easier to glue and clamp it to the lid while it's square, hold off routing the large quarter-round profile until after the molding is glued in place on the lid.

Rout the Roman ogee profile before mounting it. Mill this ogee on both edges of a strip about 3" wide and 52" long. Then, rip the strip into two 1½"-wide strips. Halve one strip, miter the ends, and glue them to the lid.

After the glue is dry and any squeeze-out cleaned up, rout the quarter-round with a ¾"-radius roundover bit. The pilot bearing will hang below the profile, so you must use an edge guide to control the cut.

When you are done, sand the molding well to remove the mill marks.

Installing the Hinges

The hand-forged hinges I chose look great and work well (see Figure 11). The leaf that mounts to the lid is 16" long, and the one that mounts to the chest has a right-angle bend. It sits on the top edge of the back and extends down the inside face. To accommodate the barrel, the chest leaf must be recessed into the chest back. Form a notch in the top rail that's about ½" deep.

Mount the hinges to the lid first. Line them up on the underside with the hinge pins parallel to the edge. (It may not be perfectly square, but that's the charm of handmade hardware.) Then, screw them in place. Set the lid and hinges on the top back edge of the chest, and mark along the hinges in the chest edge. Cut the notches. I found that I could set the lid in place, with the hinges down in the notches and the prop holding the lid open. It stayed that way, freeing my hands for drilling pilots and driving the remaining screws.

Finishing Up

I used multiple coats of Waterlox to finish my chest. I brushed on the first and second coats and then applied subsequent coats with a soft, lint-free cloth. A rubdown with fine steel wool between coats ensured a smooth finish. Clean up all the dust and debris with tack cloths before applying more finish.

This dream project was a long time in the works, but as you can see by the results, it was well worth the wait. Good luck with yours!

Figure 10: *Sliding dovetails are the perfect joint choice when wood movement is an issue. Mill these on the router table using a tall auxiliary fence to support the workpiece.*

Figure 11: *The lid prop, supported by two short dowels, holds the finished cabinet open, exposing the hand-forged hinges.*

Jelly Cupboard Reproduction

Sometimes, the best way to learn furniture design is to reproduce an antique. That's what you'll do in this project, using measurements and joints taken directly from a century-old cupboard. The original was built solely with hand tools, so for a real trip back in time, sharpen up yours and try to do the same.

by Tim Johnson

The genesis for this jelly cupboard came from a 100-year-old antique I stumbled upon in an antiques store. The fact that so many cupboards like this one have survived for a century or more is testimony to the integrity of their construction. Working with little more than planes, saws, and hammers, the builders combined common sense with efficiency and often designed their cabinets based on an ancient Greek standard of proportions. I've followed the dimensions and construction methods of the original closely in my rendition here.

Choosing Stock

Once you've bought your project lumber, set aside the best straight-grained pieces for the face frame and door frames, and choose interestingly patterned pieces for the door panels. Try to select pieces that are similar in color. Choose your next-best boards for the sides and the remaining stock for the top—a slightly crowned grain pattern on the top's front edge is a nice touch. Remember, this cabinet is so simple that the visual impact of the wood becomes an important design element.

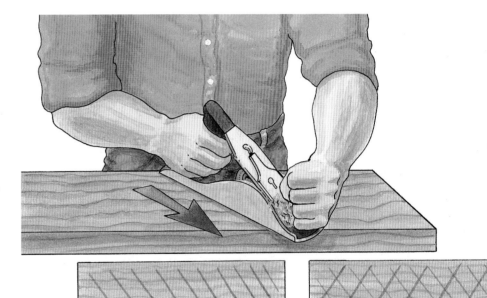

Figure 1: *If you choose to flatten your project panels with a hand plane, make diagonal passes across the panels in both directions. Finish by taking cleanup strokes along the length of the stock to remove any planing marks.*

Getting Started

Look over the Material List on page 43. Then, begin building your reproduction by milling stock and joining it into oversize panels for the shelves (pieces 1). Make a couple of shelves 12" longer than necessary so you'll have testing material when you get to the joint-fitting stage later on. After the glue dries, plane the shelves flat, first planing diagonally in one direction and then in the other to create an X pattern (see Figure 1). Be sure to plane both sides of each shelf this way. Then, smooth the surfaces by taking light passes along the grain.

Now, mill and join stock for the sides and top (pieces 2 and 3), and plane these panels just as you did the shelves. Once you've finished planing, joint one edge of each side panel and cut the panels to size. Make sure the two panels match exactly, and check their ends for squareness. Complete the same steps with the top, but rip it ¼" wider than its finished width, and then rip the panel again to a width of 15¾".

The objective is to rip the front edge off the top now so you can rout the grooves easily, and then glue it back on after the joints are completed.

Machining the Sides and Top

The construction of many older cabinets focuses on a single joinery technique. On this cupboard, the shelves connect with the sides, and the sides to the top, with barefaced, dovetailed housing joints (see the joint detail drawing on page 42). The builder of the original cupboard chose this joint because it's fairly easy to cut with hand tools.

To form the joint, start by installing a ⅝" dado blade in your table saw and plowing ⅜"-deep dadoes in the top and sides, as shown in the shelf locations drawing on page 43. Cut a few dadoes in some scrap wood, as well, for use as testing material.

Next, make three hardboard baseplates for your router, to use for cutting the dovetailed shoulders on the dadoes and the tails on the ends of the shelves and sides. Make these plates to match your router's current baseplate; for example, the round one shown in Figure 2 is for a Porter-Cable router. Now, make two ½"-wide x ¼"-thick hardwood strips to serve as baseplate fences, and drill a router bit clearance hole in each one.

Screw a baseplate to your router, and chuck a 14° dovetail bit in the collet. Lower the bit ⅜" to match the depth of the dadoes you just cut. Now, position a fence on the baseplate, as shown in Step 1 of Figure 2. When the fence is set correctly, mark its position, and glue it to the plate (5-minute epoxy works great here). Test this setup on scrap wood to see that the bit just grazes the top corner of the dado wall.

Given that dadoes that are cut on the table saw usually have slightly irregular bottoms due to the imperfections of the panels, the router bit pass will probably shave the high spots. But since the bit isn't as wide as the dadoes, you'll need to make a second pass to level the dado bottoms. Switch to the second shop-made baseplate. Glue on a fence the same way you did before, but this time position it as shown in Step 2 of Figure 2. Once the epoxy sets, rout the remaining ridges in the dado bottoms. When you've completed the routing, glue the cutoff piece from the top back to the panel, and trim its front edge to bring the top to final width.

Routing the Tails

The third baseplate makes routing the tails on the shelves and sides a breeze. Keep the dovetail bit set to the depth of the dadoes, and secure a scrap piece from a side panel in your bench vise. Now, install your adjustable router fence, and set it as shown in Figure 3. Rout the end of the scrap piece, and check the tail's fit in a dado. If it's too big or small, continue adjusting the fence until you get a perfect slip fit.

To find the exact shelf length you need, rout two pieces of side panel scrap, and then slide them into the dadoes in the top. Measure the distance between them, and add the depths of

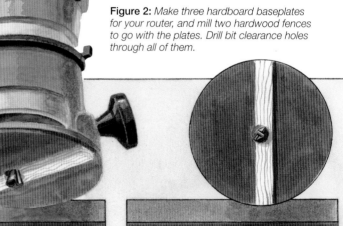

Figure 2: *Make three hardboard baseplates for your router, and mill two hardwood fences to go with the plates. Drill bit clearance holes through all of them.*

Step 1: *Mount a fence to your first baseplate to position the dovetail bit so it just grazes the upper outside corner of the dado.*

Step 2: *Mount a fence to your second baseplate so the dovetail bit just grazes the lower inside corner of the dado.*

two dadoes. The result is the perfect shelf length for your cabinet. Now, joint and rip your shelves to width, and crosscut them to the length you just calculated. Make sure the ends are square, and then rout the tails. Follow the same procedure to rout tails on the top end of each side panel.

Before assembling the carcass, cut rabbets in the sides and top for the back (pieces 4 through 6). Install a ½" dado blade in your table saw, and clamp an auxiliary face to the fence. Cut ⅜"-deep rabbets in the sides and a ½"-deep rabbet in the top. Be sure to stop the rabbet in the top 2⅞" from each end. After squaring the ends of the top rabbet with a chisel, lay out the feet pattern on the sides, following the drawings on pages 42–43. Cut out the waste with a jigsaw, and sand the edges smooth.

Assembling the Carcass

To begin assembling the carcass, have a friend hold the sides on their back edges while you slide the top onto the tails—but without using glue. This will hold the assembly steady while you glue the shelves in position. Spread a slow-setting glue, such as urea resin or hide glue, into the dadoes for one shelf and on the back 4" or so of the shelf's tails. Slide the shelf into position, tapping it with a hammer and block if necessary. Slipping ½"-thick scrap pieces into the rabbets in the sides will keep the shelves from sliding through.

Repeat this procedure for all four shelves, and then draw the assembly tight with bar clamps and cauls (see Figure 4). You can use square-headed nails to pull the joints tight if you wish. Be sure to check the cabinet for squareness and clean up any squeeze-out after the glue becomes rubbery. Allow the cabinet to sit overnight, and then glue the top to the sides.

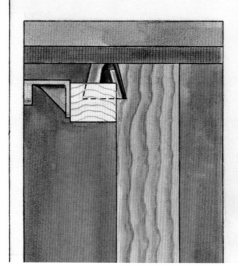

Figure 3: *To rout the tails, mount the third baseplate on your router, and guide the cut with your router's straightedge fence.*

⁷⁄₈" *The key to ending up with tight joints is to size the tails so they just barely slip into the dadoes.*

Cut the tails to fit the dadoes in the sides and top.

Plane the front edge of each shelf flush with the sides, and sand and finish the inside if you want (the old-timers usually left the inside unfinished).

Mill ½"-thick poplar for the cabinet back, and cut the back pieces to size. Next, rabbet the edges of the back pieces, as shown in the back elevation drawing on page 42. Cut tapers on the bottoms of pieces 4 to match the front stiles, as shown in the face frame elevation drawing on page 43. Glue and nail pieces 4 and 6 into place, making sure you avoid nailing through the rabbets. Now, slide the remaining panels (pieces 5) into position, center them, and drive one nail at each shelf location and at

the top rabbet. This arrangement will allow for plenty of wood movement.

Making the Cabinet Face Frame

Mill the face frame stock (pieces 7 and 8) to thickness. Then, joint and rip the stiles ¹⁄₁₆" wider than their finished dimension and the rail to actual size. Cut the pieces to length, double-checking the Material List dimensions against your carcass to determine the correct measurements. Cut the taper on the bottom of each stile, using the face frame elevation drawing on page 43.

Now, form the tongue-and-groove joints on the face frame. First, rout a groove in each stile, as shown in

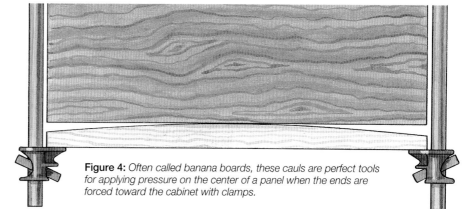

Figure 4: *Often called banana boards, these cauls are perfect tools for applying pressure on the center of a panel when the ends are forced toward the cabinet with clamps.*

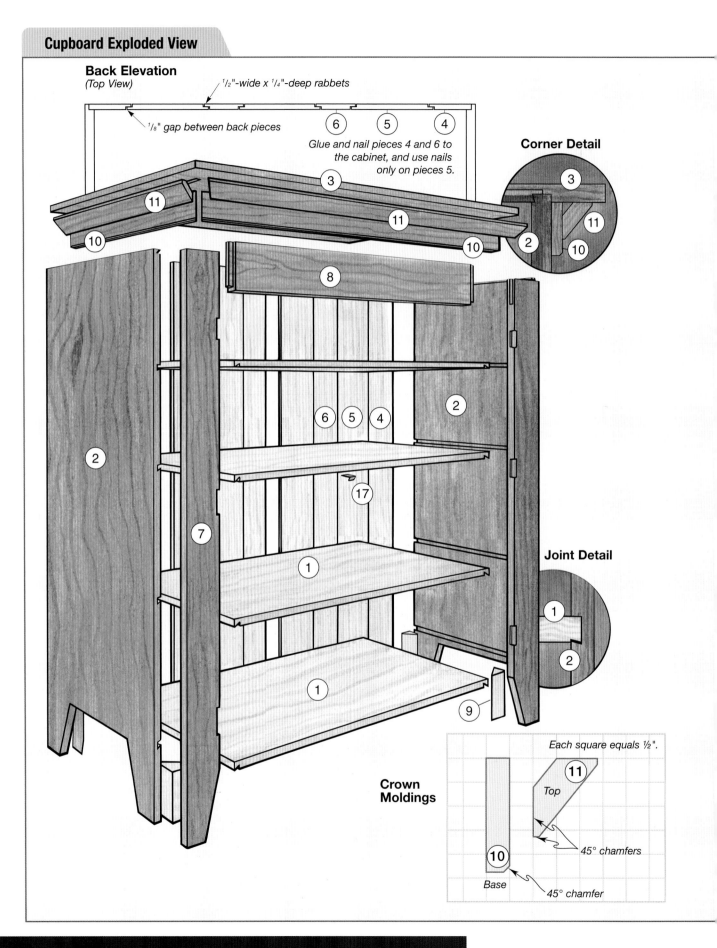

Back Elevation
(Top View)

$1/2$"-wide x $1/4$"-deep rabbets

$1/8$" gap between back pieces

6 5 4

Glue and nail pieces 4 and 6 to
the cabinet, and use nails
only on pieces 5.

Corner Detail

Joint Detail

**Crown
Moldings**

Each square equals ½".

Top

45° chamfers

Base

45° chamfer

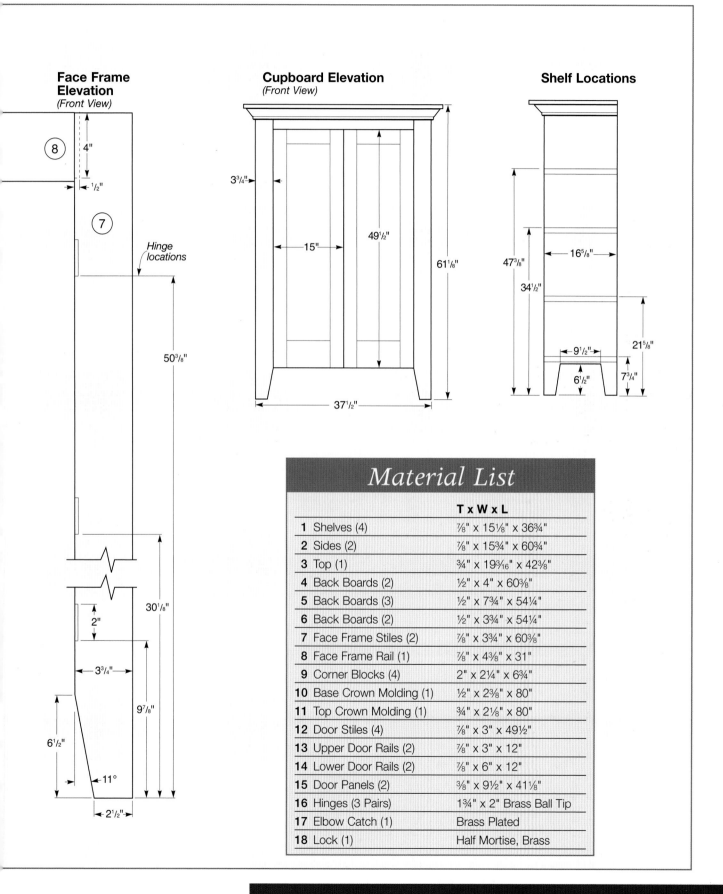

Face Frame Elevation
(Front View)

8

4"

1/2"

7

Hinge locations

50³/₈"

30¹/₈"

2"

3³/₄"

9⁷/₈"

6¹/₂"

11°

2¹/₂"

Cupboard Elevation
(Front View)

3³/₄"

15"

49¹/₂"

61¹/₈"

37¹/₂"

Shelf Locations

47³/₈"

34¹/₂"

16⁵/₈"

9¹/₂"

6¹/₂"

21⁵/₈"

7³/₄"

Material List

		T x W x L
1	Shelves (4)	⁷/₈" x 15¹/₈" x 36³/₄"
2	Sides (2)	⁷/₈" x 15³/₄" x 60³/₄"
3	Top (1)	³/₄" x 19⁹/₁₆" x 42³/₈"
4	Back Boards (2)	¹/₂" x 4" x 60³/₈"
5	Back Boards (3)	¹/₂" x 7³/₄" x 54¹/₄"
6	Back Boards (2)	¹/₂" x 3³/₄" x 54¹/₄"
7	Face Frame Stiles (2)	⁷/₈" x 3³/₄" x 60³/₈"
8	Face Frame Rail (1)	⁷/₈" x 4⁵/₈" x 31"
9	Corner Blocks (4)	2" x 2¹/₄" x 6³/₄"
10	Base Crown Molding (1)	¹/₂" x 2⁵/₈" x 80"
11	Top Crown Molding (1)	³/₄" x 2¹/₈" x 80"
12	Door Stiles (4)	⁷/₈" x 3" x 49¹/₂"
13	Upper Door Rails (2)	⁷/₈" x 3" x 12"
14	Lower Door Rails (2)	⁷/₈" x 6" x 12"
15	Door Panels (2)	³/₈" x 9¹/₂" x 41¹/₈"
16	Hinges (3 Pairs)	1³/₄" x 2" Brass Ball Tip
17	Elbow Catch (1)	Brass Plated
18	Lock (1)	Half Mortise, Brass

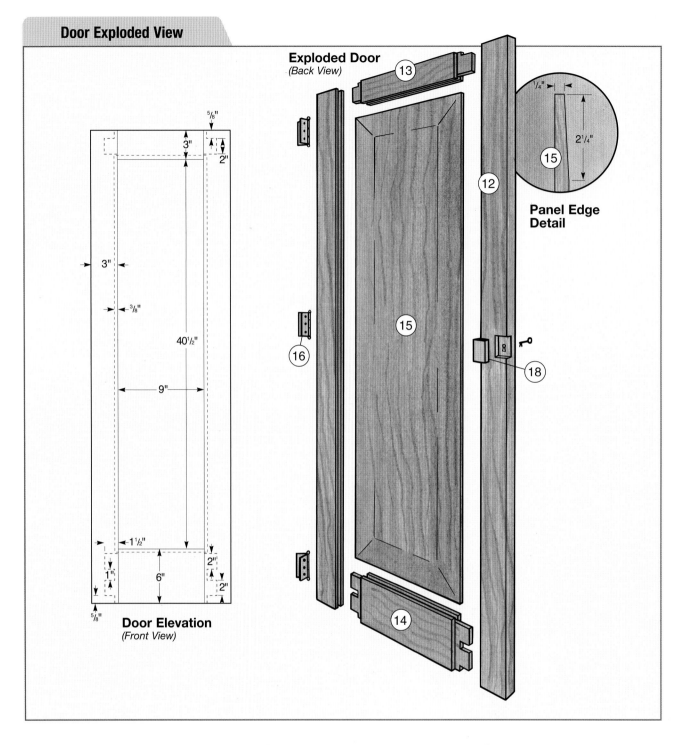

Exploded Door
(Back View)

Panel Edge Detail

5/8"
3"
2"
3"
3/8"
40 1/2"
9"
1 1/2"
2"
1"
6"
2"
2"
5/8"

Door Elevation
(Front View)

1/4"
2 1/4"

the face frame elevation drawing, and then use your table saw to cut tenons on the rail to fit the stile grooves.

Dry assemble the frame, and check its fit against the carcass—I cut a temporary lower rail that helped keep the frame square. When everything is in order, disassemble the frame, apply glue to the joints, and clamp it back together. Remember to check for squareness.

Glue the face frame to the carcass, letting the stiles stick out from each side about 1/16", and don't forget to glue the rail to the top. On the original cabinet, one nail was driven through the frame at each shelf location to stiffen the shelves. Allow the glue to cure. Then, glue blocks (pieces 9) into the corners formed by each pair of legs, and plane the stile edges flush with the sides.

Cut the crown moldings (pieces 10 and 11) to shape, as shown in the patterns and the corner detail drawing on page 42, and miter them to length. Glue and nail the front base molding to the cabinet, but for the sake of wood movement, glue only the first 4" of the side base moldings. Glue and nail the top moldings to the base molding. Be sure to glue all the miters.

Making the Doors

Mill your door frame stock to thickness, and then joint and rip the rails and stiles (pieces 12 through 14) to width. Using the table saw and a ¼" dado blade, machine the grooves for housing the panels. Set the rip fence on the saw to center the blade on your stock, and raise the blade to ⅜". Now, run the appropriate edges of the stiles and rails through the blade.

Lay out the mortises, as shown in the door elevation drawing on page 44, and then clear out the waste. Cut the door mortises using whatever method you prefer. To allow for seasonal movement, cut the lower mortises for the bottom rail tenons about ⅛" wider than called for in the door elevation.

Following the door elevation, form the rail tenons with your table saw, dado blade, and miter gauge. Make sure the cuts are square to the stock, and size the thickness of the tenons for a snug fit in the mortises. Cut the gap in the bottom rail tenons with a handsaw and chisel, as shown in Figure 5.

Now, mill and size the door panels (pieces 15), remembering to allow for seasonal movement when ripping them to width (the panel width called for in the Material List is a compromise between seasonal extremes). Use a hand plane to taper the back edges

Figure 5: *Once you've formed the tenons with your table saw, dado blade, and miter gauge, cut the gap in each lower rail tenon with a handsaw.*

of the panels, as shown in the panel edge detail drawing on page 44, until they fit into the frame grooves. This procedure is just like making old-fashioned raised panels—except in this case, the flat side will show on the front of the door.

Once the panels fit in the door frames, sand them, and then apply finish to prevent unfinished wood from becoming exposed when the panels shrink. Spread glue in the mortises, the tenon haunches, and the first 1" of the tenon cheeks, and assemble the doors, keeping them flat and square.

Mortise the doors and face frame stiles for the loose-pin butt hinges (pieces 16). Loose-pin hinges allow you to remove the doors easily during the fitting process (driving screws in and out

of the wood too many times would strip the pilot holes). Mount the doors, and then plane their overlapping edges to a perfect fit, bearing in mind the season as you establish the gap between the doors. It's easier to shave a little material off later than it is to add it back on.

Following tradition, the right door latches to the left door, and the left door latches to the cabinet. An elbow catch (piece 17) will firmly hold the left door to a shelf, and a half-mortise lock (piece 18) is ideal for the right door. Be sure to notch the left door so it can accept the lock plunger, and install an escutcheon in the keyhole. As on the original cupboard, the key to the lock acts as the pull for the doors.

Finishing Up

After sanding the cabinet thoroughly, seal it with a washcoat of shellac, and then finish with two coats of a quality varnish. In the old days, these cabinets were almost always painted, so a color finish is appropriate if you prefer to go that route instead.

Once you've constructed your own jelly cupboard, I know you'll appreciate what those old-timers accomplished with just a few hand tools. If you're lucky, someday a woodworker may happen upon your cupboard and decide that it's worth reproducing.

---

*Quick*Tip

Shop-Made Logs

Even a benchtop planer produces more shavings than one knows what to do with, and if you use a lathe, you know that the chips can form a mountain in no time. One way to put shavings and chips to one last bit of good use is to make your own shop logs. Lay a sheet of newspaper on your bench or worktable, pile on the shavings, and roll it into a tight sausage. After three or more layers of newspaper, secure the ends and center with string, and your log is ready for the fireplace.

Angler's Cabinet

If you love to fish, you're sure to have a closet full of fishing gear to contend with. This handsome pine angler's cabinet provides plenty of storage for rods, tackle boxes, waders, and anything else you might need for a day on the water.

by Rick White

When free time rolls around, you can generally find me in one of two places: in my shop doing some woodworking or on my boat doing some fishing. For me, one common denominator between woodworking and fishing is the absolute necessity of having the proper tool for the job. When I need a mortising machine or maybe a Fenwick fishing rod, I buy it. It gets troubling, however, when all those tools start to accumulate. Storing tools can be a challenge, whether it be in the workshop or in the den with those trophy-fishing mounts.

Hence, this storage cabinet, specifically designed to hide—er, store—my ever-growing collection of fishing tackle. I chose knotty pine lumber and plywood for this project to reflect my Northwoods heritage, and I lined the interior of the cabinet with ¼" tongue-and-groove pine paneling to add visual interest.

Storage Is the Key

By making use of every inch of interior space, I am able to store a ton of stuff in this cabinet and retain a relatively small footprint. Each door is a swinging cabinet of its own, holding rods, reels, nets, stringers, and other gear. The trade-off is that this unit is very tall—just a few inches

short of an 8' ceiling. (Check your ceiling's height before you build; you may need to adjust the cabinet's height.) The shelves are adjustable and include a couple of full-extension drawers for monofilament line (to keep it out of the light, since it can break down from ultraviolet rays) and other smaller items such as special reels and tools. To build the interlocking drawer joints, I even bought a new drawer lock router bit—more about that in the exploded view drawing on page 52.

The casework design for this cabinet is basically two big boxes that share a base and decorative top. Heavy-duty wraparound piano hinges support the doors, and some fancy, fish-shaped pulls dress the unit. If you have a well-outfitted shop and a measure of determination, you might be able to polish off this piece in a long weekend.

Constructing the Big Boxes

Review the Material List on page 49. Then, slice up your sheet stock first, cutting the four sides and their tops and bottoms (pieces 1 and 2) from knotty pine plywood (see Cutting Diagram for ¾" Knotty Pine Plywood on page 52). I chose to make one large box for each compartment of the cabinet. After you assemble each box, slice the

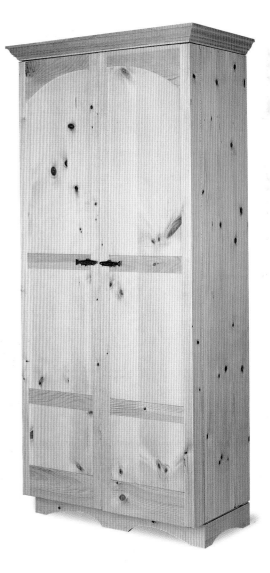

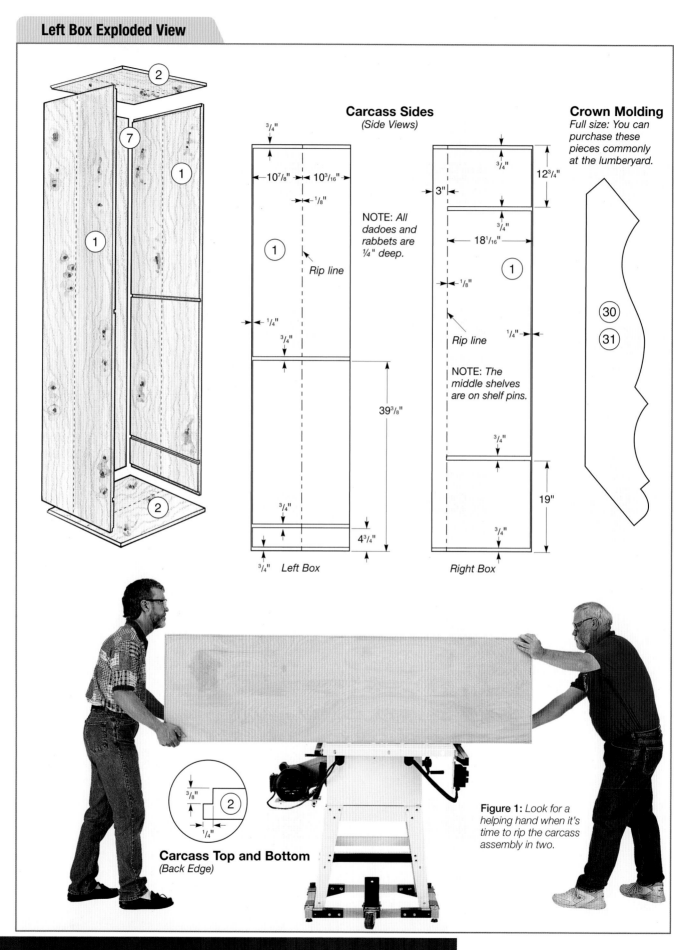

Carcass Sides
(Side Views)

3/4"

10⁷/₈" 10³/₁₆"

1/8"

NOTE: *All dadoes and rabbets are ¼" deep.*

1

Rip line

1/4"

3/4"

39³/₈"

3/4"

3/4" Left Box 4³/₄"

Crown Molding
Full size: You can purchase these pieces commonly at the lumberyard.

12³/₄"

3/4"

3"

3/4"

18¹/₁₆"

1

1/8"

Rip line

1/4"

NOTE: *The middle shelves are on shelf pins.*

3/4"

19"

3/4"

Right Box

30

31

3/8"

2

1/4"

Carcass Top and Bottom
(Back Edge)

Figure 1: *Look for a helping hand when it's time to rip the carcass assembly in two.*

Material List – Carcass and Doors

		T x W x L
1	Carcass Sides (4)	¾" x 21³⁄₁₆" x 84"
2	Carcass Tops and Bottoms (4)	¾" x 21³⁄₁₆" x 19"
3	Fixed Shelves (2)	¾" x 18" x 19"
4	Divider Shelves (6)	¾" x 17" x 19"
5	Rod Base Shelves (2)	¾" x 10⅝" x 19"
6	Rod Divider Shelves (2)	¾" x 10⅝" x 19"
7	Carcass Backs (2)	¼" x 19" x 83¼"
8	Pine Edging (1)	⅛" x ¾" x 75'
9	Door Stiles (4)	¾" x 2" x 84"
10	Middle Rails (4)	¾" x 3" x 16¾"
11	Bottom Rails (2)	¾" x 6" x 16¾"
12	Top Rails (2)	¾" x 8" x 16¾"
13	Bottom Panels (2)	¼" x 17" x 12¾"
14	Middle Panels (2)	¼" x 17" x 24"
15	Top Panels (2)	¼" x 17" x 34¾"

Figure 2: *Use a ¼" slot cutter in your router table to help make the symmetrically curved top door rails. The rails provide a nice bit of visual interest to this tall, slender cabinet.*

door sections off the front of each one, ensuring perfectly matched doors and cabinet sections. Before you start assembly, however, look to the elevation drawings on page 48 for the locations of the dadoes and rabbets that you'll need to plow for the shelves, backs, tops, and bottoms.

Be sure to check the actual thickness of your lumber and plywood before you start the various machining operations—manufactured stock varies in thickness. Once you've completed your machining, join the sides, tops, and bottoms with glue and screws set into counterbored holes. (Plug the holes later with flat-topped pine plugs.)

Now, make the fixed shelves and divider shelves (pieces 3 and 4) that go into the gear storage side of the cabinet. On the rod-holding side, you will need to make matching pairs of rod base and rod divider shelves (pieces 5 and 6). The drawings on page 52 show the shapes and machining details for these solid-lumber pieces. Next, mount the plywood backs (pieces 7) into the compartments, making sure the units are square before the glue cures.

More Than Just Making the Doors

When it comes time to cut the door sections off the large boxes, ask a friend to lend a hand (see Figure 1); it's safer and easier than doing it yourself. Making the doors this way not only ensures a perfect fit to the carcass, but it also keeps the figure pattern intact on the side panels. After the door sections are removed, glue the fixed shelves and the rod holders in place. Then, apply ⅛"-thick pine edging (piece 8) to hide the exposed edges of the plywood.

The front of each of the door sections is closed up with a classic frame-and-panel assembly, accented with symmetrically arched top rails. Make the flat door panels with ¼" knotty pine plywood.

Select straight pine lumber to make the stiles and rails (pieces 9 through 12), and cut these pieces to size. Tight knots are acceptable, as they add to the overall rustic look of the cabinet. Start the machining by plowing a ¼"-wide x ⅜"-deep groove down the length of the stiles' inside edges, using a ¼" dado head. Do the same to the appropriate edges of the middle and bottom rails. Now, set up your miter gauge, and employ the same dado head to form the full-width tenons

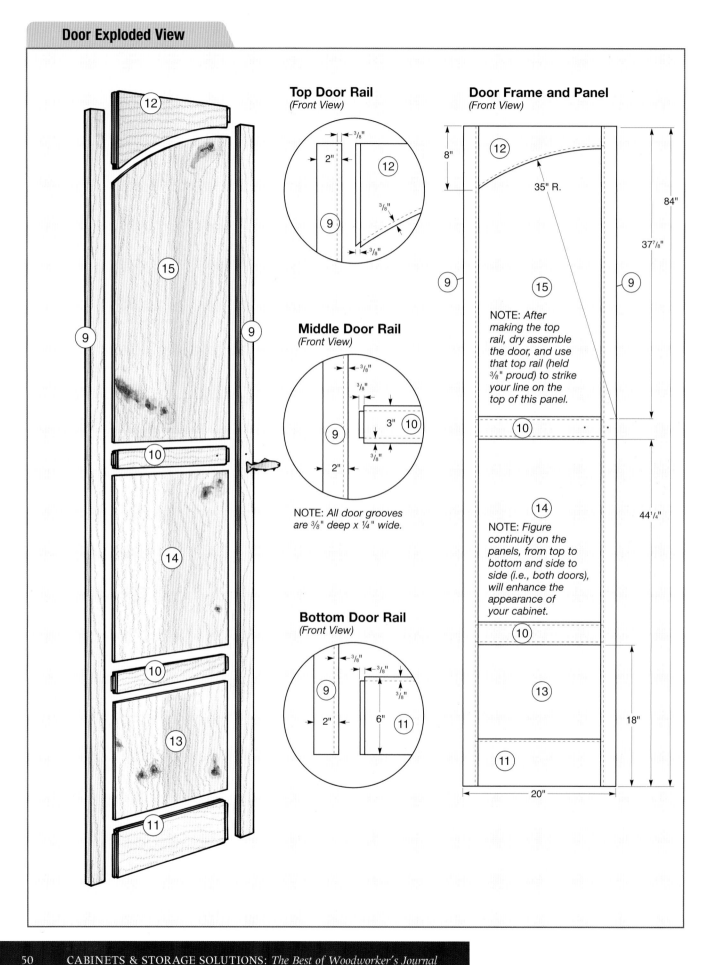

Top Door Rail
(Front View)

³/₈"
2"
12
9
³/₈"
³/₈"

Middle Door Rail
(Front View)

³/₈"
³/₈"
9
3"
10
³/₈"
2"

NOTE: *All door grooves are ³/₈" deep x ¹/₄" wide.*

Bottom Door Rail
(Front View)

³/₈"
³/₈"
9
³/₈"
2"
6"
11

Door Frame and Panel
(Front View)

8"
12
35" R.
84"
37⁷/₈"
9
15
9

NOTE: *After making the top rail, dry assemble the door, and use that top rail (held ³/₈" proud) to strike your line on the top of this panel.*

10
44¹/₄"
14

NOTE: *Figure continuity on the panels, from top to bottom and side to side (i.e., both doors), will enhance the appearance of your cabinet.*

10
18"
13
11
20"

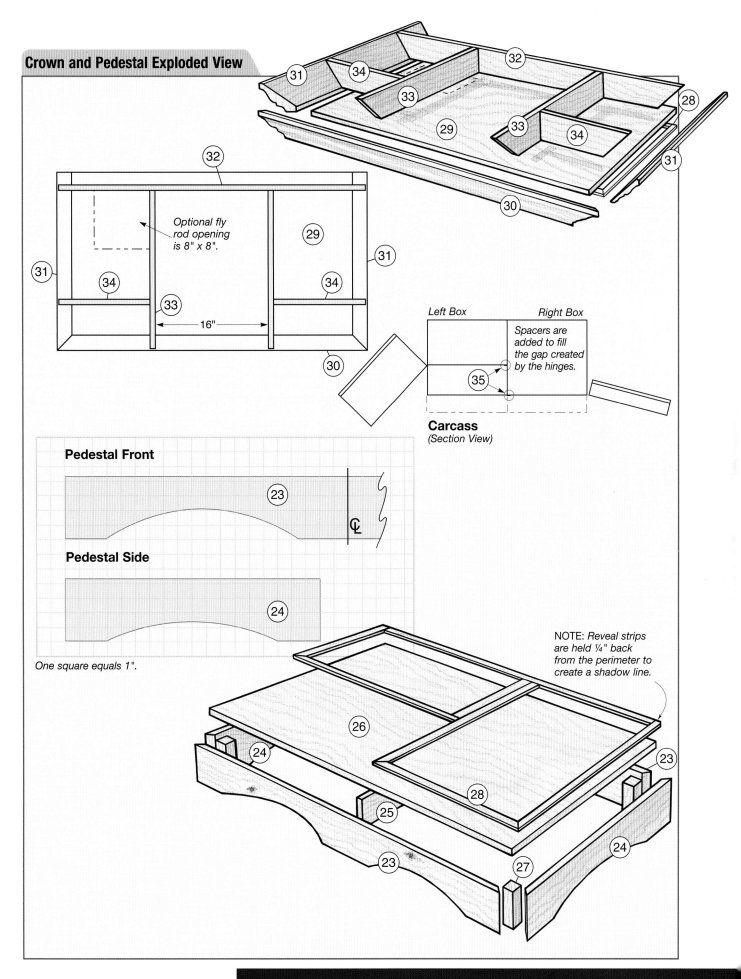

Optional fly rod opening is 8" x 8".

16"

Left Box

Right Box

Spacers are added to fill the gap created by the hinges.

Carcass
(Section View)

Pedestal Front

Pedestal Side

One square equals 1".

NOTE: Reveal strips are held ¼" back from the perimeter to create a shadow line.

Cutting Diagram for ¾" Knotty Pine Plywood

Knotty pine plywood is a good choice for this cabinet because it has the stability of regular plywood combined with the beauty of knotty pine lumber. You will need to purchase this plywood at a full-service lumberyard—one that commonly deals with cabinet-grade hardwood and plywood. While you're there, pick up the crown molding. Use the cutting diagrams at right for sizing down each sheet of plywood.

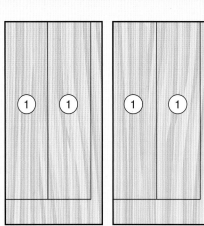

Drawer Exploded View

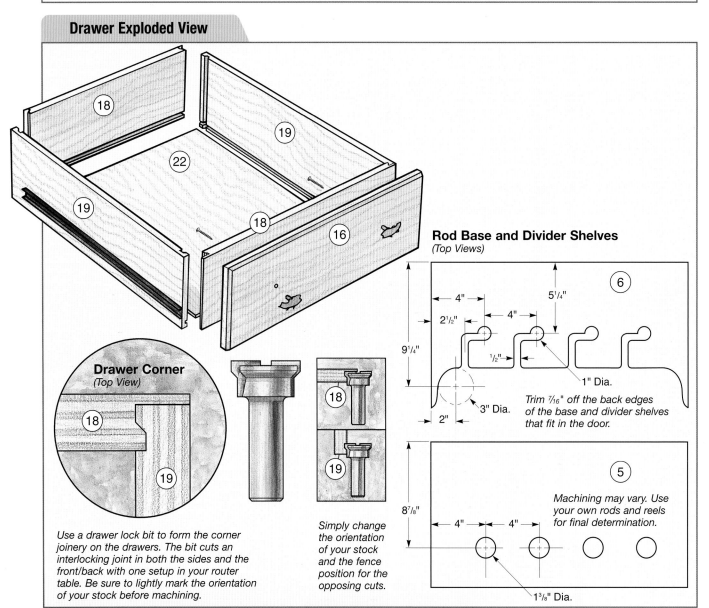

Drawer Corner
(Top View)

Use a drawer lock bit to form the corner joinery on the drawers. The bit cuts an interlocking joint in both the sides and the front/back with one setup in your router table. Be sure to lightly mark the orientation of your stock before machining.

Simply change the orientation of your stock and the fence position for the opposing cuts.

Rod Base and Divider Shelves
(Top Views)

4"

5¼"

2½"

4"

9¼"

½"

1" Dia.

3" Dia.

2"

6

Trim ⁷⁄₁₆" off the back edges of the base and divider shelves that fit in the door.

8⁷⁄₈"

4"

4"

5

Machining may vary. Use your own rods and reels for final determination.

1³⁄₈" Dia.

at the ends of all the rails. The top rails remain rectangular for the moment.

On a large, flat work surface, temporarily clamp the stiles and rails together as they will appear on the front of the cabinet. You don't need the panels during this test assembly. Make sure the clamp-up is square and true. At the center seam, measure down 37⅞", and strike a 35" radius across the top rails to create their gentle curve. Disassemble the clamp-up, and take the top rails over to your band saw. Cut the arcs, and then sand the rough saw marks smooth while holding the rails together as a pair. Chuck a ¼" bearing-guided slot cutter in your router table, and plow a groove centered along the curved edge of each rail (see Figure 2 on page 49).

With that done, you're ready to cut up your ¼" knotty pine plywood to form the flat panel sections (pieces 13 through 15) of the door. The key here is to select material in such a way that the grain flows visually across the front of both doors and through the rails. Test fit the door assemblies together, leaving off the curved top rails. Lay the curved rails on

top of the assemblies (but hold them ⅜" proud of the top of the door stiles), and use the curved bottom edge to strike a pencil line onto the upper door panel. Take the top panels to the band saw, and cut the curve right on the pencil line. You may want to scribe the line with a shop knife to prevent grain tearout. Do one final test fit before you glue and clamp the door subassemblies together. Then, secure the door fronts to the cutoff door assemblies with glue and finish nails. Scrape and sand the doors smooth, and you're ready to move on to making the drawers.

Making the Drawers, Index Holes, and Top Opening

Now, look over the Material List on page 54. The two drawers are made mostly of ½" material (pieces 16 through 21) with ¼" plywood bottoms (pieces 22). I used a drawer lock router bit (see the drawings on page 52) to form the drawers' corner joints. It works slick: Just cut the sides, fronts, and backs to size; plow the ¼" bottom dadoes (¼" up from the bottoms); and use the bit to rout the corner joints

Figure 3: *A little hardware splurge adds a rustic touch and some identity to this angler's cabinet.*

on your router table. A small amount of test fitting on some scrap lumber is all the setup that's required.

Once the drawer boxes are glued up, mount them in the cabinet on full-extension drawer slides, and use double-sided tape to fit the faces to the fronts of the drawers. With the drawers ready to go, move on to drilling the index holes for the shelf support pegs.

If you're a fly fisher, one last detail you may want to include is the opening at the top of the rod holder side of the cabinet. I bored it so my fly rods could extend out through the top. You may not need this detail, as the interior height is sufficient for most ordinary fishing rods. But if you do, make this opening with a jigsaw, and cover the exposed plywood with your ⅛" pine edging.

Adding the Crowning Touches

This cabinet sits on a separate pedestal and is capped off with store-bought crown molding that is held in place with some bracing. The pedestal is framed up with a front, a back, and two side pieces, as well as a center support beam (pieces 23 through 25). See the exploded view drawing on page 51 for construction details.

Band saw the exposed front and side members of the pedestal with the decorative curves shown in the pattern drawings on page 51. Glue and screw the base together, and drop the base top (piece 26) in place to square up the subassembly. Glue cleats (pieces 27) in each corner to provide a little extra

Figure 4: *Tongue-and-groove pine paneling is a final detail in this Northwoods fishing cabinet. Finished with orange shellac, this project will look great in your den, cabin, or vacation home.*

support. Now, trim out the pedestal with ¼"-thick reveal strips (piece 28) mitered around the top edge, holding them back ¼". These strips separate the carcass from the base (and later, the crown molding) and create a pleasing shadow line. They also allow the large doors to swing freely.

Next, create the crown molding subassembly. Wrap the crown molding around a ¾" plywood cap (pieces 29 through 31). On the underside of the cap, secure more of the reveal strip with glue and small brads. Next, cut an opening to match the fly rod hole in the top of the rod holder side of the cabinet (if you didn't include this detail, ignore this step). Finally, install bracing (pieces 32 through 34) to add support to the top's crown molding (see the drawings on page 51).

A word to the wise: Because the cabinet is so tall, install the base and top after you've placed the cabinet in your room. This will make it a lot easier to set the cabinet upright in a typical house with its 8' ceilings. If you mount the subassemblies prematurely, the cabinet may not fit.

Adding Some Fishy Hardware

With most of the work done, temporarily mount the pedestal and base to the cabinet. Then, hang the doors, using wraparound piano hinges for strength and durability. You will have to notch the wrapping aspect of the hinges to fit around the fixed shelves. To accommodate the thickness of the hinges, glue several small spacers (pieces 35) in place.

Now, add pulls for the doors and drawers. I bought specialty fish-shaped pulls (see Figure 3 on page 53) from Rockler Woodworking and Hardware (800-279-4441, *www.rockler. com*). Next, mount magnetic catches to hold the doors shut. Finally, to add to the Northwoods theme, cut and fit ¼" pine tongue-and-groove paneling (piece 36) inside the cabinet and doors. Glue it in place (see Figure 4 on page 53), and add a few small brads for insurance.

Finishing Up with Shellac

After the paneling is in place, it's time for a thorough sanding inside and out (always a pain!), followed by several coats of orange shellac. Sand lightly after the first coat to remove any dust nibs. After that, you can apply the remaining coats without sanding—shellac partially dissolves the layer of finish underneath and fuses to it for a good bond without sanding. You just can't beat orange shellac as a finish on pine lumber. It brings out the beauty of the grain and knots and adds a real warmth to the wood. As an alternative to shellac, you can use polyurethane varnish, as described in Finishing with Polyurethane on page 55.

Now, all you have to do is figure out a way to quietly get all your fishing gear into the cabinet without anyone noticing how much stuff you actually own!

Material List – Drawers, Pedestal, and Crown

		T x W x L
16	Small Drawer Face (1)	½" x 6" x 18¼"
17	Large Drawer Face (1)	½" x 12" x 18¼"
18	Small Drawer Front and Back (2)	½" x 6" x 17¼"
19	Small Drawer Sides (2)	½" x 6" x 17"
20	Large Drawer Front and Back (2)	½" x 12" x 17¼"
21	Large Drawer Sides (2)	½" x 12" x 17"
22	Drawer Bottoms (2)	¼" x 16½" x 17"
23	Pedestal Front and Back (2)	¾" x 4¼" x 40"
24	Pedestal Sides (2)	¾" x 4¼" x 18"
25	Pedestal Support Beam (1)	¾" x 3½" x 16½"
26	Pedestal Top (1)	¾" x 16½" x 38½"
27	Support Cleats (4)	¾" x ¾" x 3½"
28	Reveal Strip (1)	¼" x ¾" x 250"
29	Crown Cap (1)	¾" x 21¹¹⁄₁₆" x 39½"
30	Crown Front Molding (1)	¾" x 3⅝" x 45"
31	Crown Side Moldings (2)	¾" x 3⅝" x 22"
32	Crown Long Brace (1)	¾" x 2" x 43¾"
33	Crown Medium Braces (2)	¾" x 2" x 21⅞"
34	Crown Short Braces (2)	¾" x 2" x 13³⁄₁₆"
35	Door Spacers (6)	⅛" x ¾" x 2"
36	Pine Paneling (1)	¼" x 40 Sq. Ft.

Finishing with Polyurethane

Follow these tips to help prevent dust problems before applying a polyurethane finish.

- Never sand the wood and apply the finish in the same room without allowing time for the dust to settle first.
- Wet mop the shop floor before finishing, and avoid wearing dusty clothes.
- Always strain the finish if it's dirty or has formed a surface skin.
- Hit your brush against your hand to shake out any loose bristles.
- Wipe the wood with a tack cloth just before you begin brushing.

Pour polyurethane into a clean container, and add paint thinner, if needed, to create smoother flow-out without bubbles. After brushing on a coat, tip off the excess with the brush held at about 45°. This will smooth away drips and blend in bristle marks.

Looking for the most durable finish you can apply with a brush? You can't beat polyurethane. It's very resistant to scratches, heat, water, solvents, and alkalies. Its main drawback, however, is the same as with all varnishes. It cures so slowly that dust has time to settle in the finish.

Polyurethane is an alkyd-resin varnish with polyurethane resin added. The polyurethane resin increases the toughness and durability of the varnish. You may hear polyurethane called urethane, leaving you to wonder if there are two different finishes. Actually, both names apply to the same finish, with polyurethane being the more accurate description.

Polyurethane is available in gloss, semigloss, and satin sheens. Stirring is essential for all but gloss polyurethane to keep the flatting agent mixed in the liquid. The effect of the flatting agent is cumulative—each additional coat dulls the surface more. To control the glossiness of your finish, you can mix sheens, either between cans or coats.

Polyurethane Myths

Contrary to popular belief, polyurethane doesn't last forever, although it's more durable than most finishes. On floors, polyurethane is vulnerable to wear, as dirt carried on the soles of shoes acts like sandpaper. To increase the life of the finish, wax your floors to reduce friction. Around sinks, polyurethane holds up well unless water finds a way through a crack and under the finish. The water then causes the finish to

peel. You can extend the life of the finish by coating the ends of boards (especially under the sink), and then adding more coats to the top whenever cracks begin to appear. When you add coats of polyurethane, be sure the surface is clean and sanded lightly with 280-grit or finer sandpaper to get a good bond.

If treated correctly, polyurethane will resist cracking for decades. More than anything else, this means keeping your finished piece out of direct sunlight. Strong light causes finishes to deteriorate faster than any other element, and polyurethane is especially vulnerable on projects left outdoors and exposed to sunlight.

There's no advantage to using a sanding sealer under polyurethane, because polyurethane sands fairly easily. In fact, sanding sealers may weaken the bond since they contain stearate, a soap-like substance that has poor adhesion to polyurethane.

A common complaint about polyurethane is that it looks more plastic than other finishes. In fact, it is a plastic, as are all film finishes except for shellac (which is a natural material). Another misleading generalization is that you should never shake the can, or you'll get bubbles in the finish. Bubbles are really caused by the air introduced while brushing on the finish. You can prevent bubbles from curing in the film by adding about 10% paint thinner, which slows the curing enough to allow the bubbles to pop out and the film to level out more completely.

Applying Polyurethane

For your first coat, pour some polyurethane into a clean container, such as a wide-mouthed jar or coffee can, and stir in 50% paint thinner. Apply the mixture with a good-quality bristle or foam brush, going with the grain. Allow the finish to cure overnight, and then sand the surface smooth using 280-grit sandpaper. Remove the dust with a vacuum or tack cloth.

For the next two or three coats, again working from a clean container, brush the polyurethane (full strength or reduced 10%) in any direction, and then tip off the wet finish, brushing with the grain and, with the brush held at 45°, dragging it lightly over the surface.

Applying polyurethane to a vertical surface should be done as thinly as possible, so it won't sag or run. It helps to wipe your brush over the edge of a clean jar after each tipping-off stroke to squeeze out any excess finish. Continue to tip off until the finish stops sagging.

Allow each coat to cure overnight. If the weather is cold or damp, this may take longer. Test the finish by pushing your fingernail into an inconspicuous place—if it gives, you need to wait a while longer. If more than a week goes by before you apply the next coat, it's wise to abrade the entire surface with 0000 steel wool or a 3M Scotch-Brite pad. This scratches the surface and adds "tooth" for better adhesion.

Early American Dresser

Walk a mile in the shoes of a colonial cabinetmaker, and you'll learn a lot about how an heirloom is made. This piece even has a not-so-secret drawer.

by Stuart Barron

Building this dresser may mark a number of firsts for you. It may be the first time you build a piece of early American furniture. It may be your first large solid-wood casework project. And it may be your first shot at cutting dovetails by hand, if you so choose. But jumping these hurdles will surely open up creative possibilities while helping you build a truly classic dresser.

Inspiration for this project came when I visited a small antiques shop. Just inside the front door sat an unusual old dresser made of clear pine with an orange shellac finish. It had all the telltale signs of age— fine joints, nicked feet, a beautiful patina, and a crazed finish—although I could tell

by all the plugged pilot holes in the drawer fronts that the hardware wasn't original. What really caught my eye was the curved top molding, which turned out to be the front of a drawer. After doing a little research, I found that hidden drawers like this one were used for storing documents, although it's hard to imagine how the drawer remained secret for very long. Working from some basic measurements and a photo of the dresser, I made some detailed drawings and set out to construct this dresser just like the original antique.

Selecting Wood and Gluing Panels

Country craftsmen traditionally chose local woods for their projects, such as cherry and pine, and they left the imported woods to urban cabinetmakers, who had rich customers with an appetite for fancier furniture. I chose cherry

Figure 2: *Align the edge of the jig base with your layouts, and rout the grooves using a dovetail bit.*

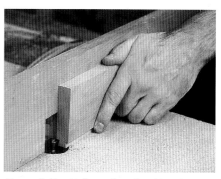

Figure 3: *Rout tails on the rails with a dovetail bit and a router table, making sure the fit is just loose enough to slide the tails into the grooves in the sides.*

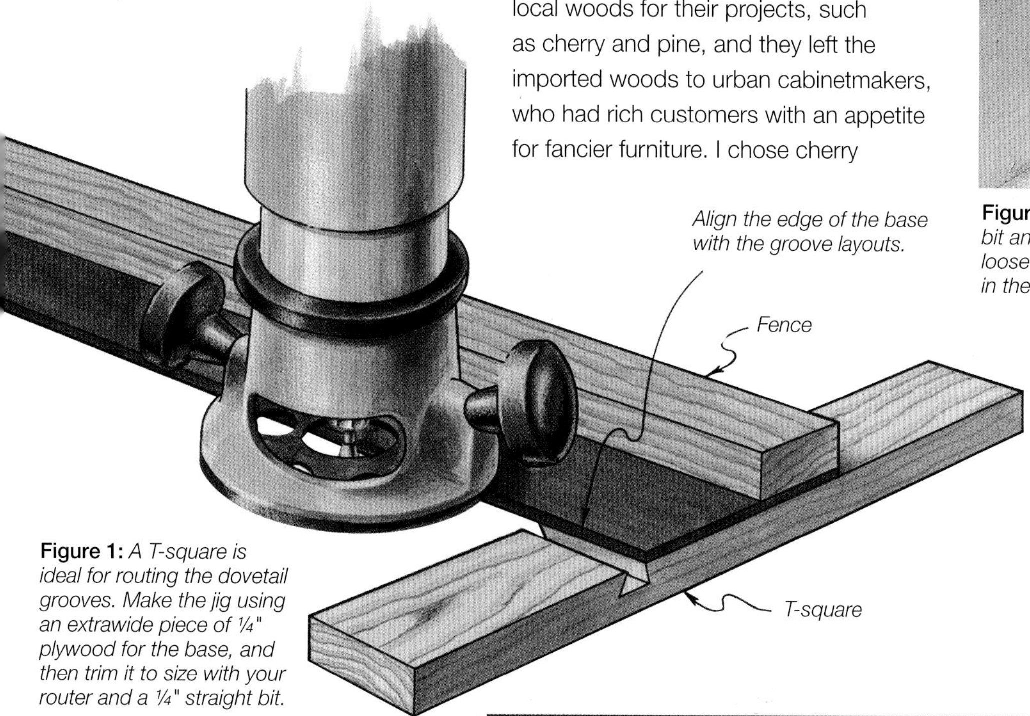

Align the edge of the base with the groove layouts.

Fence

T-square

Figure 1: *A T-square is ideal for routing the dovetail grooves. Make the jig using an extrawide piece of ¼" plywood for the base, and then trim it to size with your router and a ¼" straight bit.*

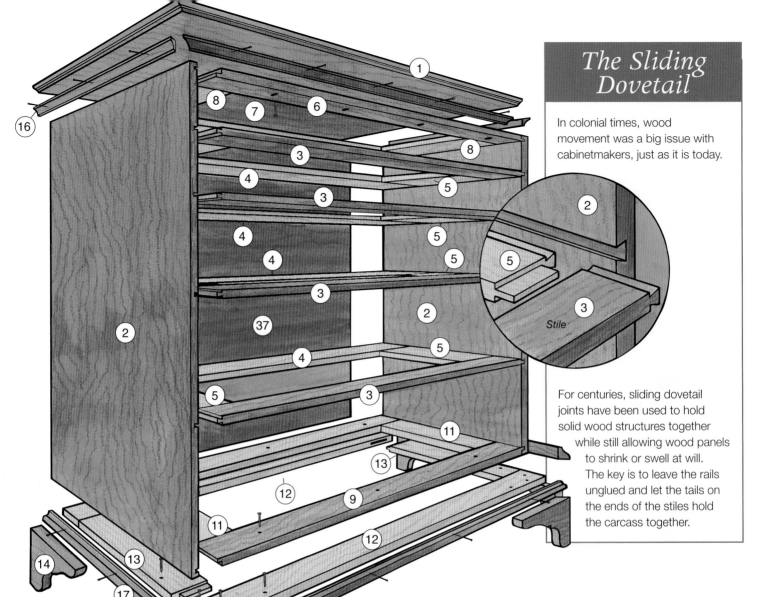

In colonial times, wood movement was a big issue with cabinetmakers, just as it is today.

Stile

For centuries, sliding dovetail joints have been used to hold solid wood structures together while still allowing wood panels to shrink or swell at will. The key is to leave the rails unglued and let the tails on the ends of the stiles hold the carcass together.

Material List

		T x W x L			T x W x L
1	Top, Cherry (1)	¾" x 22" x 39"	**10**	Bottom Frame Rear Stile, Poplar (1)	¾" x 2⅞" x 35⅞"
2	Sides, Cherry (2)	¾" x 20½" x 32"	**11**	Bottom Frame Rails, Poplar (2)	¾" x 3⅜" x 15⅝"
3	Middle Frame Front Stiles, Cherry (4)	¾" x 2⅞" x 35⅞"	**12**	Base Frame Stiles, Poplar (2)	¾" x 2⅞" x 36⅝"
4	Middle Frame Rear Stiles, Poplar (4)	¾" x 2⅞" x 35⅞"	**13**	Base Frame Rails, Poplar (2)	¾" x 2⅞" x 15⅝"
5	Middle Frame Rails, Poplar (8)	¾" x 3⅜" x 15⅝"	**14**	Feet, Cherry (6)	1¾" x 6¾" x 8½"
6	Top Frame Front Stile, Cherry (1)	¾" x 2⅞" x 35⅞"	**15**	Biscuits/Splines (4/2)	#20 Biscuits/¼" Splines
7	Top Frame Rear Stile, Poplar (1)	¾" x 2⅞" x 35⅞"	**16**	Cornice Moldings, Cherry (2)	¾" x 1" x 48"
8	Top Frame Rails, Poplar (2)	¾" x 3⅜" x 15⅝"	**17**	Base Moldings, Cherry (2)	¾" x 1" x 48"
9	Bottom Frame Front Stile, Cherry (1)	¾" x 2⅞" x 35⅞"	**18**	Top Drawer Face, Cherry (1)	¾" x 4" x 36⅝"

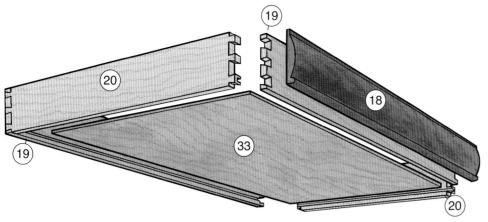

Figure 4: *Clamp a setup block to your fence to align the shoulder of your tenon layout with the ½" dado blade. Make two passes to cut each cheek.*

because it's both a handsome species and often less expensive than clear pine, another good choice for furniture like this. For the hidden parts of the dresser, such as the drawer sides and backs and the internal frames, I chose poplar. The drawer bottoms and the dresser's back panel are made of birch plywood.

Take a look at the Material List below. Set aside your best cherry boards for the drawer fronts (pieces 18, 21, 24, 27, and 30), and use your next-best stock for the top and sides (pieces 1 and 2). Joint and glue your lumber for the top and side panels, and after the glue sets up, remove the squeeze-out with a scraper or chisel. Later, plane the panels flat, and sand them to 120 grit.

Cut the side panels to size, and then lay out the sliding dovetail grooves, the dadoes, and the rabbets, as shown in the side panel elevation drawing on page 61.

Cut the dadoes and rabbets with your table saw and the appropriately sized dado blades. Then, build a jig for routing the sliding dovetail grooves (see Figure 1 on page 57). Chuck a dovetail bit in your router, and clamp the jig next to a joint layout on a panel. Set the depth of cut to ⅜", and rout the groove (see Figure 2 on page 57). Repeat this procedure for each of the sliding dovetail grooves.

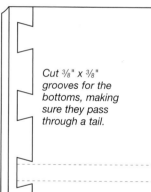

Dovetail Joint Detail

Use this layout as a guide, varying the number, spacing, and size of the dovetails on each drawer. Begin and end each joint with a half pin.

Cut ⅜" x ⅜" grooves for the bottoms, making sure they pass through a tail.

		T x W x L			T x W x L
19	Top Drawer Front/Back, Poplar (2)	¾" x 3½" x 35⅛"	28	#4 Drawer Back, Poplar (1)	¾" x 6½" x 35⅛"
20	Top Drawer Sides, Poplar (2)	¾" x 3½" x 18½"	29	#4 Drawer Sides, Poplar (2)	¾" x 6½" x 18½"
21	#2 Drawer Front, Cherry (1)	¾" x 4½" x 35⅛"	30	#5 Drawer Front, Cherry (1)	¾" x 7½" x 35⅛"
22	#2 Drawer Back, Poplar (1)	¾" x 4½" x 35⅛"	31	#5 Drawer Back, Poplar (1)	¾" x 7½" x 35⅛"
23	#2 Drawer Sides, Poplar (2)	¾" x 4½" x 18½"	32	#5 Drawer Sides, Poplar (2)	¾" x 7½" x 18½"
24	#3 Drawer Front, Cherry (1)	¾" x 5½" x 35⅛"	33	Top Drawer Bottom, Plywood (1)	⅜" x 34¼" x 17⅝"
25	#3 Drawer Back, Poplar (1)	¾" x 5½" x 35⅛"	34	Drawer Bottoms, Plywood (4)	⅜" x 34¼" x 18"
26	#3 Drawer Sides, Poplar (2)	¾" x 5½" x 18½"	35	Drawer Stops, Poplar (10)	¾" x ¾" x 2"
27	#4 Drawer Front, Cherry (1)	¾" x 6½" x 35⅛"	36	Drawer Pulls (8)	Antique Brass
			37	Back, Plywood (1)	⅜" x 36" x 33"

Top Frame Elevation

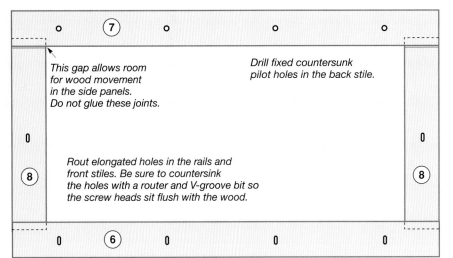

⑦

This gap allows room for wood movement in the side panels. Do not glue these joints.

Drill fixed countersunk pilot holes in the back stile.

Rout elongated holes in the rails and front stiles. Be sure to countersink the holes with a router and V-groove bit so the screw heads sit flush with the wood.

⑧   ⑧

⑥

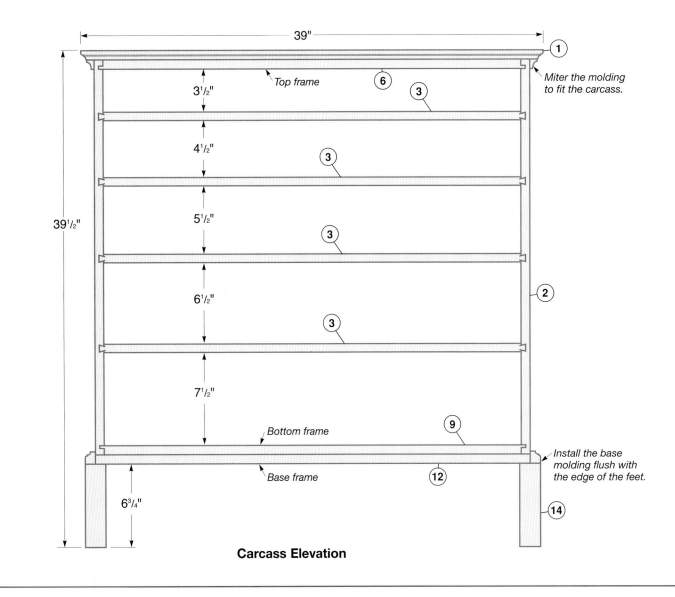

39"

①

Top frame   ⑥   ③

Miter the molding to fit the carcass.

3½"

③

4½"

③

5½"

39½"

③

6½"

②

③

7½"

⑨

Bottom frame

Base frame   ⑫

Install the base molding flush with the edge of the feet.

6¾"   ⑭

Carcass Elevation

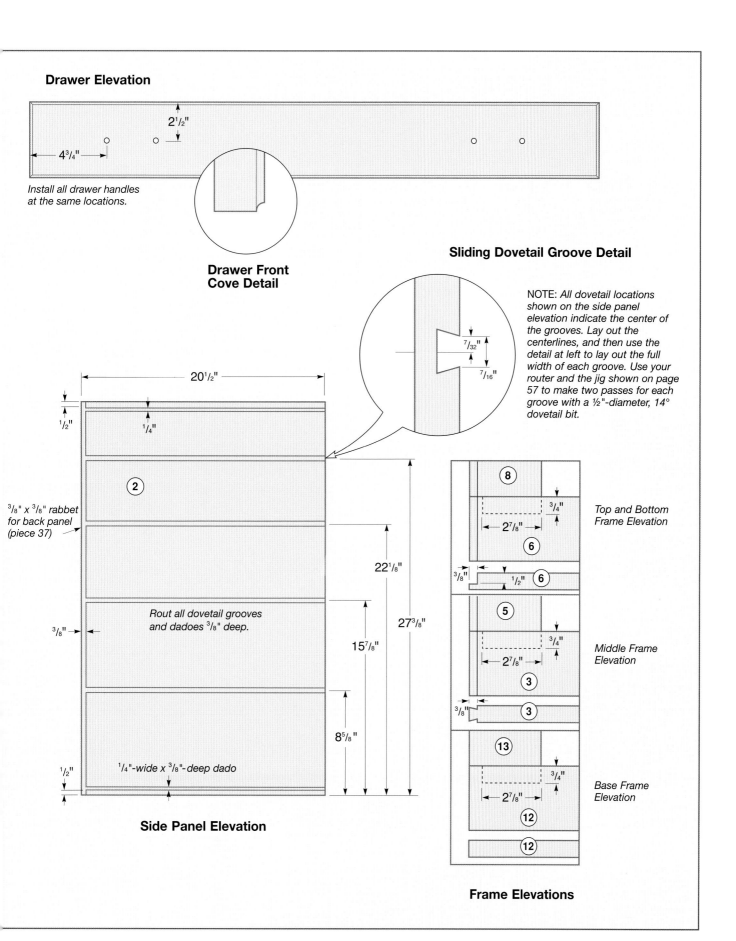

Drawer Elevation

2¹/₂"

4³/₄"

Install all drawer handles at the same locations.

Drawer Front Cove Detail

Sliding Dovetail Groove Detail

⁷/₃₂"

⁷/₁₆"

NOTE: *All dovetail locations shown on the side panel elevation indicate the center of the grooves. Lay out the centerlines, and then use the detail at left to lay out the full width of each groove. Use your router and the jig shown on page 57 to make two passes for each groove with a ½"-diameter, 14° dovetail bit.*

20¹/₂"

¹/₂"

¹/₄"

②

³/₈" x ³/₈" rabbet for back panel (piece 37)

³/₈"

Rout all dovetail grooves and dadoes ³/₈" deep.

22¹/₈"

27³/₈"

15⁷/₈"

8⁵/₈"

¹/₂"

¹/₄"-wide x ³/₈"-deep dado

Side Panel Elevation

⑧

³/₄"

2⁷/₈"

⑥

³/₈"

¹/₂"

⑥

Top and Bottom Frame Elevation

⑤

³/₄"

2⁷/₈"

③

³/₈"

③

Middle Frame Elevation

⑬

³/₄"

2⁷/₈"

⑫

⑫

Base Frame Elevation

Frame Elevations

Top Edging

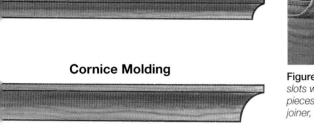

Cornice Molding

Top Drawer Face

Cut on your table saw.

Shape with a block plane.

Top Drawer Face Detail

Make a saw kerf, and then shape with a rabbet plane.

Shape with a rabbet plane.

Base Molding

Foot Bracket

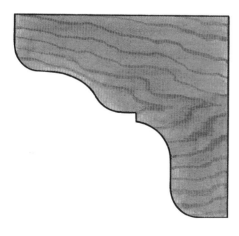

Figure 5: *After mitering the front feet, cut slots with a biscuit joiner, and then join the pieces with biscuits. If you don't have a biscuit joiner, use splines.*

Building the Carcass

Rip cherry and poplar stock for the middle frames, top frame, bottom frame, and base frame (pieces 3 through 13). After cutting the pieces to length, set up your router table with the same dovetail bit you just used for the grooves. Clamp a fence near the bit, and cut a dovetail on the edge of some poplar scrap wood to fit in the side panel grooves. You want a snug fit, just tight enough to require a few taps with a mallet before it slides into place. Adjust your setup until you get the fit just right, and then rout tails on one edge of the rails for the middle frames (see Figure 3 on page 57 and the detail drawings of the sliding dovetail groove on pages 58 and 61). Once you've finished routing tails on the rails, cut a tail on the end of another scrap piece of poplar, and test its fit in a groove. If necessary, readjust the router table setup to get a good fit on a test piece, and then rout the ends of the rear middle frame stiles. Next, test cut the end of a cherry scrap piece (the fit might change again), and rout the front middle frame stiles.

Since there isn't room for well-supported sliding dovetail joints at the ends of the side panels, join the top and bottom frames to the sides with tongues and dadoes. Install a ⅜" dado blade in your table saw, and raise the blade ½" to form the ¼" tongues on the ends of the stiles and one edge of each rail.

Now, lay out mortises on all the frame stiles for the rail-to-stile joints, as shown in the frame elevation drawings on page 61. Use a ³⁄₁₆" drill bit and your

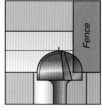
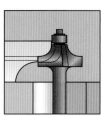

Top Edging Detail
Step 1: *With a router table and core-box bit, form a cove at the edges of a board.*
Step 2: *Install a roundover bit in your router table to complete the molding.*

Cornice Molding Detail
Rout the edges of a board with a piloted cove bit, leaving a ⅛"-wide fillet along the top of each edge.

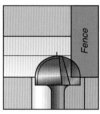
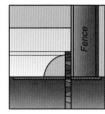

Base Molding Detail
Step 1: *With a router table and core-box bit, rout a cove along the edges of your board.*
Step 2: *Cut rabbets with your table saw.*

drill press to rough out the mortises, and then clean them up with a chisel. Next, form tenons on the ends of the rails to fit the mortises, using a table saw and a ½" dado blade (see Figure 4 on page 59).

Assembling the carcass will go a lot more smoothly if you recruit an extra pair of hands for the task, and I recommend installing one frame at a time to keep the process manageable. Start by spreading glue in the first 3" of one set of dovetail grooves in the side panels, and then slip a front stile into place. Next, set the carcass on its face, brush some glue into the front stile mortises, and slip the rails into the dovetail grooves from the back of the side panels. Be careful to avoid gluing the rails to the sides, or you'll restrict the seasonal movement of the panels. Press the rails as far forward as you can to seat the tenons in the front stile mortises. Now, brush glue in the last 2" of each dovetail groove, and tap the rear stiles into place, stopping when the rails

Figure 6: *Use a ¼" or narrower band saw blade for making the tight cuts along the outline of each foot. Set the saw guides just above the wood to keep the blade from wandering.*

Figure 7: *Trace the pattern of the top drawer face on the end of your stock, and remove some of the waste with your table saw. Shape the face with a rabbet plane and block plane.*

sit flush with the rabbets in the sides. Do not put glue in the rear stile mortises, so the side panels can move. Clamp the carcass together, and then repeat the installation procedure for the rest of the frames, including the top and bottom frames.

Constructing the Base

Glue the base frame together. Then, select thick cherry stock for the feet (pieces 14). Cut the stock for the feet to size, and miter one end of four pieces for the front foot assemblies. Make sure the miters are square to the edges of the stock. Next, cut biscuit slots or rout a spline slot in the miters (see Figure 5). Adding biscuits or splines (pieces 15) to the miter joints will greatly reinforce the foot assemblies. Now, make a full-size pattern of the foot, using the drawings on pages 60 and 62 as guides, and trace it onto your stock. Band saw the feet to shape (see Figure 6), and smooth the edges with a drum sander. Make plywood splines if you need them, and glue the mitered feet together.

After blending the corners of the two front foot assemblies with a palm sander, draw a line on the top of each foot ¾" back from the front edge. Glue and screw the base frame to the feet, aligning the outside edges of the frame with the lines you just drew on the feet; make sure the back edge of the frame is flush with the back edge of the rear feet. The ¾"-wide ledge now formed on the top of each foot will support the base molding that conceals the joint between the carcass and the base.

Adding the Moldings

To make the cornice molding (pieces 16), rout the edges of a 3" or wider board with a cove bit and roundover bit, following the cornice molding detail drawing on page 62. Miter the molding to length, and then glue and pin the front piece to the cabinet with #17 wire brads. For the side pieces, glue the first 3" only, and then pin the remaining length to the side panels with brads to allow for wood movement. Use a nail set to drive the brad heads below the wood surface, and then fill the holes with a matching wood putty.

Rout a 3" or wider piece of stock for the base molding (pieces 17) with a cove bit, and then trim the leftover waste on your table saw, as shown in the base molding detail drawings on page 62. Use a rabbet plane and sandpaper to round over the fillet on the front edge of the molding, and rip the molding off the board. Miter the molding to length, and then glue and nail the pieces to the base assembly.

Now, rout ⅛"-wide elongated holes in the front stile and rails of the top frame, and drill fixed holes in the back stile, as shown in the top frame elevation drawing on page 60. Countersink all the holes with a V-bit and router to recess the heads of your screws. These pilot holes will allow the top to move after it's screwed to the carcass.

Cut the top to size, and rout its front and side edges with the bits shown in the top edging detail drawings on page 62. Sand the top to at least 120 grit, and then position the panel

Secret drawers were common in eighteenth-century furniture and often contained a family's most important documents. Today, they serve better as sock drawers than as document hideaways.

Cutting dovetail joints isn't hard—it just takes practice and patience. However, using quality tools definitely helps. A marking gauge with a knife point, for instance, will lay out crisp joint shoulders that give your chisels a positive starting point, and a well-tuned bevel gauge will keep your pin and tail angles consistent. Stiff-bladed saws make it easier to keep your pins and tails square, and sharp chisels are essential.

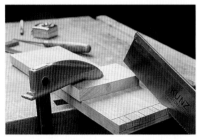

Use a fine-toothed tenon saw with a back stiffener to cut the pins and tails, always stopping just shy of the shoulder lines.

Sharp chisels make fine-tuning your dovetails possible. Without them, you'll get more tearout and sloppier-fitting joints.

A coping saw will speed up the repetitive work of removing the waste after the pins and tails are defined with the tenon saw.

on the carcass. Mark all the pilot hole locations, drill them with a ³⁄₃₂" bit, and secure the panel to the cabinet with #8 screws.

Complete the cabinet assembly by placing the carcass on the base and drilling countersunk pilot holes through the bottom frame and into the base frame. Now, drive in screws to hold the two subassemblies together.

Making the Drawers

Select a board for the top drawer front (piece 18), and rip it to width. Cut it a little longer than needed, and trace the shape of the top drawer face profile (see the drawing on page 62) onto the ends of the board. Begin the shaping process by ripping a kerf to define the inside edge of the bottom bead, as described in the top drawer face detail on page 62. Next, remove some of the waste at the top of the drawer face by tilting the table saw blade 15° and running the stock on edge through the blade. Straighten the blade to cut the small rabbet along the top edge, and then form the hump and bead of the molding by hand with a rabbeting plane and smoothing plane (see Figure 7 on page 63). Wrap up the shaping with a palm sander.

Rip and crosscut the rest of your drawer fronts to size, as well as all the sides and backs (pieces 19 through 32). Then, lay out the dovetails—half-blind dovetails on the fronts and through dovetails on the backs and top drawer box (see the exploded views on page 59). Use a marking gauge with a knife point to define the back shoulder of each joint, and use a utility knife for laying out the side shoulders of the pins and tails. Be sure to begin and end each joint with a half pin, as shown in the dovetail joint detail drawing on page 59. Cut the pins first, and then use them to trace the tail locations. A fine-toothed tenon saw works well for cutting the joints, and paring them to final fit is only possible with a very sharp chisel (see Cutting

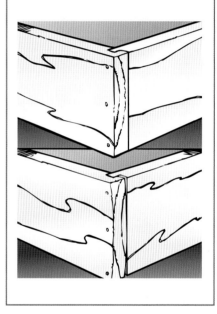

Dovetails at left). Or rout the dovetails with a router and dovetail jig.

After completing the dovetail joints, rout the ³⁄₈"-wide x ³⁄₈"-deep grooves for holding the drawer bottoms (pieces 33 and 34), as shown in the drawer elevation drawing on page 61. Notice that these grooves will run through a pair of tails in the drawer sides, but the resulting holes won't show on the backs of the drawers.

Assemble the drawers, checking for squareness as you go. Allow the glue to dry, and then trim the joint ends flush with the drawer sides and backs. Use a hand plane to carefully shave the top edges of the drawers until they fit the cabinet openings—if it's winter, leave a ³⁄₃₂" gap; in summer, a ¹⁄₃₂" gap. Next, screw the top drawer box to the drawer face. Be sure to align its ends with the sides of the dresser and leave a ¹⁄₁₆" gap between the top of the drawer face and the cornice molding.

Use a cove bit to rout the edges around all the drawer faces except the top one. Then, slide the drawers into the cabinet, and install the stops (pieces 35).

Screw the stops to the rear stiles on each frame. Now, drill pilot holes in the drawer fronts for the pulls (pieces 36).

Cut plywood for the back (piece 37), and set it into the cabinet. Then, drill countersunk pilot holes, and screw the back to the rabbets in the side panels.

Now that you've spent all this effort putting your dresser together, you get to take it apart again. Remove the back, base, and top and pull out the drawers so you can sand everything to 220 grit before applying an oil finish. With the first

coat of finish, you'll see the cherry begin to mellow, which will continue for years until the piece looks like an antique. Apply three more coats of oil finish, and polish off the project with a coat of paste wax.

There's a wealth of woodworking knowledge hidden in this dresser. By building it, you've now stepped into the shoes of the craftsman who built the original some 200 years ago. Perhaps no one else will fully recognize your achievements—except, of course, another woodworker.

QuickTip

Jig for Cutting Mitered Corners

If your table saw won't cut accurate miters, this jig can help. Start with a keyed plywood base of ¾"-thick stock. Lower the blade below the tabletop, and make sure the plywood slides smoothly along the miter slot. Raise the blade and cut the side absolutely parallel to the blade. Cut two matching sides to about 48°, and glue these to the base, holding their tips to the saw-cut parallel edge. With a steel square, mark a line on the jig at 90° to the blade, and add a fence for registering the edges of your stock. Now, tilt the blade just a bit until you have a perfect 45° angle for your cuts. Remember to reset the blade to vertical after using it.

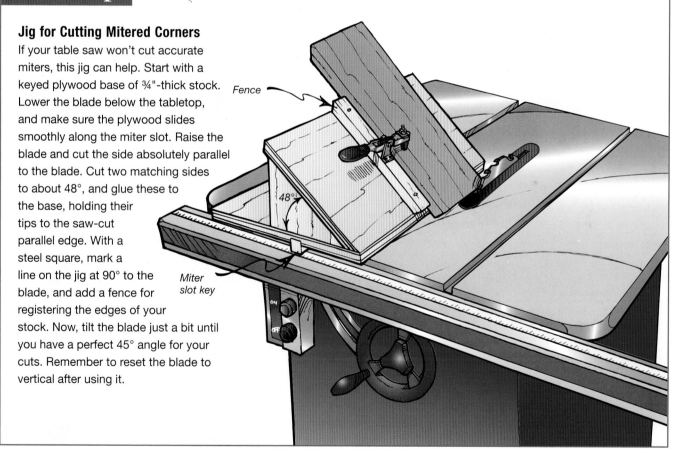

Scandinavian-Style Sideboard

A short base and a broad, low cabinet define a sideboard, and this design has a twist: Instead of the usual metal hardware, it has flush-fit drawers and doors. It also has a beveled top and sapwood veneer to make it a Scandinavian masterpiece.

by Rick White

Several years ago, *Woodworker's Journal* featured a dining room table that caused quite a stir (see Figure 1). Furniture projects have always been popular with readers, and the dining room table proved to be one of the most well liked of all. The magazine received a steady stream of pictures from folks who built the table or who took the ideas and adapted them in their own way. In the issue that followed the one featuring the dining table, the magazine offered plans for a matching dining chair. Now, here is a sideboard to complete the set.

The sideboard adheres to the Scandinavian styling of the original table and chair pieces, and the completed cabinet will provide more than enough room for all your fine china, crystal, and other servingware.

Figure 1: *The sideboard design picks up many of the details featured in this dining table and chair set. Both were feature projects in* Woodworker's Journal *some years ago.*

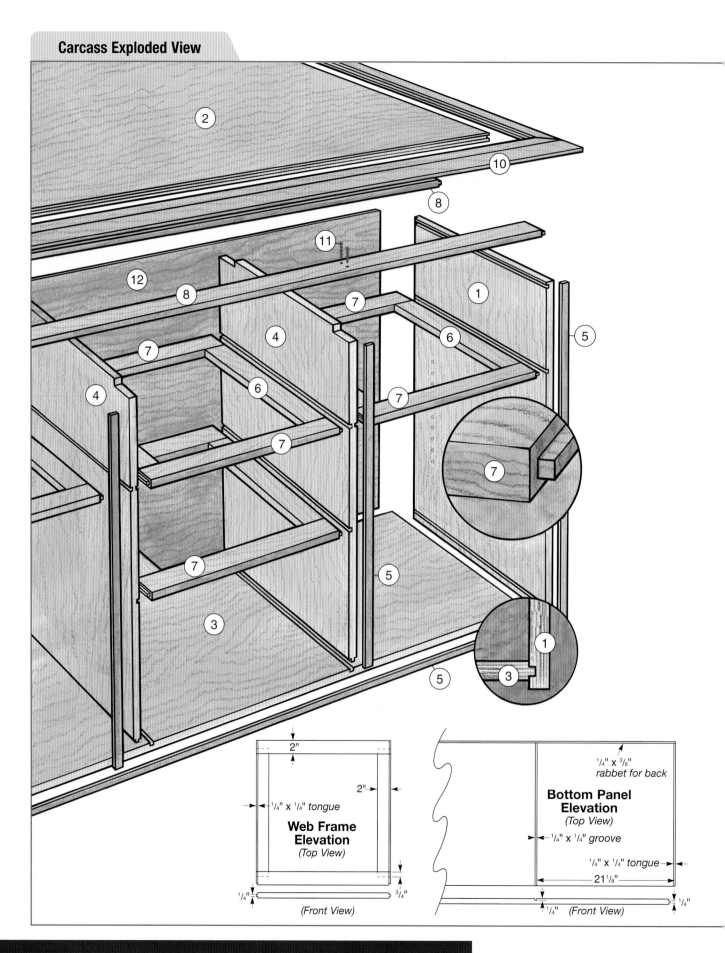

Web Frame Elevation
(Top View)

2"

2"

¹/₄" x ¹/₄" tongue

¹/₄"

³/₄"

(Front View)

Bottom Panel Elevation
(Top View)

¹/₄" x ³/₈" rabbet for back

¹/₄" x ¹/₄" groove

¹/₄" x ¹/₄" tongue

21¹/₈"

¹/₄"

¹/₄"

(Front View)

Side Panel Elevation

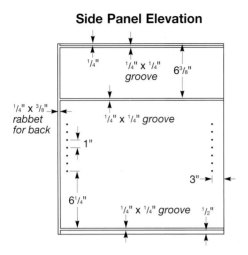

1/4"
1/4" x 1/4" groove
6³/₈"
1/4" x 3/8" rabbet for back
1/4" x 1/4" groove
1"
3"
6¹/₄"
1/4" x 1/4" groove
1/2"

Divider Panel Elevation

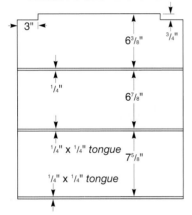

3"
6³/₈"
3/4"
1/4"
6⁷/₈"
1/4" x 1/4" tongue
7⁵/₈"
1/4" x 1/4" tongue

Material List – Cabinet

		T x W x L
1	Sides (2)	¾" x 21¾" x 24¼"
2	Top (1)	¾" x 21" x 63¾"
3	Bottom (1)	¾" x 21¾" x 64"
4	Dividers (2)	¾" x 21½" x 23½"
5	Banding Strips (6)	¼" x ¾" x 96"
6	Web Frame Rails (8)	¾" x 2" x 19¼"
7	Web Frame Stiles (8)	¾" x 2" x 21⅛"
8	Subtop Rails (2)	¾" x 3" x 63¾"
9	Shelf Supports (8)	¼" Dia. Posts
10	Top Edgings (3)	¾" x 2" x 72"
11	Screws (100)	#8-1¼"
12	Back (1)	¼" x 23⅝" x 64"
13	Adjustable Shelves (2)	¾" x 20¼" x 20½"
14	Screws (50)	#4-⅝" Oval Head

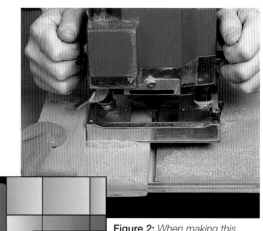

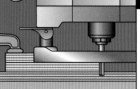

Figure 2: *When making this simple jig, leave the base a little wide, and then trim it with a ¼" bit. Now you can clamp the jig so the freshly cut edge aligns with each dado layout line.*

Cutting Your Cabinet Stock

The sideboard is made up of two parts: the cabinet and the base. It's best to build the cabinet first, so you can alter the size of the base if your cabinet ends up with slightly different dimensions than those shown in the drawings. Review the Material List at left. Then, start by cutting the sides, top panel, bottom, and dividers (pieces 1 through 4) from your sheet of cherry plywood. Label your pieces, and set aside the top panel for now. Then, make the router alignment jig shown in Figure 2. Lay out the dadoes in the sides, divider, and bottom, as shown in the panel elevation drawings at left. Then, clamp the alignment jig alongside each layout line, and rout the ¼"-wide x ¼"-deep dadoes.

Now, rip plenty of banding (pieces 5) for the project, and glue a strip to the front edge of each plywood panel (except for the top). The banding will cover all the dado joints, giving the cabinet a clean, streamlined appearance. Once the glue dries, use a chisel to clean off any glue squeeze-out from the dadoes, and then plane and scrape the banding flush with the surfaces of the plywood (see Figure 3 on page 70). You may be tempted to use a belt sander here, but it's a risky choice—if you accidentally sand through the veneer, you'll have to start over.

Wrap up this first stage of the project by cutting notches at the top corners of the two dividers, as shown in the divider panel elevation drawing. Use a jigsaw equipped with a fine-toothed blade, and set the saw at a slow speed to avoid splintering the plywood veneer.

Adding Panel Reinforcements

Each drawer opening is defined by a web frame (pieces 6 and 7), and the top is supported by two subtop rails (pieces 8). These frames and rails join the plywood panels

Figure 3: *Scribble pencil lines alongside the banding, and then, when you begin planing through the lines, you'll know it's time to switch to a scraper.*

Figure 4: *To rout the stile mortises, chuck a ¼" straight bit in your router table, and draw a line on the fence that shows where to stop the cuts.*

Figure 5: *Clamping a setup block to the fence for aligning the tenon cheek cuts will reduce the chance of a kickback.*

with tongue-and-groove joints to give the cabinet great rigidity. You'll also use this joint to connect the plywood panels to each other. In order for you to cut all the tongues as uniformly as possible, the solid stock for the web frames and subtop rails has to be the same thickness as the plywood. Since plywood is usually a little under ¾" thick, plane the lumber for the frames and subtop rails to match it. If you don't have a way to plane the solid stock, take care throughout the project to adjust each setup to get consistently snug-fitting joints with both materials.

Now, rip and crosscut the hardwood stock to size, and lay out the stile mortises for the web frames, as shown in the web frame elevation drawing on page 68. Rout the mortises with a ¼" straight bit chucked in your router table (see Figure 4), making a number of ⅛"-deep passes to reach the full ¹³⁄₁₆" depth. Be sure to draw a stop line on the fence so you know when to end the cuts. Then, square the ends of the mortises with a chisel.

After completing the mortises, set up your table saw for cutting tenons on the ends of the web frame rails and subtop rails. Install a ¼" dado blade, raise it ¼", and clamp a setup block to the saw's fence. Using the miter gauge for support, first cut the ¼"-long tenons on the subtop rails. Then, reset the fence, and make three passes to cut the ¾"-long tenons on the web frame rails (see Figure 5).

Glue the web frames together, double- and triple-checking each one for squareness as you go. An out-of-square frame will make the final carcass assembly difficult, and it will make fitting the doors and drawers a nightmare.

Allow the glue to dry, and then sand the joints flush. Recall that the web

frames and subtop rails meet the sides and dividers with tongue-and-groove joints, and the bottom panel is attached to the sides and dividers with the same joint. To cut the tongues, switch to a ¼" dado blade, and clamp a wood auxiliary face to your table saw fence. Raise the blade a hair under ¼", and set the fence so it just grazes the blade. Now, cut tongues on pieces of scrap hardwood and plywood, and check their fit in a dado. Once you've made any necessary setup adjustments, cut all the tongues for a snug fit (remember to readjust your blade height if your stock varies in thickness). While you're at it, cut the ¼" x ⅜" rabbets along the back edge of the sides and bottom for installing the back.

Complete preliminary construction of the cabinet by cutting ¼" x ¼" notches at the front corner of each tongue. The notches will allow the front edges of these pieces to slide in flush with the rest of the carcass assembly.

Assembling the Cabinet

A willing helper will make a big difference while putting this carcass together. Begin by organizing all the parts in some sort of order so you can join them efficiently. Then, spread glue in the grooves in one side panel, one divider, and the bottom. Join these pieces together along with a web frame, and then add the second divider and two more web frames. Wrap up the assembly by installing the last web frame, the subtop rails, and the other side panel. Use bar clamps and cambered bearers to spread out the clamping pressure along the entire length of each joint (see Figure 6 on page 72), checking the cabinet for squareness as you go. Drill countersunk pilot holes, and screw the subtop rails to

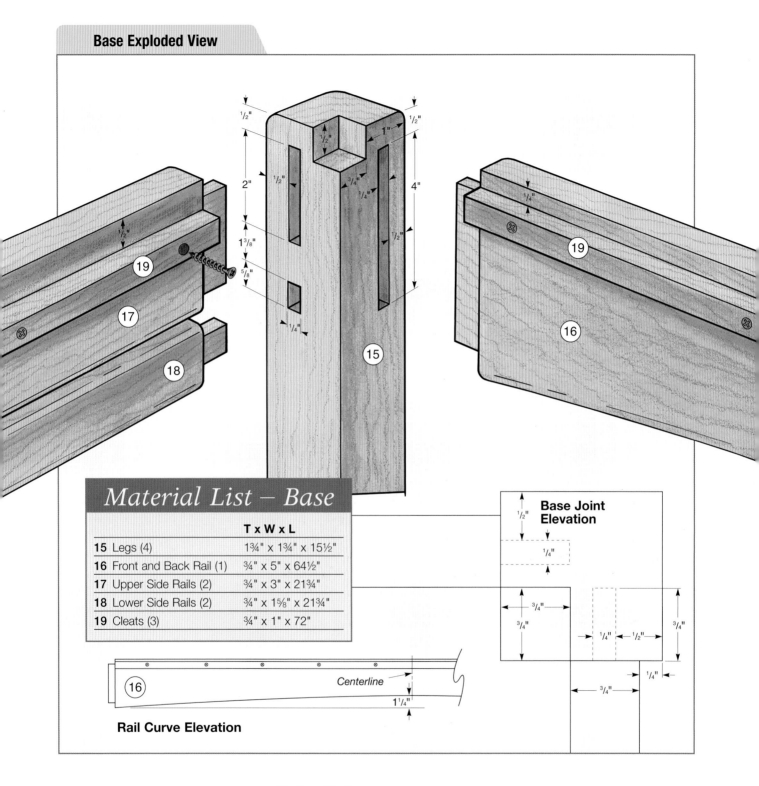

Material List – Base

		T x W x L
15	Legs (4)	1¾" x 1¾" x 15½"
16	Front and Back Rail (1)	¾" x 5" x 64½"
17	Upper Side Rails (2)	¾" x 3" x 21¾"
18	Lower Side Rails (2)	¾" x 1⅝" x 21¾"
19	Cleats (3)	¾" x 1" x 72"

Base Joint Elevation

Centerline

Rail Curve Elevation

the dividers. Then, use a scrap piece of pegboard as a guide for drilling holes in the sides and dividers for the adjustable shelf supports (pieces 9), as shown in the panel elevation drawings. Locate the pegboard carefully on each cabinet panel so the holes align all across.

Making the Top
You've already cut the plywood top to size, so now you can prepare it for joining the edging (pieces 10). Use your router and a ¼" slot-cutting bit with the appropriately sized bearing to plow a ¼"-deep groove into all four edges of

the panel; be sure you center the slots on the edges.

Next, rip stock to width for the edging, letting the pieces run a few inches long for the time being. After you've ripped enough stock, install a ¼" dado blade in your table saw, and raise

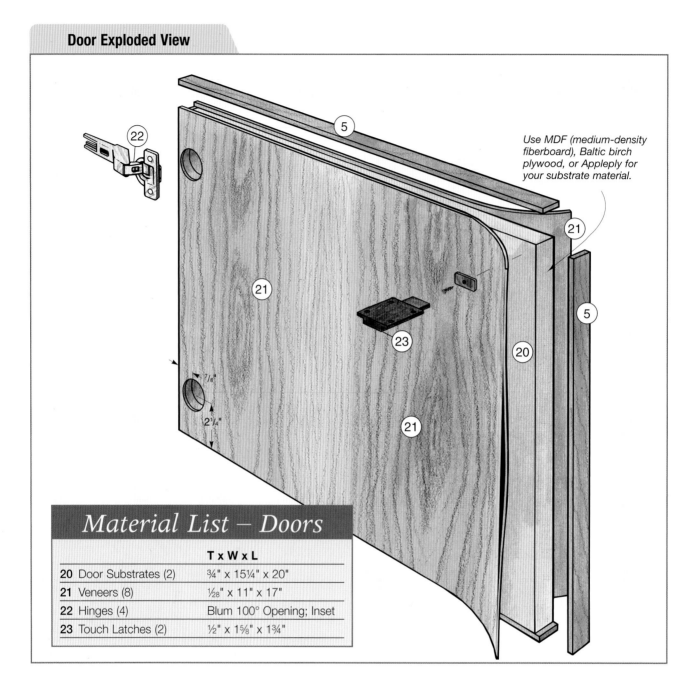

Door Exploded View

Use MDF (medium-density fiberboard), Baltic birch plywood, or Appleply for your substrate material.

⁷/₈"

2¼"

Material List – Doors

		T x W x L
20	Door Substrates (2)	¾" x 15¼" x 20"
21	Veneers (8)	¹/₂₈" x 11" x 17"
22	Hinges (4)	Blum 100° Opening; Inset
23	Touch Latches (2)	½" x 1⅝" x 1¾"

Figure 6: *Cambered bearers are always useful for clamping a large assembly. The curved 2" x 4"s spread out the clamping pressure so that joints at the center of a wide panel are just as tight as those along the edge.*

the blade ¼" to form the tongues, as shown in Figure 7. Clamp a wood face to the fence, and slide the fence right next to the blade. Now, form a tongue on a piece of scrap wood, test its fit in the grooves of the plywood top, and form the tongues on the edging.

For the final step in shaping the edging, rip a 22½° bevel on the top face of each piece. Now, return the blade to 0°, angle the table saw's miter gauge 45°, and miter the edging to length.

Figure 7: *To make the edging, form tongues with a ¼" dado blade, and rip a bevel on the top surfaces. Miter the pieces to length when you're done.*

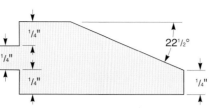

Glue the edging to the top panel, and use a hand plane and scraper to level the joints flush.

Now, position the completed top on the carcass—and you'll get a good sense of where your project is heading. As long as you have the pieces in place, drill countersunk pilot holes through the subtop rails for the hold-down screws.

Wrap up this stage of the cabinet construction by cutting the back and adjustable shelves to size (pieces 12 and 13). Glue banding to the front edge of each shelf, and secure the back to the cabinet with screws (pieces 14).

Building the Base

Unlike the cabinet, the base is made entirely of solid wood. Review the Material List on page 71, and begin the base construction by cutting 1¾"-thick stock for the legs (pieces 15) and ¾"-thick lumber for the front and back rails, as well as the upper and lower side rails (pieces 16 through 18). If you can find an interestingly grained piece of wood for the front rail, it will add a nice touch to the project.

With the pieces cut to size, you can turn your attention to the mortise-and-tenon joints. First, lay out the leg mortises, as shown in the base exploded view on page 71. Then, plow out the waste with your plunge router, using the router's fence attachment and a ¼" straight bit. Set the depth of cut for 1¾16", but take shallow passes to reach that full depth. Square the ends of the mortises with a ¼" chisel.

Now, set up your table saw with a ¾" dado blade, and cut tenons on

the ends of all the base rails, as shown in the base exploded view and base joint elevation drawing on page 71. You may need an outboard support for cutting tenons on the long front and back rails.

Cut the edge shoulders with a handsaw, and then fit the tenons into the leg mortises. If you like the way everything fits together, take the base apart, and lay out the long curves on the front and back rails, using the rail curve elevation drawing on page 71. Cut the curves with a jigsaw or band saw.

To seat the cabinet in the base, the top inside corner of each leg must be notched. Lay out the notches, and cut them with a handsaw and chisel —work carefully here when chopping with the grain, or you may split a leg.

Many of the edges on the base are eased with a router using a ⅜" roundover bit. Rout all the rail edges except those that make contact with the cabinet, and on the legs, rout the top outside edges and front corner.

Sand the parts for the base, and glue them together, cleaning up any squeeze-out after the glue sets to a rubbery consistency. Next, cut the cleats (pieces 19), and screw them to the inside of the upper side rails, front rail, and back rail, as shown in the base exploded view.

Veneering the Doors

Because this sideboard is designed to go with the table and chairs, it picks up many of the same details. Especially important was matching the sapwood in the splat of the chair. You can either follow this design

How to Veneer Doors

When veneering with contact cement, use a stable substrate such as MDF (medium-density fiberboard) or Baltic birch plywood. To keep the substrate balanced, lay the veneer perpendicular to the grain of the plywood surfaces.

Step 1: *Joint the edges, and hold them together with masking tape. Then, flip the veneer over and apply veneer tape to the seam.*

Step 2: *Remove the masking tape, and spread white glue on the seam. Then, unfold the veneer, and place it under pressure while the joint dries.*

Step 3: *Apply contact cement to both the veneer and the substrate, and let it dry. Use stickers to position the veneer over the substrate.*

Step 4: *Carefully pull out the stickers, lay the veneer on the substrate, and then tamp the surface with a hammer and scrap wood block.*

How to Shape the Drawer Handles

Make the sculpted drawer handles in pairs out of ¾" x 3¼" x 22" cherry stock. For a safe operation, keep the support bridges intact at the center and outside edges as you shape the handle pulls.

Step 1: *Draw the pattern for a pair of handles on ¾" stock, and, adjusting the blade height for each cut, rip the waste from the pull areas.*

Step 2: *Tilt the blade 45°, and cut a shallow V on the top surface of the stock. These cuts begin to form the drop on the front edge of each handle.*

Step 3: *Once the shaping is completed, rip off the outside bridges, leaving perfect surfaces for gluing the handles to the drawer faces.*

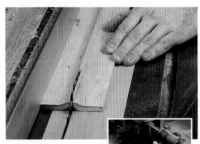

Step 4: *Split the handles apart (above), and then band saw the top profiles (right).*

½"-thick poplar, and cut the dovetail joints (I routed them with the help of a Leigh jig). Once the dovetails are cut, plow ¼" x ¼" grooves ¼" up from the bottom edge of each box wall for holding the bottom panels (pieces 30), as shown in the drawer exploded view on page 75. Cut the bottoms to size, and glue the boxes together.

After sanding the joints flush, lay out the drawer slide positions on the drawer boxes and in the cabinet. Install the slides (pieces 31), and slip the drawers into place. Now, cut the drawer faces to size (pieces 32 through 34), and position them on the boxes so they're flush with the bottom of each opening. Drill countersunk pilot holes through the box fronts, and secure the faces with screws (pieces 11).

Fashion the handles (pieces 35) with a table saw, as shown in How to Shape the Drawer Handles at left. You'll find the end and top profiles for the handles in the drawings on page 75. Glue the handles to the top edge of each drawer face, and blend the handles into the faces with sandpaper after the glue dries.

Finishing Your Sideboard

Remove the back and all the hardware from the cabinet, and separate the cabinet from the base. Sand all the parts up to 220 grit, making sure to ease any sharp corners and blend in the roundovers. Wipe down the project with a tack cloth to clean off the dust, and then rub on four coats of oil finish. Sand lightly between each coat, and continue cleaning off the dust each time with the tack cloth. Four coats should do the job, but you can add more if you want to produce a glossier sheen.

Let the last coat of finish dry for several days, and then rub on a coat of paste wax to protect the finish from water spots. Buffing the wax out will produce a beautiful satin sheen that completes this classic sideboard.

choice or use veneer with a regular grain pattern running across it.

See the Material List on page 72. Cut the plywood to size for the door substrates (pieces 20), and band the edges with ¼"-thick solid stock, as shown in the door exploded view on page 72. Next, cut eight oversize pieces of veneer (pieces 21). Joint the edges, and follow How to Veneer Doors on page 73 to bond the veneer to the plywood substrates.

Blum hinges (pieces 22) are perfect for mounting these doors in the cabinet. They're adjustable in three directions, so you can center the doors perfectly in the openings, and they're hidden when the doors are closed. Drill holes in the back of each door for the hinge cups,

and secure the mounting plates in the cabinet. Slide the hinge arms onto the mounting plates, and make adjustments to center the doors in the openings.

Magnetic touch latches (pieces 23) provide an ideal complement to the hinges on this project. They eliminate the need for door handles to preserve the contemporary styling of the piece. Install the latches, and then move on to building the drawers.

Constructing the Drawers

On high-quality furniture like this sideboard, dovetails are the only way to go when joining the drawer boxes. Referring to the Material List on page 75, cut the box fronts, backs, and sides (pieces 24 through 29) to size from

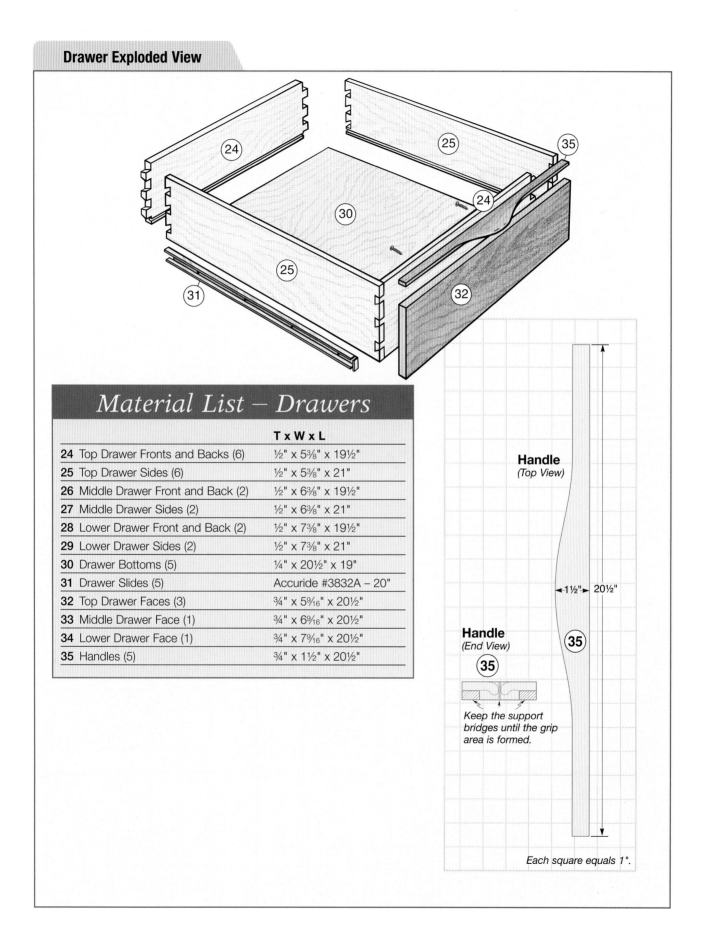

Material List – Drawers

	T x W x L
24 Top Drawer Fronts and Backs (6)	½" x 5⅜" x 19½"
25 Top Drawer Sides (6)	½" x 5⅜" x 21"
26 Middle Drawer Front and Back (2)	½" x 6⅜" x 19½"
27 Middle Drawer Sides (2)	½" x 6⅜" x 21"
28 Lower Drawer Front and Back (2)	½" x 7⅜" x 19½"
29 Lower Drawer Sides (2)	½" x 7⅜" x 21"
30 Drawer Bottoms (5)	¼" x 20½" x 19"
31 Drawer Slides (5)	Accuride #3832A – 20"
32 Top Drawer Faces (3)	¾" x 5⁹⁄₁₆" x 20½"
33 Middle Drawer Face (1)	¾" x 6⁹⁄₁₆" x 20½"
34 Lower Drawer Face (1)	¾" x 7⁹⁄₁₆" x 20½"
35 Handles (5)	¾" x 1½" x 20½"

Handle
(Top View)

◄1½"► 20½"

Handle
(End View)

35

Keep the support bridges until the grip area is formed.

Each square equals 1".

Bowfront Bureau

Bending wood can be a challenge, but don't let the graceful curves of this bureau put you off. By using a combination of easy-to-build bending jigs and bendable plywood, you'll ease right through the tricky parts.

by Rick White

This bowfront bureau is simpler to construct than you might at first think. A single template lets you lay out the long, lazy arches for the top of the mirror, the leading edge of the tabletop, and the bowed drawer fronts. The color scheme is white ash accented by dark walnut trim.

Building a Bending Form

This project begins with the top of the mirror frame, because the curve established here is used to create all the other curves in the dresser. The arched top is made up of several thin laminations that are face glued together and clamped to a bowed form to dry.

The first step in the form's construction is to lay it out with pencil lines on ¾" plywood (see A Simple Bending Jig on page 78 and the curved arch bending jig layout on page 81). Drive an 8d finish nail into the plywood at each end, 65½" apart. Connect the nails with a pencil line, and draw a second, intersecting line halfway along it, at 90°. Drive a third nail exactly 2¹⁵⁄₁₆" up this line. Bend a strip of thin hardwood (or plywood) so it touches all three nails—you might need help here—and draw a curved line along the bottom edge. Extend the line a few inches past each nail.

Clamp a second piece of ¾" plywood below the first, and then jigsaw

both pieces at the same time, staying just outside your layout line. Leave the clamps in place, and belt sand precisely to the line. Keep the sander moving so you don't create any flat spots.

Predrill for screws, and then glue and screw several 3" spacers between the two sheets of plywood. Use a square to make sure the bowed edges line up perfectly as you drive the screws home.

Laminating the Arch

The mirror arch is made up of five ⅜"-thick boards (see the Material List on page 79). Four of these (pieces 1) are ash, while the top one (piece 2) is walnut.

It's a good idea to spread a single layer of wax paper along the form before you start gluing. This will prevent the laminated arch from sticking to the form. You should also make sure you have enough clamps on hand before you start gluing. You'll need about 20—one placed every 6" or 8" on both top and bottom.

Leave the laminations about 3" longer and ¼" wider than their finished size, and then spread the glue with a brush or roller to get even and complete coverage. Work quickly, or the glue will begin to set. Make sure the laminations' edges all line up as closely as possible, and then start applying clamps from the center out. If you see a small gap, move the clamps closer together.

Let the glued assembly dry for at least 24 hours before removing any clamps. While it's drying, you can make the mirror posts.

Making the Mirror Posts

Like the arch, the large posts (pieces 3) that frame the mirror are also laminated. This makes them more stable than a single large piece of stock that might twist or split over the years. It's also easier to find ¾" clear stock than 2¼"-thick boards.

Leave the laminations about 1" longer and ⅛" wider than their final size, and laminate three boards together to make each post. After the glue dries, remove your clamps, and dress one laminated face of each post on the jointer. Then, place the jointed face against the table saw fence, and rip each post to a hair over its final dimension. Make one final pass per post on the jointer, to clean up the ripped face, and then square off the bottom of each post on the miter saw.

Transfer the radius of the arch to the top of each post, and band saw it to shape. Keep in mind that you'll need a right and a left post. Then, sand the cuts smooth.

Milling the Arch

Before assembling the arch on its posts, clean up its edges, trim it to length, and chamfer the bottom edge. After removing the clamps, begin by running the arch

A Simple Bending Jig

The jig to create the gently curved mirror arch is made from plywood and spacers. As you laminate the arch, the jig will be subjected to a lot of stress, so be sure to use plenty of glue and screws when you make it.

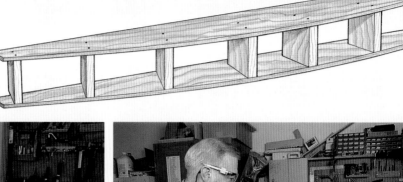

To begin making the bending jig, strike the gentle curve of the mirror arch onto a piece of plywood. This curve must be fair and true.

After using a band saw or handheld jigsaw to rough cut the curve, carefully sand right to the line with your belt sander.

across the jointer to clean one side, and then rip it 1/16" oversize on the table saw before jointing the other side (see Figure 1). Trim it to length so the bottom edge is 67⅜" long.

The chamfering is done with a 45° bearing-guided router bit. To reduce tearout, chamfer the ends first and then the front—along the bottom edge only. Then, switch to a rabbeting bit to plow the stopped rabbet along the bottom edge of the back. Stay with this bit to rabbet the inside back edge of each post, remembering that they're mirror images, not identical shapes.

Make sure the back edges are flush as you connect the arch to the posts with 3" flathead wood screws, driven into counterbored pilot holes.

The final arch lamination, the walnut cap (piece 2), can be applied now. Glue and clamp it in place. After the glue dries, remove the clamps, and trim the edges flush with the ash. A bearing-guided, flush-trimming bit works well on the sides, but use a belt sander on the ends to prevent tearout.

Use the bending form to lay out the curves on the arched walnut trim

Figure 1: *While the arched mirror top may seem to present a machining challenge, simply take the curved piece in stride.*

piece (piece 4) that backs up the mirror frame. Miter the ends of this piece while it's still rectangular, and then cut it to size and shape on the band saw. Cut the straight trim for the sides and bottom (pieces 5 and 6) to size, and miter the remaining corners to fit. Test fit the pieces into the rabbets you just made in the post and arch subassembly.

Making the Mirror Frame

The arched mirror will be surrounded by an ash frame. This frame is glued in front of the walnut trim that you just made. Making the frame is very similar to the process used to make the walnut trim. Begin by striking the curve for the arched top of the frame (piece 7), and then miter its ends before band sawing it to shape. Cut the remaining parts—the sides and bottom (pieces 8 and 9)—to size, miter their corners, and add biscuit mortises for even more stability. Form the rabbets on the back edges of the frame (see the mirror frame detail drawing at right) to accept the trim and mirror back (piece 10). Now is also the time to chamfer the forward edges of the frame. Sand all four parts, dry fit them to the mirror assembly to check their fit, and then assemble with glue and biscuits. Before you go any further, clamp a straightedge in place to guide your router while you mill four dadoes for the walnut inlays (pieces 11) in the frame. Glue the inserts in place, and sand them flush after the glue dries.

Install the back with glue and clamps. When this subassembly is dry, glue and clamp the mirror frame in place, centering it on the walnut trim. At this point, you're ready to order your mirror glass (piece 12), so the glazier can be working on it while you get busy building the dresser carcass.

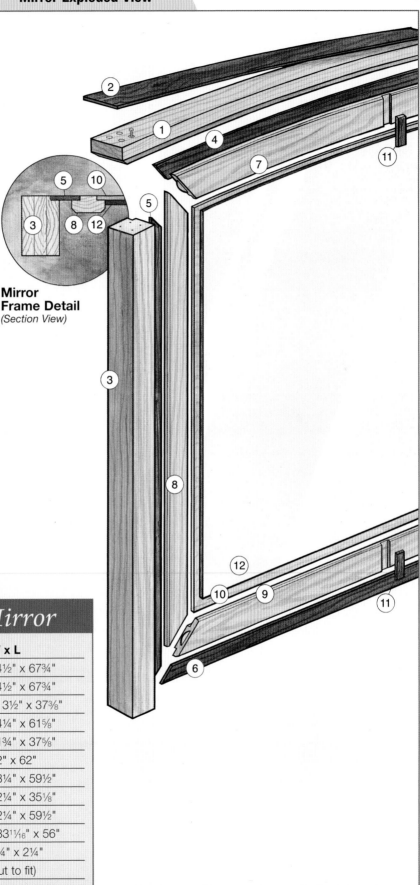

Mirror Exploded View

Mirror Frame Detail
(Section View)

Material List – Mirror

	T x W x L
1 Arch Laminations, Ash (4)	³⁄₈" x 4½" x 67¾"
2 Arch Lamination, Walnut (1)	³⁄₈" x 4½" x 67¾"
3 Mirror Posts (2)	2¼" x 3½" x 37⅜"
4 Walnut Trim, Top (1)	¼" x 4¼" x 61⅝"
5 Walnut Trim, Sides (2)	¼" x 1¾" x 37⅝"
6 Walnut Trim, Bottom (1)	¼" x 2" x 62"
7 Mirror Frame, Top (1)	¾" x 3¼" x 59½"
8 Mirror Frame, Sides (2)	¾" x 2¼" x 35⅛"
9 Mirror Frame, Bottom (1)	¾" x 2¼" x 59½"
10 Mirror Back (1)	¼" x 33¹¹⁄₁₆" x 56"
11 Walnut Frame Inserts (4)	¼" x ¾" x 2¼"
12 Mirror (1)	¼" (Cut to fit)

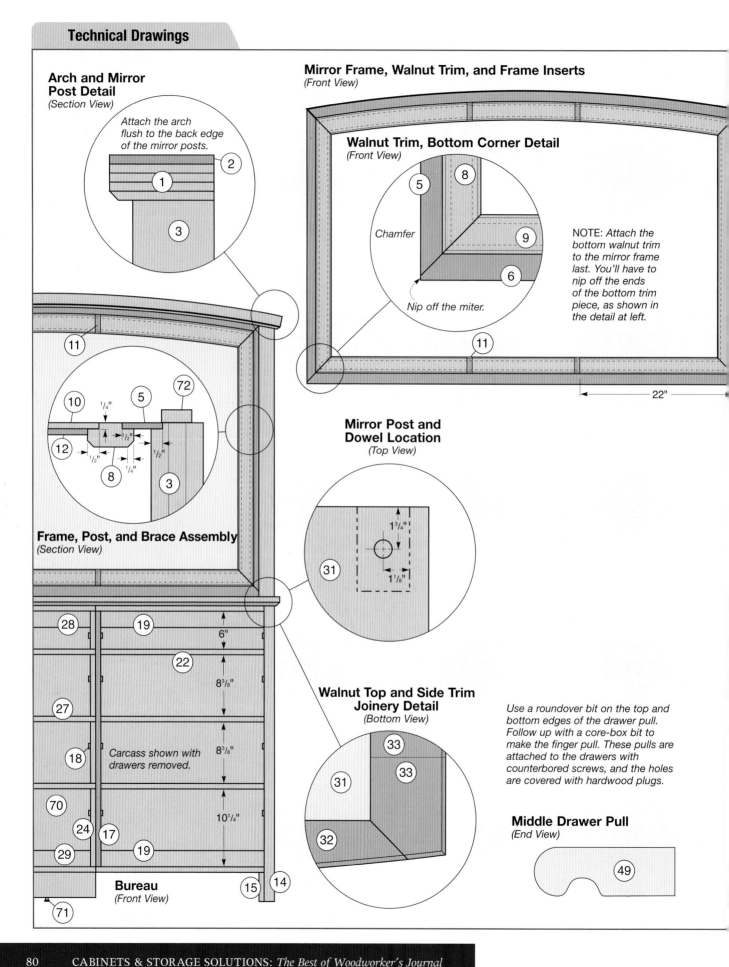

Arch and Mirror Post Detail
(Section View)

Attach the arch flush to the back edge of the mirror posts.

Mirror Frame, Walnut Trim, and Frame Inserts
(Front View)

Walnut Trim, Bottom Corner Detail
(Front View)

Chamfer

Nip off the miter.

NOTE: *Attach the bottom walnut trim to the mirror frame last. You'll have to nip off the ends of the bottom trim piece, as shown in the detail at left.*

22"

Frame, Post, and Brace Assembly
(Section View)

1/4"

1/2"

1/2"

1/2"

1/4"

Mirror Post and Dowel Location
(Top View)

1 3/4"

1 1/8"

Walnut Top and Side Trim Joinery Detail
(Bottom View)

6"

8 3/8"

8 3/8"

10 1/4"

Carcass shown with drawers removed.

Use a roundover bit on the top and bottom edges of the drawer pull. Follow up with a core-box bit to make the finger pull. These pulls are attached to the drawers with counterbored screws, and the holes are covered with hardwood plugs.

Middle Drawer Pull
(End View)

Bureau
(Front View)

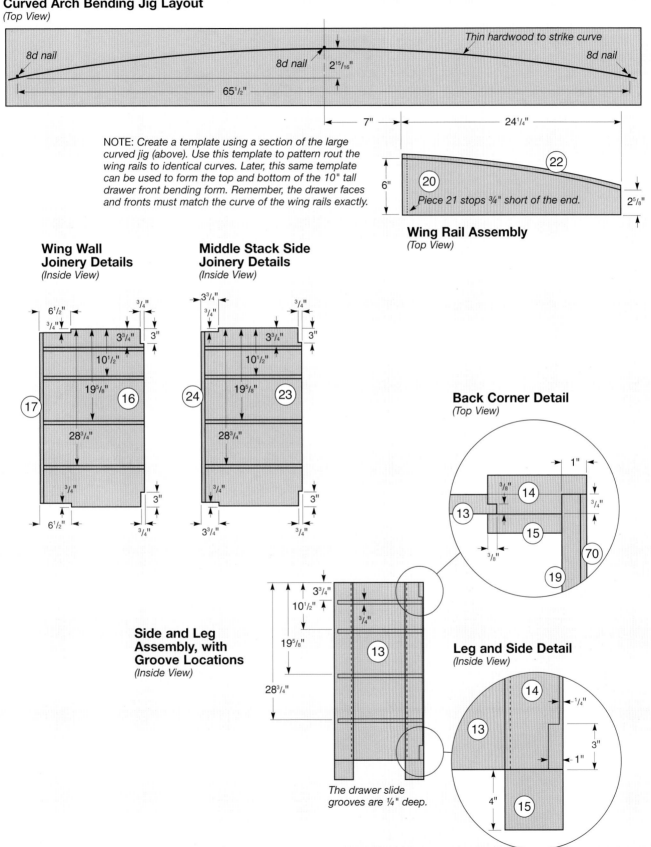

Curved Arch Bending Jig Layout
(Top View)

8d nail

Thin hardwood to strike curve

8d nail

8d nail

$2^{15}/_{16}$"

$65^{1}/_{2}$"

NOTE: Create a template using a section of the large curved jig (above). Use this template to pattern rout the wing rails to identical curves. Later, this same template can be used to form the top and bottom of the 10" tall drawer front bending form. Remember, the drawer faces and fronts must match the curve of the wing rails exactly.

7"

$24^{1}/_{4}$"

6"

(20)

(22)

Piece 21 stops $^{3}/_{4}$" short of the end.

$2^{5}/_{8}$"

Wing Rail Assembly
(Top View)

Wing Wall Joinery Details
(Inside View)

$6^{1}/_{2}$"

$^{3}/_{4}$"

$^{3}/_{4}$"

$3^{3}/_{4}$"

3"

$10^{1}/_{2}$"

$19^{5}/_{8}$"

(17)   (16)

$28^{3}/_{4}$"

$^{3}/_{4}$"

3"

$6^{1}/_{2}$"

$^{3}/_{4}$"

Middle Stack Side Joinery Details
(Inside View)

$3^{3}/_{4}$"

$^{3}/_{4}$"

$^{3}/_{4}$"

$3^{3}/_{4}$"

3"

$10^{1}/_{2}$"

$19^{5}/_{8}$"

(24)   (23)

$28^{3}/_{4}$"

$^{3}/_{4}$"

3"

$3^{3}/_{4}$"

$^{3}/_{4}$"

Back Corner Detail
(Top View)

1"

$^{3}/_{8}$"

(14)

$^{3}/_{4}$"

(13)

(15)

$^{3}/_{8}$"

(70)

(19)

Side and Leg Assembly, with Groove Locations
(Inside View)

$3^{3}/_{4}$"

$10^{1}/_{2}$"

$^{3}/_{4}$"

$19^{5}/_{8}$"

(13)

$28^{3}/_{4}$"

The drawer slide grooves are $^{1}/_{4}$" deep.

Leg and Side Detail
(Inside View)

(14)

$^{1}/_{4}$"

(13)

3"

(15)

1"

4"

Building Three Drawer Stacks

There are 12 drawers in the bureau—three stacks with four drawers each—and the logical way to build such a large piece is to break it into these three separate subassemblies. Because the two wing units are mirror images of each other, you can build both at the same time.

Refer to the Material List on page 85. Cut the bureau sides (pieces 13) to size. These are ¾" ash-veneered plywood, as their outer faces will be visible. Plow the rabbet in each long edge, and set the sides aside. Next, cut the legs and leg blocks (pieces 14 and 15) from solid-ash lumber. With your portable router, mill grooves to receive the bureau sides, and create a rabbet down the rear legs' back edge to receive the bureau's back later. Glue and clamp them together, but be sure to make a right and a left panel.

Next, cut the wing walls (pieces 16) to size, notching all four corners, as shown in the drawings on page 81. These walls will be hidden, so a less-expensive grade of plywood will do nicely. Trim the front edge of each wall with solid-walnut stock (pieces 17). Chuck a ¾" straight bit into your router, and plow stopped dadoes into the inside faces of the walls and sides to hold the drawer slides (pieces 18). This is a good time to form the small rabbets on the back legs to accept the back stringers (pieces 19). Then, glue and clamp the drawer slides into all four panels next. Cut these from hardwood.

Making the Curved Rails

Each of the wings features drawer fronts that pick up the curve of the mirror. You can use that bending form as a template to lay out the curves on the wing rails and intermediate wing rails (pieces 20 and 21). I used a jig and a pattern-routing bit (see Figure 2) to be sure the front edges of each of these curved rails were identical. Apply solid-ash trim (piece 22) to the front of each rail, using glue and clamps to secure it. This is a very gentle curve, so the ash will have no problem bending around it, but leave the clamps on overnight just to give the glue ample time to reach full strength.

The curved rails are secured to the bureau sides with pocket hole joints on the ends that butt into the front legs. Glue these joints, as well. Assemble the wings upside down on a flat work surface, and make sure each subassembly is square and plumb as you work. A few clamps will help keep everything in position while the glue dries.

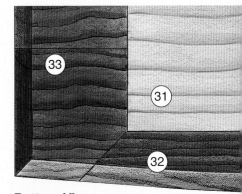

Carcass Exploded View

Front View

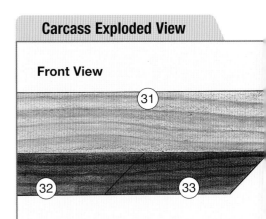

Chamfered Shadow Lines

An elegant shadow line along the front of the bureau is emphasized by adding walnut accents. To create the same look along the sides, glue up short lengths of walnut, and apply them with the end grain exposed. That way, the accent wood can move in concert with the top during seasonal humidity changes.

Bottom View

Figure 2: *The arc of the curved rails on the wing sections must be identical. To achieve this, cut the rails to within ¹⁄₁₆" of their shape, and remove the last bit of stock with a jig and template-routing bit.*

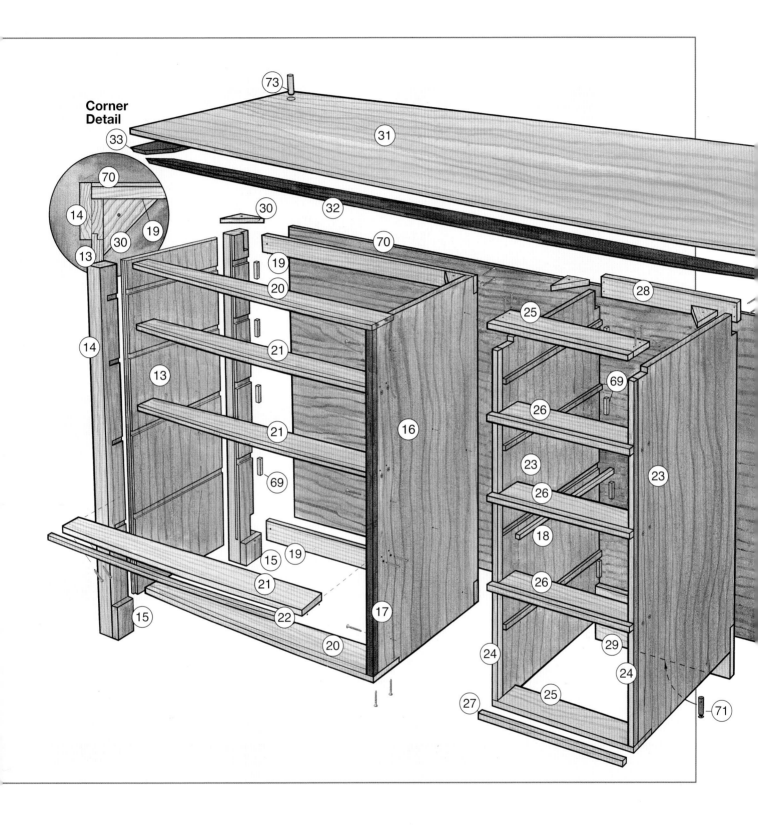

Corner Detail

Constructing the Third Drawer Stack

The middle of the three drawer stacks is more economical to build. Its sides (pieces 23) are totally hidden, so there's no need to use ash-veneered plywood here. Cut the sides to size, and then lay out the notches at all four corners of each. Cut these with a jigsaw, keeping in mind that you need a left and a right panel that are mirror images of each other. Plow the dadoes for the drawer slide stock (piece 18) with a router and straight bit or dado blade on the table saw, and then cut the ash trim for the front edges (piece 24) to size. Next, glue and clamp the trim and drawer slides in place.

As with the outer stacks, the middle stack's top and bottom rails (pieces 25) are a tad longer than the intermediate ones (pieces 26). They're not curved, however, so you can cut all five rails to size on the table saw. Apply solid-ash trim (piece 27) to the front edge of each. Cut the rear upper and lower stringers (pieces 28 and 29) to size. Note that the lower stringer is much wider than the upper, which allows you to place an adjustable leg into its edge. While this center support may not be necessary, it's better to be safe than sorry. Glue and screw the middle stack together, as you did with the wings. The screw locations are not critical, as they will all be hidden.

After the glue dries, sand all three drawer stacks down through the grits to 220. Now, assemble the carcass. Glue and screw the wings to the middle stack, lining them up properly from front to back. Again, this is best done upside down on a flat surface. After assembly, glue and screw the corner blocks (pieces 30) in place. They should be predrilled to attach the top.

Figure 3: *The finger pulls on the curved drawer handles are plowed on the router table with a core-box bit. Use a rounded "point fence" to get an extra measure of control as you move the curved piece across the router table from right to left.*

Making the Bureau Top

This is the least complicated subassembly in the entire project, and yet it may well be the most critical. Such a large expanse of ash is bound to attract admiring—and critical—glances. Begin making the top (piece 31) by selecting your best ash boards. Any width from 3" to 6" is acceptable. After jointing them, alternate their growth rings as you edge glue the boards to make a panel. Sand the panel flat with a belt sander, or take it to a cabinet shop and have it sanded on a panel sander for best results. Then, trim the top to size, but keep it as a rectangle for

---

Tricks for Building Curved Drawers

Featuring curved fronts and sides of differing lengths, these drawers are not your typical cabinet fare.

After creating the drawer sides, use an angled dado head to form the dadoes for the fronts. Remember that you have to make right and left versions.

Fit the bottom to the curved fronts by tracing their curve and trimming to match. The curved fronts are glued up on premade jigs. You'll find details in the elevation drawings on page 81 to help with this.

After a quick belt sanding to extend the gentle curve of the drawer front through the corner joints, turn to the table saw to form the notches that are designed to accept the curved drawer pulls.

now. Next, glue and clamp the walnut accents (pieces 32 and 33) in place, mitering the corners. Note the unusual orientation of piece 33 on each end. This keeps expansion and contraction issues to a minimum. Cut and fit the back spacer (piece 34), and glue it in place. After the glue has cured, use the original bending form as a template to lay out the curve on the front edge of the dresser top. Band saw close to the curved edge, and clean it up with your belt sander.

Switch to a chamfering bit to create the relief along the bottom edge of the top; the walnut lends an elegant effect to the dresser top when it's trimmed back in this manner. Work across the grain first and then along it to minimize chipping and tearout.

Constructing the Drawers and Pulls

Eight of these drawers have curved fronts, while the four drawers in the middle stack are pretty standard fare. Let's begin with the center ones. All of these grooves, rabbets, and dadoes can be milled on the table saw with a dado head set to the correct width. See the technical drawings for complete part dimensions.

All four middle drawers are constructed in the same manner; only their heights differ (see the Material List on page 87). Cut the sides (pieces 35 through 37) to size, and then plow a groove on the outside of each for the drawer slide. Follow up with a groove along the inside for the drawer bottom, and mill two dadoes across the inside for the drawer back and front.

The backs (pieces 38 through 40) require a ¼" groove for the drawer bottoms. Plow this same groove in the drawer fronts (pieces 41 through 43), and then rabbet the ends of each drawer front. Cut the drawer bottoms (pieces 44) to size, and assemble the drawers with glue and clamps. Don't glue the bottoms in their grooves; they should be free to move a little, to accommodate changes in humidity. After the glue dries, remove your clamps and slide each drawer into its opening to make sure it's a good fit before you make and mount the drawer faces (pieces 45 through 47). The grain on the faces runs vertically, so crosscut a single piece of ash plywood to yield all four faces. This will give you continuous grain from top to bottom. Glue or iron on ash-veneer edge tape (piece 48) to the vertical edges of each drawer face to cover the plywood edges. Trim the tape flush with a sharp utility knife, and turn to the drawer pulls next.

All four drawer pulls (pieces 49) can be cut from a single length of molding. Rip 60" of ½" solid ash to a width of 1¾", and then use a bullnose bit to round over the front edges. Next, chuck a 5⁄16"-radius core-box bit in your router, and plow the finger groove in the bottom of the molding. Sand to 220 grit, and crosscut the molding to make the four pulls. Install them with glue and counterbored screws. Plug the borings with ash plugs (pieces 50) made on your drill press with a plug cutter.

Material List – Carcass

		T x W x L
13	Bureau Sides (2)	¾" x 12⅜" x 36¾"
14	Legs (4)	1½" x 4" x 40¾"
15	Leg Blocks (4)	¾" x 4" x 4"
16	Wing Walls (2)	¾" x 21½" x 36¾"
17	Wing Wall Trim, Walnut (2)	¾" x ¾" x 35¼"
18	Drawer Slides (24)	½" x ¾" x 21½"
19	Back Stringers (4)	¾" x 3" x 25"
20	Wing Rails (4)	¾" x 6" x 24¼"
21	Intermediate Wing Rails (6)	¾" x 6" x 23½"
22	Rail Trim (1)	½" x ¾" x 250"
23	Middle Stack Sides (2)	¾" x 20¾" x 36¾"
24	Middle Stack Side Trim (2)	¾" x ¾" x 35¼"
25	Middle Stack Rails (2)	¾" x 3" x 14"
26	Middle Stack Intermediate Rails (3)	¾" x 3" x 12½"
27	Ash Rail Trim (1)	¾" x ¾" x 75"
28	Middle Upper Stringer (1)	¾" x 3" x 14"
29	Middle Lower Stringer (1)	¾" x 6½" x 14"
30	Corner Blocks (6)	¾" x 4" x 4"
31	Bureau Top (1)	¾" x 25" x 70"
32	Walnut Front Bureau Top Trim (1)	½" x 5" x 70"
33	Walnut Side Bureau Top Trim (2)	½" x 22" x 5"
34	Trim Spacer (1)	½" x 2" x 60"

Forming Bowfront Drawers with Bendable Plywood

The drawers in the wing units are constructed in exactly the same manner as the middle drawers, except that the fronts and faces are bowed. Note that eight of the sides (pieces 51 through 53) are shorter than the other eight (pieces 54 through 56). You should also keep in mind that you're making two stacks of drawers that are mirror images of each other, so mark the pieces as you go.

Cut all eight drawer backs (pieces 57 through 59) to size. Then, use your original bending form to lay out the curve for the drawer fronts and faces (pieces 60 through 65). You'll need to build a new bending form for the drawers, as they're taller than the original arch. If you make this form large enough to handle the bottom drawer (10¾" high), then it can be used for all eight.

Make each drawer front with three laminations of ¼" bending plywood, glued and clamped in place. It's a good idea to work with slightly oversize stock at this point and then trim it to final dimensions after the glue dries. See Tricks for Building Curved Drawers on page 84, as well as the technical drawings, for more details on the curved drawer construction.

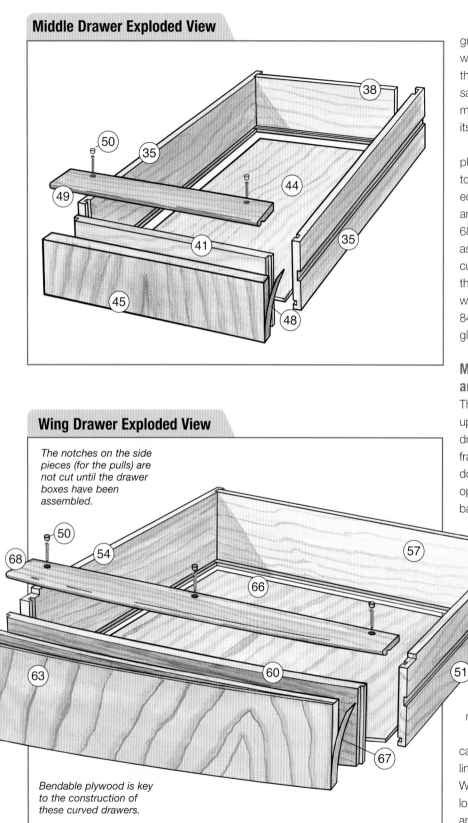

Middle Drawer Exploded View

38

50

35

49

44

41

35

45

48

Wing Drawer Exploded View

The notches on the side pieces (for the pulls) are not cut until the drawer boxes have been assembled.

50

68

54

57

66

63

60

51

67

Bendable plywood is key to the construction of these curved drawers.

Mill the dadoes for the backs and the grooves for the drawer bottoms (pieces 66) with the dado head reset to 90°. Then, cut the bottoms to size and shape on the table saw and band saw. Assemble the drawers, making sure they're square. Test fit each in its cavity after the glue dries.

Use two laminations of bending plywood and one of ash-veneered plywood to make the curved drawer faces. Trim the edges with ash-veneer edge tape (piece 67), and you're ready to make the pulls (pieces 68). These are created exactly the same way as the middle drawer pulls, except they're curved. Band saw them to shape, bullnose the front edges, plow the finger grooves with a core-box bit (see Figure 3 on page 84), and secure the pulls to the drawers with glue and plugged screws.

Making the Drawer Stops and Bureau Back

This is one piece of furniture where lining up the drawers is easy. You'll want each drawer front to line up perfectly with the face frame of the dresser, and all you have to do to achieve this is to pop them into their openings, line them up, and then go around back and put a pencil mark on the slide at the back of each drawer. Then, you can glue and screw stops (pieces 69) in place to limit each drawer's travel.

With the stops in place, cut the bureau back (piece 70) to size, and then secure it in place with brads every 6" or so around the edge and up along the back edges of the middle stack sides. Now, install the adjustable middle support (piece 71).

Slide the drawers into their various cavities, and use double-sided tape to line up the drawer faces in their openings. When you're satisfied with their fit, mark the locations with a pencil, remove the tape, and secure the faces to the drawer boxes with countersunk screws driven through the inside of the drawer fronts.

Material List – Drawers

		T x W x L
35	Top Middle Drawer Sides (2)	¾" x 5⅜" x 21¼"
36	Intermediate Middle Drawer Sides (4)	¾" x 8" x 21¼"
37	Bottom Middle Drawer Sides (2)	¾" x 9⅝" x 21¼"
38	Top Middle Drawer Back (1)	¾" x 5⅜" x 11⅝"
39	Intermediate Middle Drawer Backs (2)	¾" x 8" x 11⅝"
40	Bottom Middle Drawer Back (1)	¾" x 9⅝" x 11⅝"
41	Top Middle Drawer Front (1)	¾" x 5⅜" x 1⅝"
42	Intermediate Middle Drawer Fronts (2)	¾" x 8" x 11⅝"
43	Bottom Middle Drawer Front (1)	¾" x 9⅝" x 11⅝"
44	Middle Drawer Bottoms (4)	¾" x 11⅝" x 20½"
45	Top Middle Drawer Face (1)	¾" x 13¹⁵⁄₁₆" x 5¼"
46	Intermediate Middle Drawer Faces (2)	¾" x 13¹⁵⁄₁₆" x 8"
47	Bottom Middle Drawer Face (1)	¾" x 13¹⁵⁄₁₆" x 9⅝"
48	Middle Drawer Face Tape (1)	¹⁄₁₆" x ¾" x 70"
49	Middle Drawer Pull Molding (1)	½" x 1½" x 75"
50	Screw Plugs (48)	⅜" Dia.
51	Top Wing Drawers, Short Sides (2)	¾" x 5¼" x 18¼"
52	Intermediate Wing Drawers, Short Sides (4)	¾" x 8" x 18¼"
53	Bottom Wing Drawers, Short Sides (2)	¾" x 9⅝" x 18¼"
54	Top Wing Drawers, Long Sides (2)	¾" x 5¼" x 21"
55	Intermediate Wing Drawers, Long Sides (4)	¾" x 8" x 21"
56	Bottom Wing Drawers, Long Sides (2)	¾" x 9⅝" x 21"
57	Top Wing Drawers, Backs (2)	¾" x 5¼" x 22⅝"
58	Intermediate Wing Drawers, Backs (4)	¾" x 8" x 22⅝"
59	Bottom Wing Drawers, Backs (2)	¾" x 9⅝" x 22⅝"
60	Top Wing Drawers, Fronts (2)	¾" x 5¼" x 22¾"
61	Intermediate Wing Drawers, Fronts (4)	¾" x 8" x 22¾"
62	Bottom Wing Drawers, Fronts (2)	¾" x 9⅝" x 22¾"
63	Top Wing Drawer, Faces (2)	¾" x 23⅝" x 5½"
64	Intermediate Wing Drawer Faces (4)	¾" x 23⅝" x 8"
65	Bottom Wing Drawer Faces (2)	¾" x 23⅝" x 9⅝"
66	Wing Drawer Bottoms (8)	¼" x 22⅝" x 19¼"
67	Wing Drawer Face Tape (1)	¹⁄₁₆" x ¾" x 140"
68	Wing Drawer Pulls, Molding (1)	½" x 2½" x 195"

Odds and Ends

69	Drawer Stops (24)	½" x ½" x 2½"
70	Bureau Back (1)	¼" x 36¾" x 64"
71	Adjustable Support (1)	¾" Dia.
72	Mirror Braces (2)	½" x 1¼" x 60"
73	Dowels (2)	¾" Dia. x 5"

Some Final Thoughts

Sand the entire dresser, including the mirror frame, to 220 grit, and then apply several coats of oil finish according to the manufacturer's instructions. After the finish dries, move the dresser to its new home before you mount the mirror. This can be done with two braces (pieces 72), coupled with ¾" dowels (pieces 73). The braces are screwed into the mirror and the base, and the dowels locate and secure the mirror posts on the top (see the mirror post and dowel location detail drawing on page 80 to ensure accurate location of the dowel holes). Finally, use glazier's mastic to secure the mirror to the mirror back.

Now all that remains is to justify to your wife why you need the majority of the drawers. It's probably a battle you'll lose before it even begins.

Backyard Barbecue Cart

Barbecuing is a great pastime, but the prep work is a chore—lugging everything from the utensils and hot pads to the charcoal and lighter fluid out to the grill. Build this barbecue cart as a way of saving some effort. It's sturdy enough to wheel around outside and large enough to store a couple of bags of charcoal. It will prove to be a capable assistant to your family's chief outdoor cook—even if that person is you!

by David Larson

The cart you see here is made of soft, clear redwood panels framed with hardy white oak. Both species stand up well to the elements. I also used stainless-steel screws, waterproof polyurethane glue, and some forged-iron hardware with an exterior-grade finish. It's all topped off with an outdoor wood sealant. A couple of notes about redwood: First, there are three grades available—construction, construction heart, and all heart. All heart is the most expensive, but it's also knot

Figure 1: *Just about all the tongues and grooves can be cut on the router table with a single fence adjustment.*

free. Second, ¾" redwood is a nominal dimension—it's frequently ¹¹⁄₁₆" thick, and sometimes even ⅝". So make sure you adjust your milling setups accordingly.

Starting with the Oak Frames

This project is primarily an exercise in frame-and-panel construction. Once the pieces are cut to size (see the Material List on page 90), all the remaining milling can be done with a table-mounted router.

The cart's carcass consists of a door frame, a top frame, and three frame-and-panel subassemblies—the back, the short end (near the wheels), and the long end (with the handle). All five carcass frames (pieces 1 through 8) and the door frames (pieces 27 through 29) are cut from white oak, while the panels (pieces 10 through 14, 30, and 31) are made of free-floating tongue-and-groove redwood boards.

Tongue-and-groove construction also holds the frames together. Begin by cutting all the grooves first, as it's easier to adjust the thickness of the tongues than the width of the grooves. Install a ¼"

Figure 2: *Cut a tongue or groove on all four edges of the redwood panel pieces, and follow up with a chamfering bit.*

straight bit in your router table, locating its center ⅜" from the fence; this will center each groove in the edge of the stiles and rails. Set the depth of cut to ¼". For the locations of the grooves, consult the technical drawings on pages 94–95.

Several of the grooves in the frame pieces are stopped, while others run the full length of the piece. Cut all the grooves (see Figure 1), and then follow up by making the tongues (a tight fit is essential here). While you're cutting tongues in the frame pieces, you can also cut them on

Material List – Carcass and Doors

		T x W x L
1	End Rails (4)	¾" x 2" x 13¼"
2	Front and Back Rails (4)	¾" x 2" x 31"
3	Short End Stiles (2)	¾" x 1⅝" x 33½"
4	Long End Stiles (2)	¾" x 1⅝" x 34½"
5	Short Front and Back Stiles (2)	¾" x 2" x 33½"
6	Long Front and Back Stiles (2)	¾" x 2" x 34½"
7	Top Stiles (2)	¾" x 2½" x 36¾"
8	Top Rails (2)	¾" x 2½" x 15½"
9	Leg Braces (4)	¾" x 3" x 5¾"
10	Middle End Panels (2)	¾" x 2½" x 26"
11	Outer End Panels (4)	¾" x 5½" x 26"
12	Back Panel – A (1)	¾" x 4⅜" x 26"
13	Back Panels – B (6)	¾" x 4" x 26"
14	Back Panel – C (1)	¾" x 4⅛" x 26"
15	Bottom Stretchers (3)	¾" x 2" x 15"
16	Bottom Boards (3)	¾" x 5" x 32¾"
17	Wheels (2)	5½" Dia.
18	Axles (2)	⅜" x 2½" Carriage Bolts
19	Axle Nuts (2)	⅜"-Dia. Locking Nuts
20	Cutting Board Panel (1)	¾" x 12¼" x 22½"
21	Cutting Board Ends (2)	¾" x 1¼" x 12¼"
22	Cutting Board Slides (2)	2" x 1¾" x 32¾"
23	Towel Rack Sides (2)	¾" x 4" x 9"
24	Towel Rack Handle (1)	1¼"-Dia. Dowel
25	Corian Top (1)	½" x 15" x 32¾"
26	Bottle Opener (1)	Solid Brass
27	Door Rails (4)	¾" x 2" x 11¾"
28	Door Stiles (3)	¾" x 2" x 26"
29	Door Lip Stile (1)	¾" x 2⅜" x 26"
30	Middle Door Panels (2)	¾" x 2½" x 21½"
31	Outer Door Panels (4)	¾" x 4⅞" x 21½"
32	Strap Hinges (4)	9" Forged Iron
33	Door Latch (1)	Forged Iron
34	Magnetic Catch (1)	⁵⁄₁₆" x 2" x ¹³⁄₁₆"
35	Door Knobs (2)	1⅜"-Dia. Forged Iron
36	Utensil Hooks (4)	Forged Iron

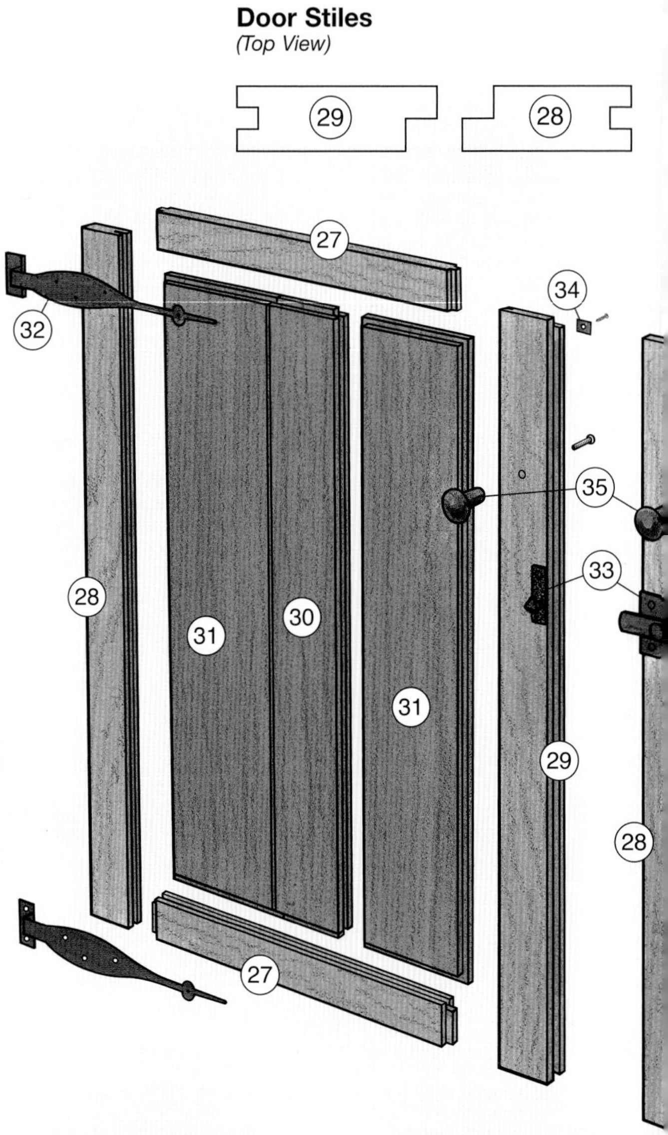

Door Stiles
(Top View)

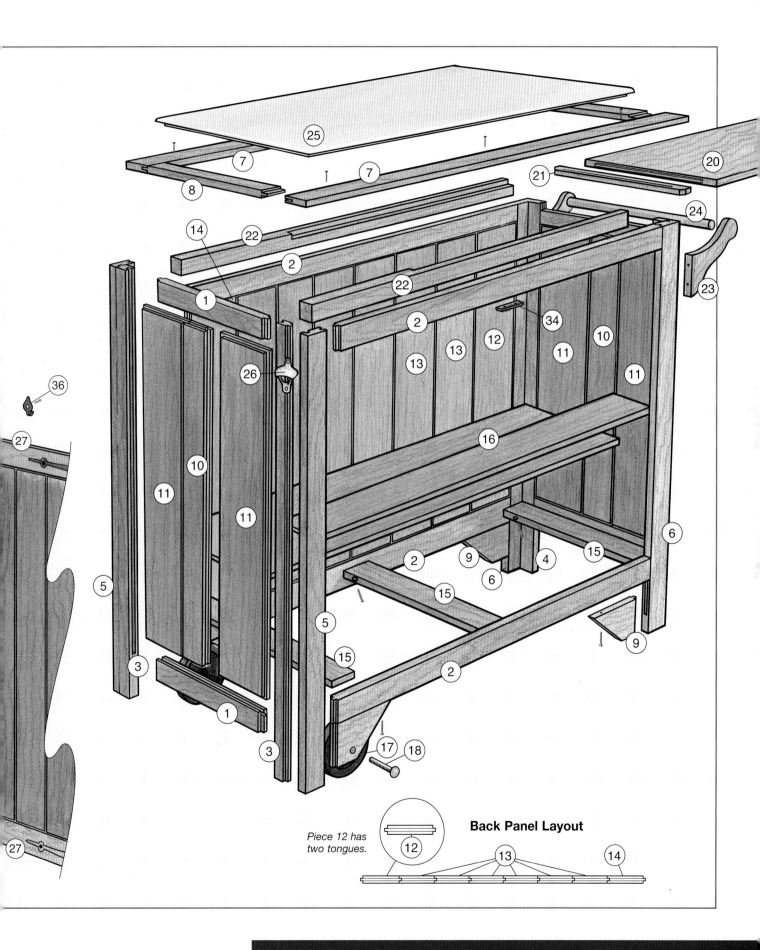

Piece 12 has two tongues.

Back Panel Layout

the leg braces (pieces 9). The tongues and grooves on the top frame are 1" long, so make these cuts in several passes.

Milling the Redwood Panels

Stick with your ¼" straight bit to create the tongues and grooves on the redwood panels (pieces 10 through 14, 30, and 31). Since ¾" nominal redwood comes in various thicknesses, adjust your router table's fence accordingly to make certain that you're centering the grooves in your stock.

Figure 3: *Use a pocket hole jig to create the hidden pilot holes in the three stretcher pieces.*

Again, check the technical drawings to determine where the tongues and grooves are cut. Just as you did on the frame pieces, start with the grooves, and test your setups on scraps of the same thickness. As these won't be glued together, a loose fit is appropriate. Start milling the edges (see Figure 2 on page 89), and then, without changing your setup, move on to the tops and bottoms of the panel pieces, which also have to fit into a frame. Finish the milling process on the redwood panels by chucking a 90° V-groove bit in your router to cut the decorative chamfers on all sides of the panel faces, as shown in the technical drawings on page 95.

Working with Corian

Corian is the most popular brand of a family of products called solid-surface materials — plastics with color patterns that permeate the material. Corian usually comes in ¼", ½", and ¾" thicknesses. Originally, it was used just for countertops. But innovative fabricators have found many new uses for Corian: from shower surrounds and plaques to cutting boards and wall panels.

Carbide bits are essential when routing Corian, which is three times as dense as most hardwoods.

Corian is relatively easy to work. Standard woodshop equipment is quite adequate, but to provide quality work, you must equip your machines with carbide blades or bits. Sharp cutters are essential to prevent chatter and surface irregularities, because Corian is three times as dense as most hardwoods.

Cutting straight lines in Corian is best done with a router. If you use a table saw, the cut will have kerf marks that will have to be removed with a router anyway, so you may as well use the right tool from the start.

Also, when using a router and straightedge, the tool moves across the surface of the material. A table saw, on the other hand, requires that you push the entire surface of the workpiece across the tabletop, which makes it prone to scratching.

Wearing protective gear is a must with Corian and similar products. Although the dust is chemically nontoxic, it can be pervasive and constitutes a mechanical nuisance. Eye protection is also recommended by the DuPont Corporation, which manufactures Corian. The product, though extremely durable, is somewhat brittle, so particles can fly under certain circumstances. It's also heavy, so use proper lifting techniques. And that density prompts one more piece of advice: When routing a decorative edge, or using a router to cut Corian, make several passes rather than trying to remove all the waste in a single pass. This is easier on your tools and improves the quality of the cut.

Achieving a matte finish on Corian is also easy. Start sanding with 180-grit paper, and work your way through 400-grit paper. Use a silicon carbide open-coat paper, and change papers often, as the fine dust tends to clog even open coats rather quickly. Wash off the excess dust with cold water, and buff with a Scotch-Brite pad.

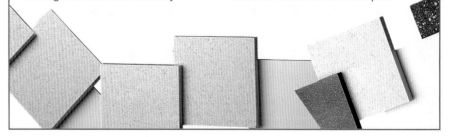

Assemble the Frames and Panels

After you've milled all the frame and panel pieces, it's time to glue and clamp each frame-and-panel assembly together. Before you do, rip one of the end rails (pieces 1) to 1⅛", and remember that one stile on one of the doors (piece 29) is wider than the others. Spread your glue sparingly, and don't glue the redwood panels to each other or to the frames—they float freely. Make sure each panel is square by measuring diagonally.

After the glue has dried in each subframe, dry fit the four frames that create the cart's carcass (where pieces 3 and 5 and pieces 6 and 4 meet). If everything fits, apply your glue to the mating tongues and grooves, and use web clamps to hold them together. You may need a couple of extra hands for this step, but polyurethane glue has a long open time, so there's no rush.

Cutting Rabbets on the Doors

There are two final milling steps on the doors, after they've been assembled. The doors are offset, so rabbets must be cut on their inside edges, and a lip must be cut on one door where they overlap. These two steps are handled on the router table with a ½" straight bit, following the dimensions shown in the technical drawings. Cut the rabbet around the inside edge of all the rails and stiles except the wide lip stile (piece 29), which gets a rabbet on the outside edge.

Figure 4: *After rounding over the top edge of the Corian with a ¼" roundover bit, create a rabbet in the bottom edge with a straight bit.*

Making the Bottom

Stretchers (pieces 15) are installed between the lower front and back rails to support the redwood bottom boards (pieces 16). If you'd prefer not to see any screws or screw hole plugs on the cart's exterior, you can use a pocket hole jig to drill screw holes diagonally through the sides of the stretchers and into the rails (see Figure 3).

After the bottom redwood boards are cut to size, set them loosely in place. It will make cleanup easier; if charcoal spills, just lift out the boards and brush them off.

This is also a good time to glue and screw the braces to the legs below the lower rails. Before you attach them, drill holes (see the technical drawings for locations) for the carriage bolts that serve as axles for the wheels (pieces 17 through 19).

Cutting Board

This cart includes a reversible cutting board that pulls out for cleanup in the kitchen sink. Create the panel (piece 20) by gluing up pieces of white oak. While the glue is drying, rout a ¼"-wide x ⅜"-deep stopped groove (see the technical drawings) in each cutting board end (pieces 21). After the glue has dried in the panel, route a corresponding tongue on each of its ends.

Assemble the cutting board, using screws instead of glue to allow for the expansion and contraction you'll surely get with this outdoor piece of furniture. You'll find the oversize screw hole locations and dimensions on the technical drawings. Wrap up by covering the screws with plugs.

With the cutting board panel assembled, use a 90° V-groove bit to route finger pulls on both sides of both ends. Finish the cutting board by drilling a ⅛" drain hole through the middle of each finger pull.

The cutting board is held in the cart by two oak slides (pieces 22) that have stopped rabbets cut in them (see the

technical drawings). After the rabbets are cut, simply glue and clamp the slides to the carcass.

Towel Rack/Handle

Enlarge the pattern for the towel rack side (pieces 23) on page 94, and cut out the pattern on your band saw. Clean up the saw marks with a drum sander.

After you have shaped the sides, use a Forstner bit to cut 1¼" holes that will hold the handle (piece 24). Attach the sides to the frame stiles with screws and glue, making sure the cutting board has enough room to slide out.

The Corian Top

Screw the top frame you built earlier to the cutting board slides now. This top frame will hold the Corian panel (piece 25). There are two milling steps involving the Corian: rounding the top edge with a ¼" roundover bit and creating a rabbet on the bottom edge (see Figure 4) to hide the screws in the top frame. If you've never worked with Corian, be sure to follow the tips in Working with Corian on page 92. It's not the same as wood.

I used Olympic WaterGuard to seal this project. It's a waterproofing sealant that resists mildew growth and blocks the sun's ultraviolet rays. Apply three coats to everything but the cutting board, sanding lightly between coats. Give the cutting board a couple of liberal coats of salad bowl finish, since it will come in contact with food. Paint the carriage bolt heads with black enamel so they match the forged-iron hardware.

After the finish dries, attach the bottle opener, hinges, door latch, magnetic catch, knobs, and utensil hooks (pieces 32 through 36). To keep your charcoal dry, apply silicone caulking around the top frame before setting down the Corian top. Then, start getting ready for that next big cookout!

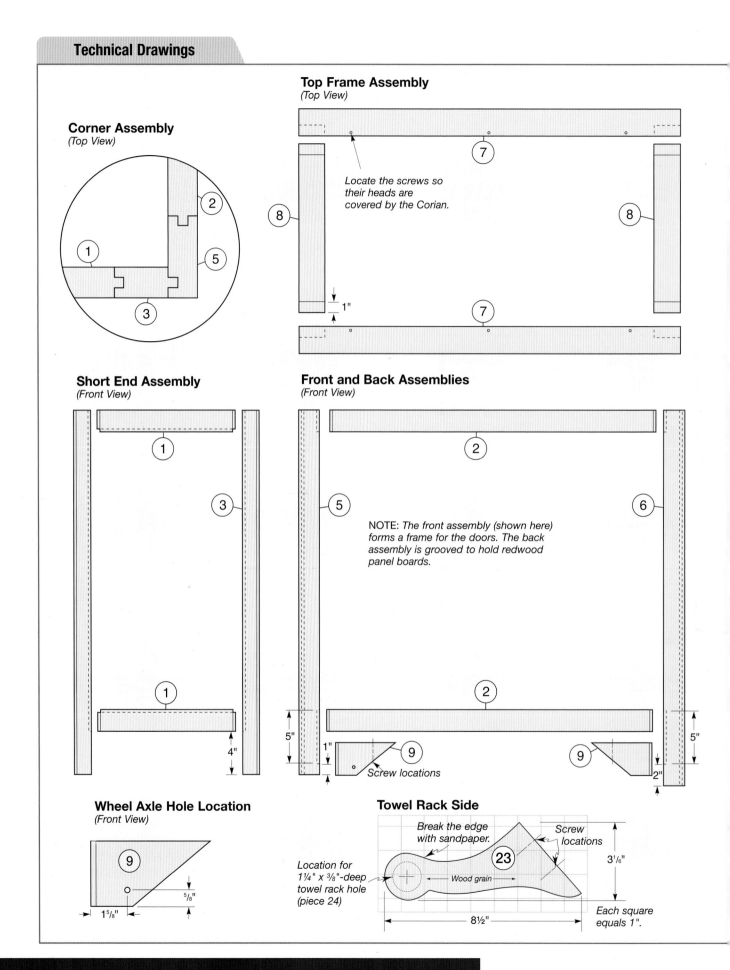

Corner Assembly
(Top View)

1
2
5
3

Top Frame Assembly
(Top View)

8
7
8
7

Locate the screws so
their heads are
covered by the Corian.

1"

Short End Assembly
(Front View)

1
3
1
4"

Front and Back Assemblies
(Front View)

2
5
6

NOTE: *The front assembly (shown here)
forms a frame for the doors. The back
assembly is grooved to hold redwood
panel boards.*

2
5"
1"
9
Screw locations
9
5"
2"

Wheel Axle Hole Location
(Front View)

9
⁵⁄₈"
1⁵⁄₈"

Towel Rack Side

Break the edge
with sandpaper.

Screw
locations

23

3¹⁄₆"

Location for
1¼" x ³⁄₈"-deep
towel rack hole
(piece 24)

Wood grain

8½"

Each square
equals 1".

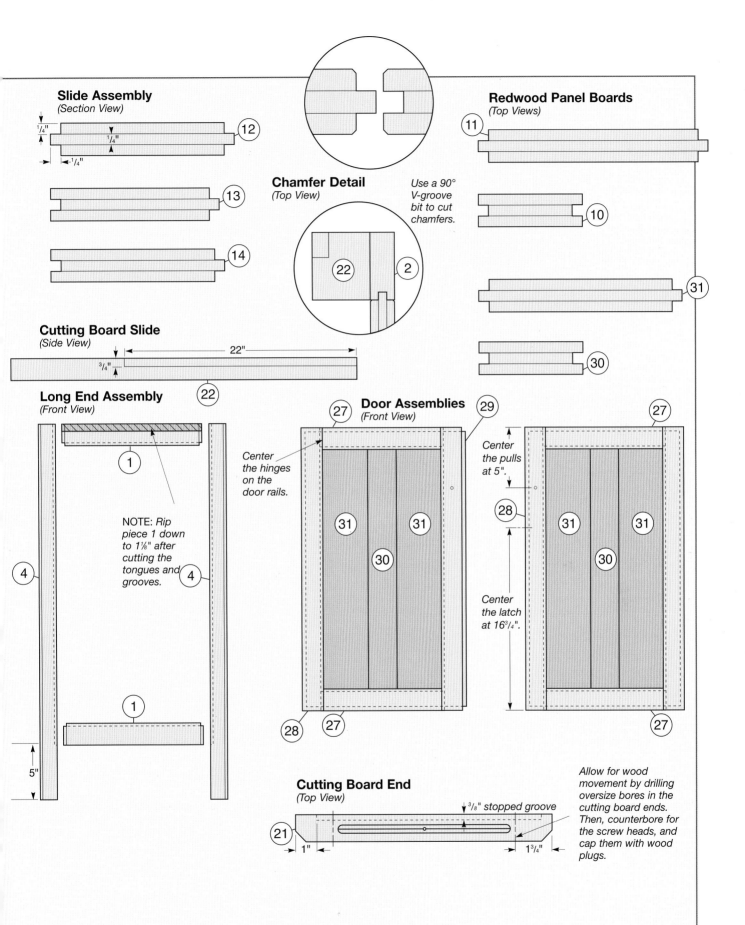

Slide Assembly
(Section View)

12

13

14

Chamfer Detail
(Top View)

Use a 90° V-groove bit to cut chamfers.

22

2

Redwood Panel Boards
(Top Views)

11

10

31

30

Cutting Board Slide
(Side View)

22"

³/₄"

22

Long End Assembly
(Front View)

1

4

4

1

NOTE: *Rip piece 1 down to 1⅛" after cutting the tongues and grooves.*

5"

Door Assemblies
(Front View)

27

29

Center the hinges on the door rails.

31

31

30

28

27

Center the pulls at 5".

28

Center the latch at 16³/₄".

27

31

31

30

27

Allow for wood movement by drilling oversize bores in the cutting board ends. Then, counterbore for the screw heads, and cap them with wood plugs.

Cutting Board End
(Top View)

³/₈" stopped groove

21

1"

1³/₄"

Arts and Crafts Hutch

Building an exquisite piece like this is a labor of love. This hutch is not a reproduction, but a totally new design that incorporates many elements found on traditional mission-era furniture.

by Bruce Kieffer

I have been building furniture for more than 25 years, and I always feel lucky when I get a commission of this caliber. At first glance, this hutch may look fairly simple to build, but don't be fooled: It's a complex piece. If you decide to build one for yourself, be prepared to devote about 200 hours to complete the job. During the construction, there's a lot to ponder. I found myself scratching my head often, even though I designed the piece! If you take it slow, things will work out fine.

This piece belongs to a very nice couple who live in downtown St. Paul, Minnesota. They are redecorating their home with newly manufactured mission-style pieces. They were looking for a top-notch small hutch to be the centerpiece of their remodel, but they couldn't find one they liked. That's when they called me. We spent a lot of time designing this piece. All of us think it turned out great.

Design Details

The hutch consists of a bookcase attached to a cabinet. They're built as two separate pieces that are joined during the final assembly of the hutch. This makes it easier to move around and work on the smaller sections.

The sides and doors of the cabinet are frame-and-panel construction. The panels are veneered with book-matched "tiger ray" white oak with the rays oriented about 45° to the grain. The

results are stunning panels with chevron-patterned figure. I bought my veneer from *wood-veneers.com*. They e-mailed pictures of the sheets to me so I could see them before I bought them, which was great.

This hutch is made mostly from solid quarter-sawn white-oak lumber. The interior panels of the cabinet are rift-sawn white-oak plywood edged with solid white oak. The cabinet back and drawer bottoms are also rift-sawn plywood. Many of the parts are attached with hidden screws so the pieces can float when the wood changes size from seasonal humidity changes. The bookcase's upper

The pulls on the hutch are handcrafted by Gerry Rucks (586-772-1939, *www.arts-n-craftshardware.com*). The style I chose is Square Cutouts. You'll need to ask for them by name. The hinges are ball tipped, loose pin, and solid brass, darkened with liquid gun blue.

rail is attached with screws and desktop fasteners, but no glue. This allows that rail to expand and contract without exposing any gaps or unfinished areas and without causing a crack in the piece.

The bookcase back is 15 pieces of tongue-and-groove, straight-grained, rift-sawn white-oak lumber. I enhanced the vertical lines by creating faux V-grooves by chamfering the edges of the tongue-and-groove joints. Five different widths are used to make the back pieces, but they look equally sized when installed. The drawer sides and backs are solid rift-sawn white oak, too.

The doors and drawers are set back ⅛" into the cabinet to create shadow lines. To make the doors look and operate properly, the cabinet hinges need to be mounted on ¼" strips of oak, where they can be mortised just like flush-mounted doors. It's more work but much more forgiving if a mistake is made.

The drawers are guided by under-drawer, center-mounted tracks and guides. The tracks are complex fabrications that are assembled loose in the web frames. The guides are just strips of wood glued to the drawer bottoms. The tracks are not locked in place until the drawers are finished. It's easier to align them that way. Also, the drawers are stopped using small flipper-style drawer stops recessed into the underside of the upper web frame.

Seven Steps to Veneering Success

Making your own veneered panels adds another dimension to your woodworking arsenal, and it's fun to do. The woodworking techniques used for veneering are similar to those used with solid wood. Saw, joint, glue, clamp, trim, and sand are all familiar woodworking tasks. In this case, narrow sheets of veneer are edge joined to make wider sheets that are then applied to a substrate (the core the veneer is glued to). I prefer MDF (medium-density fiberboard) for my substrates since it's smooth, flat, and very stable. I find it easiest

to use wood glue, cauls (flat panels that spread the clamp pressure), and clamps. For small veneered panels like these, I use slow-setting yellow glue. Getting the glue on fast enough is always a problem, so glue up one panel at a time, and get some help.

You must make balanced panels (a core with veneer on both faces, in this case), and you need to put both pieces of veneer on the core at the same time. Oversize the veneer pieces so you can cut them to their finished sizes after the veneers are glued to the substrates.

STEP 1: *Use a veneer saw and straightedge to cut the lengths and widths slightly oversize (cut the substrates oversize, too). Cut to their finished sizes after the veneers are glued to their substrates.*

STEP 2: *Use a jointer and a jig to joint the edges of the veneer sheets.*

STEP 3: *Lay the veneer sheets faceup, pull the book-matched edges together, and temporarily join the sheets with masking tape.*

STEP 4: *Flip the joined sheets over, and apply a piece of gum-backed veneer tape down the joint. Lay a scrap flat panel over the taped sheet so it dries flat. Remove the masking tape.*

Veneering Sandwich Exploded View

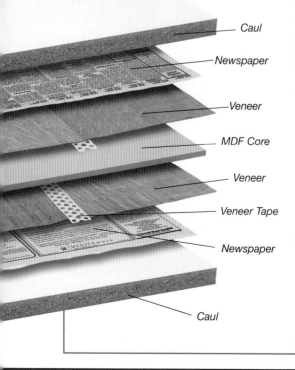

- Caul
- Newspaper
- Veneer
- MDF Core
- Veneer
- Veneer Tape
- Newspaper
- Caul

STEP 5: *Lay the sheet with the tape side down over the edge of your table. Open and glue the joint. Lay the sheet flat again to close the joint, and place sticks aside the joint to hold it flat.*

STEP 6: *Assemble the glue-up sandwich as shown in the exploded view at left. Using a narrow paint roller, apply a moderate coat of slow-setting glue to both sides of the core and to each veneer.*

STEP 7: *The glue-up requires a few deep-reach clamps. They are very important because the clamping pressure needs to be applied to the center first so no excess glue gets trapped there. Let the glue cure 24 hours before removing the clamps and trimming the panels to their finished sizes.*

There are edging pieces attached to the fronts of the under-drawer web frames $\frac{1}{16}$" below the level of those frames. This prevents the wear areas that most inset wood-on-wood tracked drawers exhibit when the bottoms of the drawer sides rub on the wood piece below the drawer. By moving the edging down, I created a $\frac{1}{16}$" reveal under the drawer, eliminating the rub areas and, as a bonus, creating a lip to align the door latch blocks to later.

Construction Notes

Careful wood selection has a huge effect on the final results. I picked my best pieces for the wide front rails and the drawer faces. I selected stock to ensure that the ray pattern was balanced, with the flakes displaying equally in both directions. I also carefully picked the wood for the corbels so their rays were at 45° pointing down and out, to match the door panels. It also made them mirror images of each other. I started by resawing some 8/4 boards to try to get a book-matched look for the corbels, but I found that unpredictable. So instead, I searched through all of my 4/4 stock until I found the right pieces. It helped to have my corbel template made with lines drawn on each side indicating the pattern I wanted.

I made sure that the show edges of the edging pieces used on the cabinet bottom, uprights, and web frames were plain sawn to match the edges of the quarter-sawn legs and top.

All of the casework joinery is done with $\frac{1}{4}$"-deep blind dadoes. I used a shop-made template and a guide bushing to rout the dadoes (see Figure 1). All the dadoes are stopped $\frac{1}{2}$" back from the

Figure 1: Rout the blind dadoes using a $\frac{1}{2}$" straight bit, a guide bushing, and shop-made templates. One template is used to fit the solid-wood parts, and another for the plywood parts.

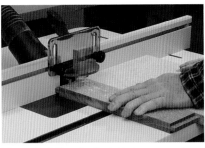

Figure 2: A Freud adjustable tongue-and-groove router bit set was used to cut the cabinet frame-and-panel joints and the bookcase back slat joints.

front edges except the dadoes for the web frames under the drawers. Those are stopped $1\frac{7}{16}$" from the front edges of the cabinet sides and uprights. The web frame edging pieces are fit and attached after the cabinet is assembled.

Assembling this bookcase and cabinet can be a nightmare if you don't anticipate the effects of cumulative error and deal with $\frac{3}{4}$"-thick plywood that's really closer to $1\frac{1}{16}$" thick (one of my pet peeves). Oversizing the interior pieces slightly and fitting them during the assembly was my solution. When dry fitting the parts, you'll have to hold the panels back from the front edges a bit since the blind notches aren't cut yet. I always use a joint-cutting and dry-fitting sequence of inside to outside, and then top to bottom. Once everything fits right, the notches can be cut on the front edges to complete the blind dadoes.

The cabinet's lower curved front and rear curved rails are glued to the bottom and screwed to the sides. I used my mortising machine to chop square holes in the sides so I could cover the assembly screws with square end-grain plugs. This worked great until I applied the stain and the plugs essentially disappeared! Even so, the only way to make them show up better under the dark stain would be to use a darker species of wood, and I would never do that. So it is what it is.

I made sure to elongate any screw holes where I knew there could be movement of the joined parts. For the

Figure 3: Use the band saw to cut the notches at the fronts of the shelf and web frame pieces that fit in the dadoes.

bookcase and cabinet tops, I held them tight at their front edges and let their back edges expand and contract. For the bookcase's upper rail and the cabinet's lower curved rails, I secured them at their top edges, letting the bottoms float.

This hutch is stained with a mission brown, non-grain-raising dye stain. It's a very rich, dark hue. I applied three coats of Danish oil for the topcoat.

Building the Cabinet

Review the Material List on page 100. Make the veneered panels for the sides and doors (see Seven Steps to Veneering Success on page 98), and then make the sides of the cabinet. I used a Freud adjustable tongue-and-groove router bit set to rout the joints (see Figure 2). It worked great, but what's unusual about it is that it cuts $\frac{7}{16}$" deep. The dimensions for the tenoned rails and the bookcase back slats all include this 7/16" dimension. If you use another method to cut the tongue-and-groove joints, you may need to compensate for the change. I found the Freud tongue-and-groove set worked best if I made a shallow scoring pass first, and then a full-depth pass to cut the remainder of the joint. I also left the rails slightly wide, cut the end tenons first, and then cut the rails to their final widths. Only then did I cut the rail grooves.

The grooves in the legs (pieces 3) are stopped short of the leg bottoms. Similarly, the tenon bottom ends of the side lower rails (pieces 4) are cut off so that when the sides are assembled, there is no visible joint (it's called a blind tenon). Wait to cut the curved shape of the side lower rails until after cutting the tongue-and-groove joints.

Next, assemble the rest of the casework parts for the cabinet. Don't forget to set the drawer tracks (pieces 21) loose in the web frames as they're assembled. Cut the blind dadoes in the sides, bottom, and upper web frame. Remember that the

Cabinet Exploded View

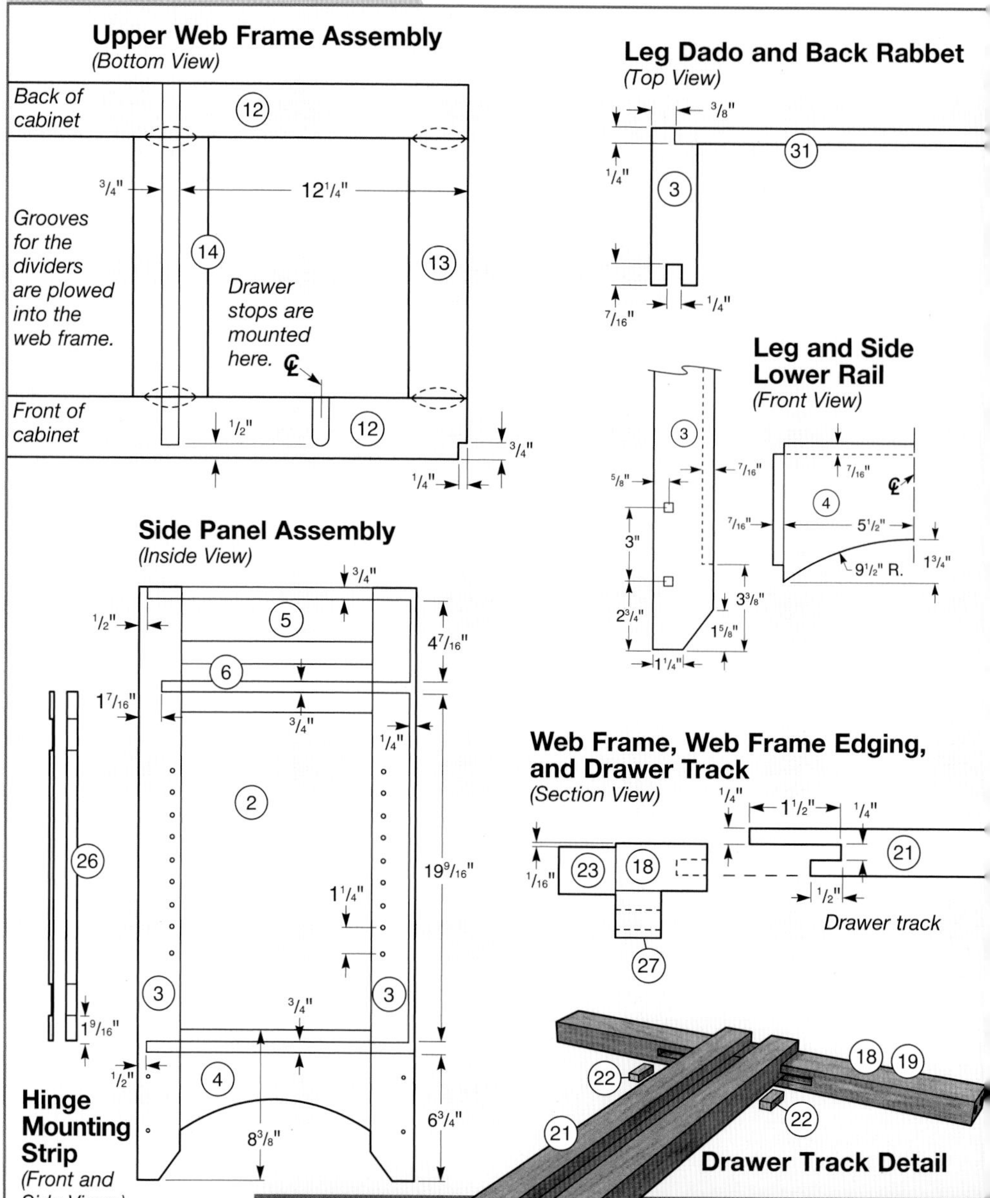

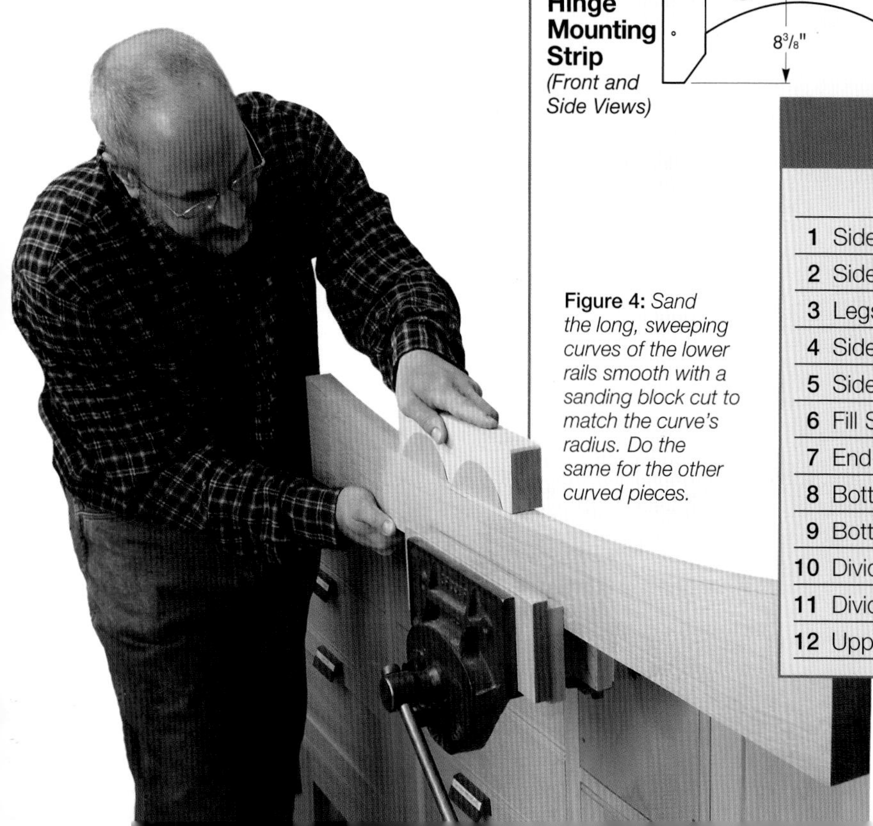

Upper Web Frame Assembly
(Bottom View)

Back of cabinet

Grooves for the dividers are plowed into the web frame.

Drawer stops are mounted here.

Front of cabinet

Leg Dado and Back Rabbet
(Top View)

Leg and Side Lower Rail
(Front View)

Side Panel Assembly
(Inside View)

Web Frame, Web Frame Edging, and Drawer Track
(Section View)

Drawer track

Hinge Mounting Strip
(Front and Side Views)

Drawer Track Detail

Figure 4: *Sand the long, sweeping curves of the lower rails smooth with a sanding block cut to match the curve's radius. Do the same for the other curved pieces.*

		T x W x L
1	Side Panel MDF Substrates (2)	¼" x 11⅞" x 22½"
2	Side Panel Veeners (4)	1/32" x 11⅞" x 22½"
3	Legs (4)	¾" x 2½" x 33"
4	Side Lower Rails (2)	¾" x 5⅝" x 11⅞"
5	Side Upper Rails (2)	¾" x 3" x 11⅞"
6	Fill Strips (2)	¼" x 2¼" x 11"
7	End-Grain Plugs (8)	⅜" x ⅜" x ¼"
8	Bottom (1)	¾" x 15" x 44"
9	Bottom Edging (1)	¾" x ¾" x 43½"
10	Dividers (2)	¾" x 15" x 25¼"
11	Divider Edgings (2)	¾" x ¾" x 24¾"
12	Upper Web Frame Stiles (2)	¾" x 2½" x 44"

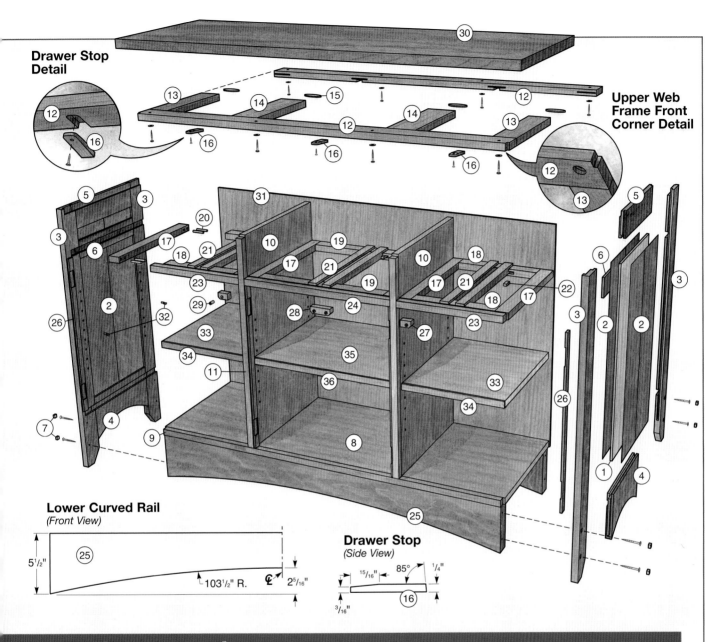

Drawer Stop Detail

Upper Web Frame Front Corner Detail

Lower Curved Rail
(Front View)

5½"
103½" R.
2⁵⁄₁₆"

Drawer Stop
(Side View)

¹⁵⁄₁₆"   85°   ¼"
³⁄₁₆"

Material List – Cabinet

		T x W x L			T x W x L
13	Upper Web Frame End Rails (2)	¾" x 2½" x 10¾"	**25**	Lower Curved Rails (2)	1½" x 5½" x 43½"
14	Upper Web Frame Middle Rails (2)	¾" x 3¼" x 10¾"	**26**	Hinge Mounting Strips (4)	¾" x ¼" x 19½"
15	Biscuits (8)	#20	**27**	Single Door Latch Blocks (2)	¾" x ¾" x 1¼"
16	Drawer Stops (3)	¼" x ¾" x 2½"	**28**	Double Door Latch Blocks (1)	¾" x ¾" x 2½"
17	Lower Web Frame Stiles (6)	¾" x 1½" x 14¹³⁄₁₆"	**29**	Magnetic Door Catches (4)	⁵⁄₁₆" Dia.
18	Lower Web Frame Rails (4)	¾" x 1½" x 9½"	**30**	Top (1)	1" x 16¾" x 47"
19	Lower Web Frame Middle Rails (2)	¾" x 1½" x 15½"	**31**	Back (1)	¼" x 44¼" x 26¼"
20	Dowel Pins (24)	¼" Dia. x 1½"	**32**	Antique Brass Shelf Pins (40)	5 mm
21	Drawer Tracks (3)	¾" x 2¾" x 14¾"	**33**	Small Shelves (2)	¾" x 14⁹⁄₁₆" x 11⅞"
22	Drawer Track Locks (12)	¼" x ¹³⁄₁₆" x 1"	**34**	Small Shelf Edgings (2)	¼" x ¾" x 11⅞"
23	Short Web Frame Edgings (2)	¾" x ¹⁵⁄₁₆" x 12"	**35**	Shelf (1)	¾" x 14⁹⁄₁₆" x 17⅞"
24	Web Frame Edging (1)	¾" x ¹⁵⁄₁₆" x 18"	**36**	Shelf Edging (1)	¼" x ¾" x 17⅞"

fronts of the under-drawer web frames are set back farther than the rest of the parts. Rout the rabbets in the sides for the back and the upper web frame. Dry fit the parts, and make the necessary adjustments. Then, go ahead and cut the notches on the front ends of the web frames, dividers, and bottom to complete the blind dado joints (see Figure 3 on page 99).

Fabricate the drawer stops (pieces 16), rout their grooves in the underside of the upper frame, and mount them to see that they work correctly. Cut the curved shapes of the lower curved rails (pieces 25), and sand them smooth (see Figure 4 on page 100). Drill the screw assembly holes in the sides for the lower rails, as well as those in the web frame to attach the top (piece 30). Chop the square holes for the plugs (pieces 7) that cover the screws that attach the lower curved rails.

Drill the shelf pin holes. Finish sand the show surfaces of the interior cabinet parts, and assemble the cabinet casework. Fit and attach the web frame edgings (pieces 23 and 24), positioning them 1/16" down from the top of the under-drawer web frames. Cut the back (piece

Figure 6: *Desktop fasteners hold the upper rail tight to the bookcase uprights but allow it to float with movement caused by humidity changes.*

31), and screw it to the cabinet. Make the door latch blocks (pieces 27 and 28), and glue them in place. Make and attach the top (piece 30), and make the shelves (pieces 33 through 36).

Building the Bookcase

For this part of the project, review the Material List on page 103. When making the bookcase, keep in mind that the upper rail and the corbels (pieces 41 and 44) are set back 1/8" from the front edges of the sides (pieces 39) and that the lower rail (piece 43) is set back 1/4" from the front edges of the sides. The front edges of the dividers (pieces 40) are flush with the front of the lower rail.

Edge glue boards together to make the sides, top, bottom, and uprights of the bookcase. Make the upper and lower rails. Glue the lower rail to the bottom. Rout the blind dado grooves and the rabbets for the back slats (pieces 46 through 50). Drill the shelf pin holes and the screw assembly holes in the top, bottom, and sides. Cut the biscuit groove for and in the corbels.

Form the notches on the upper ends of the sides and bottom ends of the uprights for the blind dadoes. Also cut the

Figure 5: *Notches are hand chopped in the back of the upper rail to allow it to expand and contract without showing evidence of that movement.*

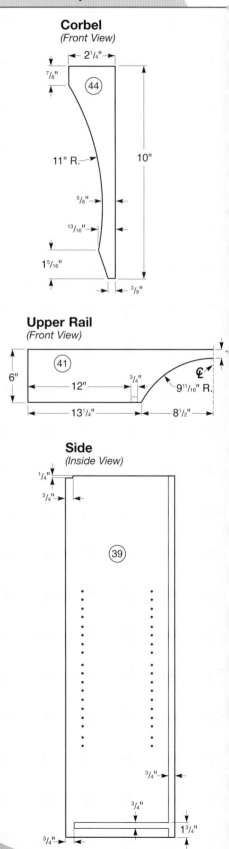

Corbel
(Front View)

2 1/4"

7/8"

(44)

11" R.

10"

5/8"

13/16"

1 5/16"

3/8"

Upper Rail
(Front View)

(41)

6"

12"

3/4"

9 11/16" R.

13 1/4"

8 1/2"

Side
(Inside View)

1/4"

3/4"

(39)

3/4"

3/4"

3/4"

1 3/4"

3/4"

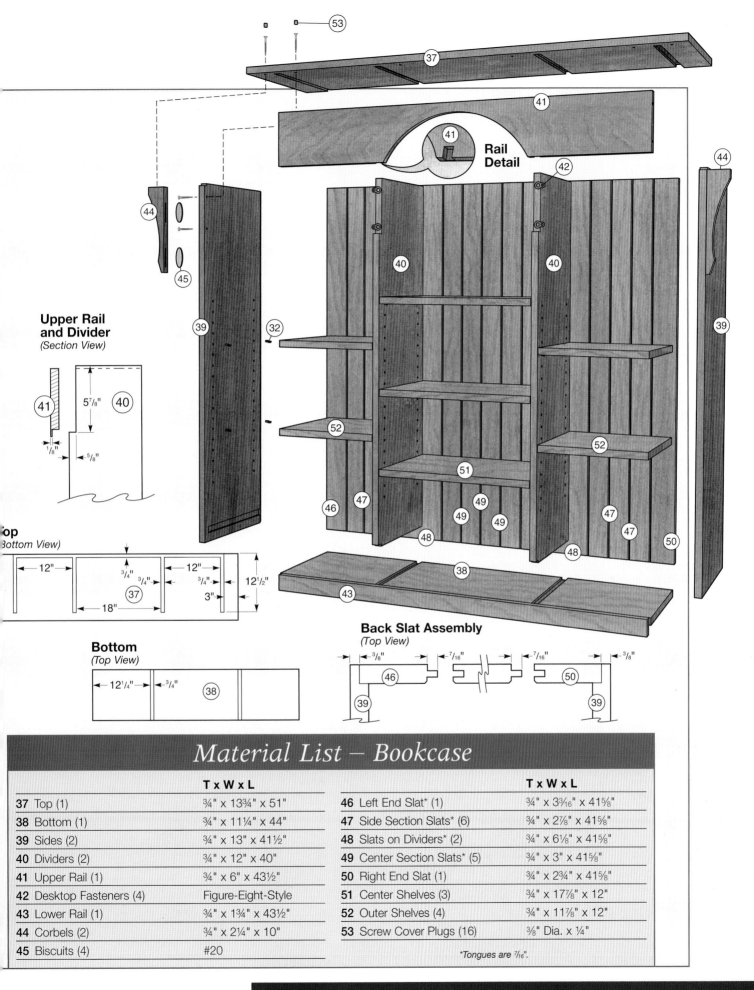

Rail Detail

Upper Rail and Divider
(Section View)

5⁷⁄₈"

⅛"   ⅝"

41   40

Top
(Bottom View)

12"   12"
¾" ¾"
¾"
18"   3"   12½"
37

Bottom
(Top View)

12¼"   ¾"
38

Back Slat Assembly
(Top View)

⅜"   ⁷⁄₁₆"   ⁷⁄₁₆"   ⅜"
46   50
39   39

Material List – Bookcase				
	T x W x L			**T x W x L**
37 Top (1)	¾" x 13¾" x 51"		**46** Left End Slat* (1)	¾" x 3³⁄₁₆" x 41⅝"
38 Bottom (1)	¾" x 11¼" x 44"		**47** Side Section Slats* (6)	¾" x 2⅞" x 41⅝"
39 Sides (2)	¾" x 13" x 41½"		**48** Slats on Dividers* (2)	¾" x 6⅛" x 41⅝"
40 Dividers (2)	¾" x 12" x 40"		**49** Center Section Slats* (5)	¾" x 3" x 41⅝"
41 Upper Rail (1)	¾" x 6" x 43½"		**50** Right End Slat (1)	¾" x 2¾" x 41⅝"
42 Desktop Fasteners (4)	Figure-Eight-Style		**51** Center Shelves (3)	¾" x 17⅞" x 12"
43 Lower Rail (1)	¾" x 1¾" x 43½"		**52** Outer Shelves (4)	¾" x 11⅞" x 12"
44 Corbels (2)	¾" x 2¼" x 10"		**53** Screw Cover Plugs (16)	⅜" Dia. x ¼"
45 Biscuits (4)	#20			

*Tongues are ⁷⁄₁₆".

Door and Drawer Exploded Views

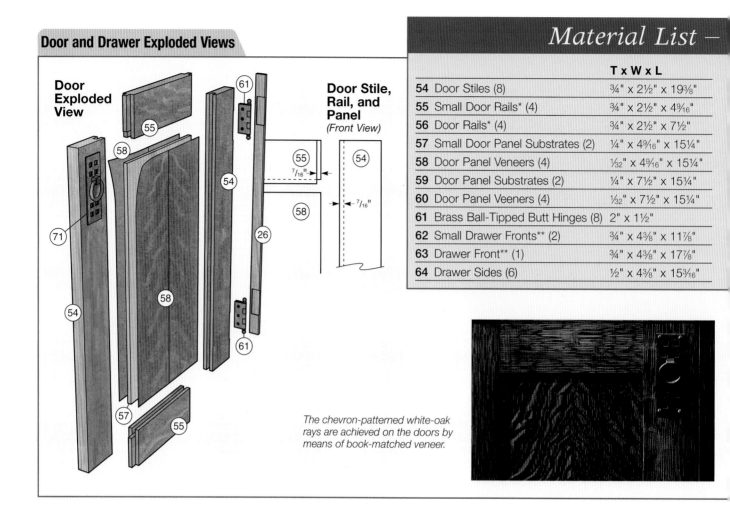

Door Exploded View

Door Stile, Rail, and Panel *(Front View)*

Material List

		T x W x L
54	Door Stiles (8)	¾" x 2½" x 19⅜"
55	Small Door Rails* (4)	¾" x 2½" x 4⁹⁄₁₆"
56	Door Rails* (4)	¾" x 2½" x 7½"
57	Small Door Panel Substrates (2)	¼" x 4⁹⁄₁₆" x 15¼"
58	Door Panel Veneers (4)	¹⁄₃₂" x 4⁹⁄₁₆" x 15¼"
59	Door Panel Substrates (2)	¼" x 7½" x 15¼"
60	Door Panel Veeners (4)	¹⁄₃₂" x 7½" x 15¼"
61	Brass Ball-Tipped Butt Hinges (8)	2" x 1½"
62	Small Drawer Fronts** (2)	¾" x 4⅜" x 11⅞"
63	Drawer Front** (1)	¾" x 4⅜" x 17⅞"
64	Drawer Sides (6)	½" x 4⅜" x 15³⁄₁₆"

The chevron-patterned white-oak rays are achieved on the doors by means of book-matched veneer.

notches at the tops of the uprights for the upper rail. Dry assemble the bookcase, fit the upper rail, and mark where the uprights land on its back. Chop the deep, short grooves in the back of the upper rail (see Figure 5 on page 102). Finish sand everything, and assemble the bookcase. Attach the upper rail with desktop fasteners, but without any glue (see Figure 6 on page 102). Glue and screw the top on, and plug the screw holes (pieces 53). Fabricate the back slats, and fit the entire back so there are ¹⁄₃₂" expansion gaps between each back slat. Screw the back in place. Place screws at the top and bottom of each slat, on the edges of the end slats, and in the center of the slats that bridge the dividers. Make the shelves (pieces 51 and 52).

Making the Doors and Drawers

All I can say is, if you've gotten this far, making the doors and drawers should be a snap. The doors are made just like the cabinet sides. Make them slightly large so there's something to trim when you fit them in the cabinet (see the Material List above). I cut the hinge mortises with a router and a template (see Figure 7). To make the hinge mounting strips (pieces 26), I routed the hinge mortises on the edge of a wide board that was ¾" thick. Then, I sliced off the ¼"-wide strips. Glue the hinge mounting strips in place, and attach the hinges and doors. The loose

Figure 7: *I used a router with a bottom-bearing hinge-mortising bit and a hinge template to rout the hinge mortises. Before removing the template, I chopped the mortise corners square using the template as a guide.*

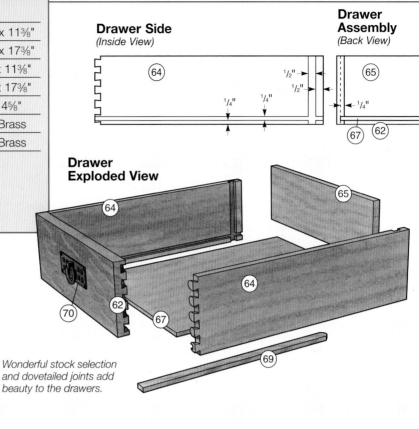

		T x W x L
65	Small Drawer Backs*** (2)	½" x 3³⁄₁₆" x 11³⁄₈"
66	Drawer Back*** (1)	½" x 3³⁄₁₆" x 17³⁄₈"
67	Small Drawer Bottom (2)	¼" x 14⅝" x 11³⁄₈"
68	Drawer Bottom (1)	¼" x 14⅝" x 17³⁄₈"
69	Drawer Guides (3)	⁵⁄₁₆" x ¾" x 14⅝"
70	Drawer Pulls (3)	Handmade Brass
71	Door Pulls (4)	Handmade Brass

*Tenons are ⁷⁄₁₆".

**Cut from one piece.

***Cut width to fit.

Drawer Side (Inside View)

Drawer Assembly (Back View)

Drawer Exploded View

Wonderful stock selection and dovetailed joints add beauty to the drawers.

pin hinges make it easy to mount and unmount the doors during the fitting. Even so, it will take hours to get your doors to fit perfectly.

The drawer fronts are joined to the drawer sides with jig-cut, half-blind dovetails. The drawer backs are set into dadoes in the sides. I plowed grooves in the drawer fronts and sides for the drawer bottoms. The drawer guides are centered and glued to the undersides of the drawer bottoms; I made MDF (medium-density fiberboard) spacers to center them perfectly. Cut the drawer backs short to allow the drawer bottoms to slide in place. Then, screw them to the bottom edge of the drawer backs. When the drawers are finished, set them in the cabinet. Adjust them so all the gaps are right, and lock in the drawer tracks by gluing the drawer track locks (pieces 22) in place in the web frame grooves.

Staining and Finishing

Be warned: Staining a large piece like this hutch is difficult enough, but staining it with a dark dye stain is about as tough as it gets. If you've never used a dye stain like this before, then practice on some large panels until you get the feel of it. Oddly enough, dye staining an inside corner doesn't seem as hard to do as staining with oil stain, but you should practice that, as well.

To make this stain (or for that matter, any stain) look good, the wood must be sanded evenly and thoroughly. I random orbit sanded everything to 220 grit. I found the most successful method for applying the stain was to brush it on, let it soak in a bit, and then blend it in with a dye-soaked rag. I was also careful not to allow the dye to pool in the inside corners. Had that happened, I would have had trouble getting those areas colored evenly.

To finish the hutch, I applied Danish oil over the stain. I put one sealer coat on everything, two coats on the cabinet interior surfaces, and three coats on all of the outside show wood surfaces. It really popped the grain, and it is silky to the touch.

Then, I delivered the hutch to my clients and enjoyed a job well done.

Cherry China Cabinet

This china cabinet features classic clean lines, gentle arches, and hidden hardware. It's amply sized to store all your table finery, and the upper cabinet will proudly display its contents through glass doors. Made carefully, this could be the signature project for your dining room or a wonderful family gift.

by Rick White

Of all the readers' requests we've received over the years for furniture plans, the perennial leader has been requests for china cabinets. With that in mind, the design team at *Woodworker's Journal* developed this beautiful project that, with care and patience, is well within the abilities of any intermediate to advanced hobbyist. It calls for full 1"-thick solid cherry boards and ½" and ¾" cherry-veneered plywood, all of which you should source before heading for the shop.

The cabinet is made up of two distinct parts. The base houses five sliding shelves behind a pair of veneered doors. The upper section is designed to proudly display family treasures on its glass shelves, keeping them dust free behind a pair of large glass doors.

Building from the Bottom Up

For the best effect, the upper and lower units of this cabinet should flow together visually. The way to achieve this is to run continuous grain all the way up the side panels. So, the first step in construction is to edge glue enough hardwood to make the two panels, each large enough to yield both a lower and an upper side. Make each side blank 1" x 17½" x 86", and you'll have sufficient material for all the side pieces (see Figure 1).

After the glue dries, sand the two panels. Then, referring to the Material List on page 108, begin your machining by cutting the base sides (pieces 1) to size. Next, refer to the drawings on page 108 to lay out the leg cutouts. To reduce tearout, apply masking tape where the cut lines will be. On the tape, mark the locations of the two legs in each side, and then cut away the waste with a jigsaw.

There is a horizontal divider (piece 2) above the bottom shelf (piece 3) in the base cabinet. The next step is to rout stopped dadoes for both this divider and the bottom shelf in each base side, using a straightedge as a guide and referring to the drawings on page 108 for the dado locations. (The divider is cut from nominal ¾"-thick stock—you may find it's actually a hair shy of that.) After plowing the dadoes, square up their ends with a sharp chisel. Next, with your straightedge clamped in place, plow a ¾"-wide x ⅜"-deep dado across the top face of the horizontal divider—running from the front to the back—to receive the vertical divider.

Dividers, Feet, and Stringers

With the base sides completed, the next step is to lay out and cut the vertical divider (piece 4), including the notch in its back corner. Then, cut the back and

Figure 1: *Jointing a dead-straight edge on the 1"-thick glued-up side blanks is the first step in accurately machining the carcass.*

front feet (pieces 5) to size and shape, and give them a thorough sanding without softening their edges. Next is the front stringer (piece 6), which is solid hardwood. Lay out a gentle arc along its bottom edge by bending a piece of hardboard or ¼" plywood along the arc, clamping it in place, and drawing the line. Cut the arc on the band saw, and then sand it thoroughly. A large drum sander in the drill press works best for this, or you can use part of the cutoff to make an arched sanding block. The back stringer (also piece 6) has no arc, since it's not visible. Trim the front edges of the dividers with ¼" hardwood (piece 7) before you begin assembly.

Attach the feet to the stringers with biscuits, glue, and clamps, and sand

Lower Cabinet Exploded View

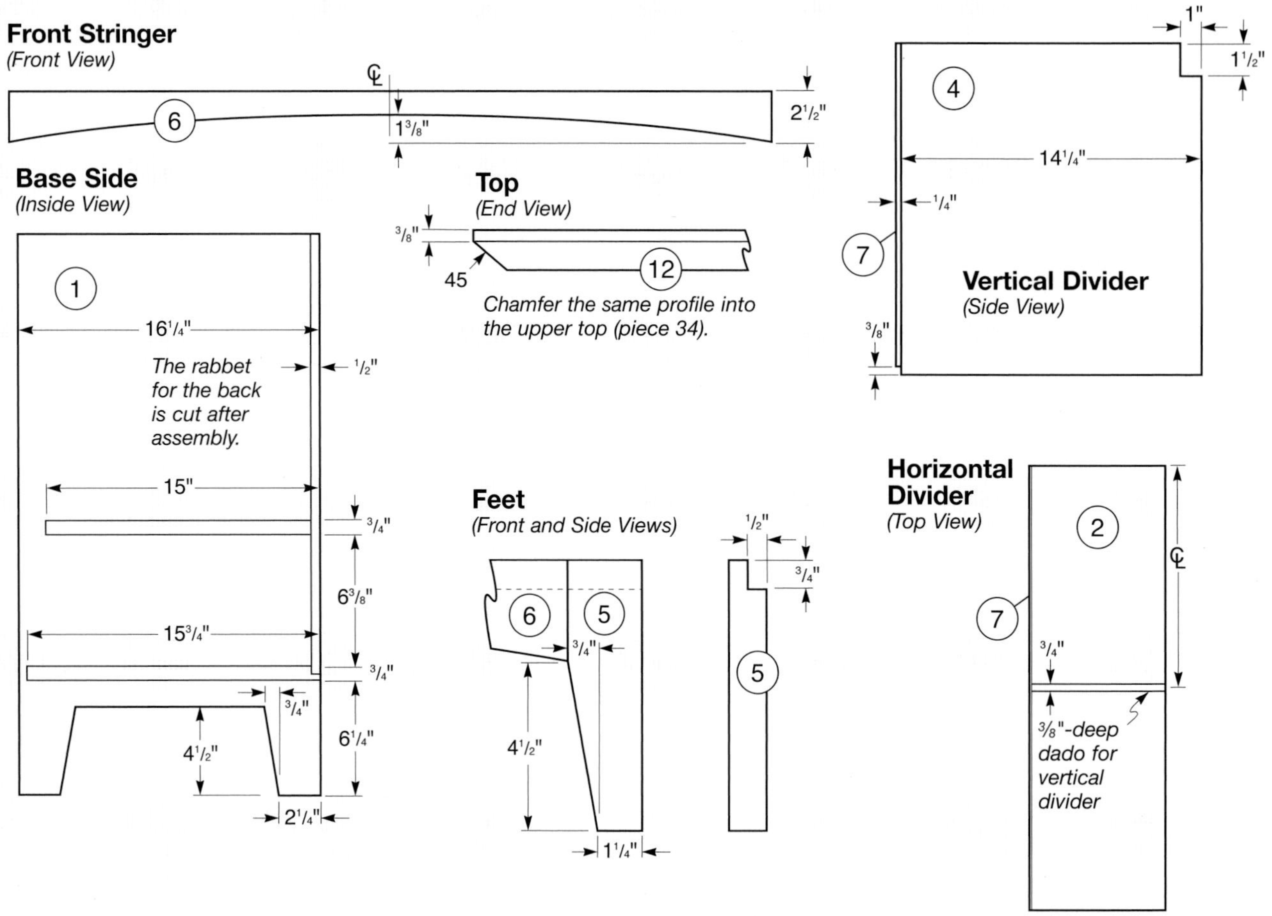
Front Stringer
(Front View)
6
1³/₈"
2¹/₂"
Base Side
(Inside View)
1
16¹/₄"
The rabbet for the back is cut after assembly.
¹/₂"
15"
³/₄"
6³/₈"
15³/₄"
³/₄"
³/₄"
6¹/₄"
4¹/₂"
2¹/₄"
Top
(End View)
³/₈"
45
12
Chamfer the same profile into the upper top (piece 34).
Feet
(Front and Side Views)
6
5
³/₄"
4¹/₂"
1¹/₄"
¹/₂"
³/₄"
5
1"
1¹/₂"
4
14¹/₄"
¹/₄"
7
Vertical Divider
(Side View)
³/₈"
Horizontal Divider
(Top View)
2
7
³/₄"
³/₈"-deep dado for vertical divider

Material List – Lower Cabinet

	T x W x L		T x W x L
1 Base Sides (2)	1" x 16¼" x 29"	**14** Small Shelf Fronts (4)	¾" x 2½" x 20⅜"
2 Horizontal Divider (1)	¾" x 14¼" x 46"	**15** Large Shelf Front (1)	¾" x 2½" x 43¼"
3 Bottom (1)	¾" x 15¼" x 46"	**16** Small Shelf Backs (4)	¾" x 2½" x 20⅜"
4 Vertical Divider (1)	¾" x 14¼" x 15¼"	**17** Large Shelf Back (1)	¾" x 2½" x 43¼"
5 Feet (4)	1" x 2" x 7"	**18** Small Shelf Bottoms (4)	¼" x 13½" x 20⅜"
6 Front and Back Stringers (2)	1" x 2½" x 41"	**19** Large Shelf Bottom (1)	¼" x 13½" x 43¼"
7 Divider Trim (1)	¼" x ¾" x 62"	**20** Small Shelf Faces (4)	¾" x 5¾" x 22⅜"
8 Top Stringers (2)	1" x 1½" x 45"	**21** Large Shelf Face (1)	¾" x 5¾" x 44⅞"
9 Top Supports (2)	1" x 1½" x 13¾"	**22** Drawer Slides (5 Pairs)	Full Extension
10 Back (1)	½" x 46" x 22"	**23** Base Door Panels (2)	¾" x 21½" x 22"
11 Glue Blocks (2)	1" x 1½" x 1½"	**24** Door Side and Top Trim (1)	¾" x 1" x 150"
12 Top (1)	1" x 19⅛" x 51"	**25** Door Bottom Trim (2)	¾" x 2½" x 22"
13 Sliding Shelf Sides (10)	¾" x 2½" x 14¼"	**26** Veneers (4)	1/32" x 24" x 27"

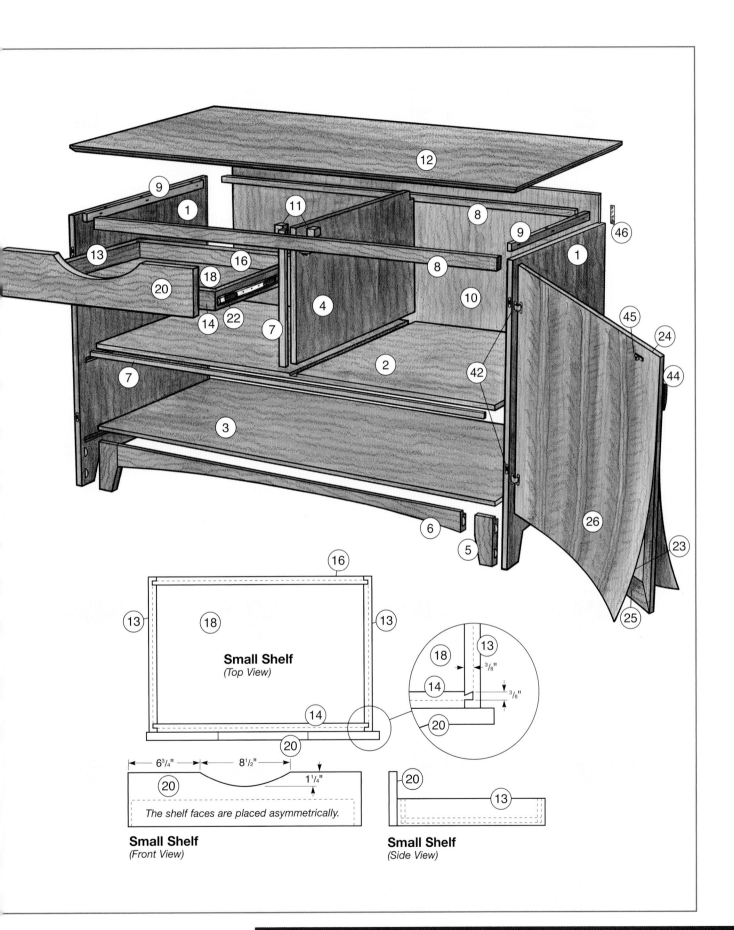

Small Shelf
(Top View)

³/₈"

³/₈"

Small Shelf
(Front View)

6³/₄"   8¹/₂"

1¹/₄"

The shelf faces are placed asymmetrically.

Small Shelf
(Side View)

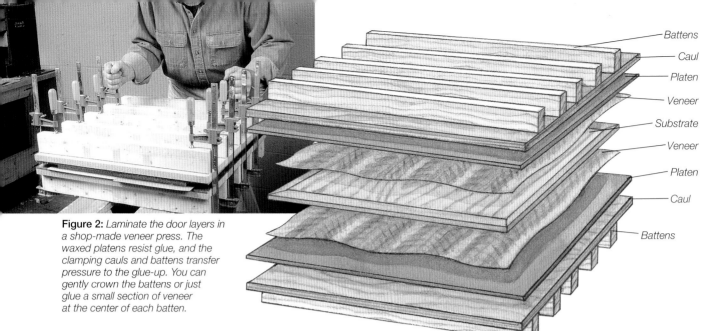

Figure 2: *Laminate the door layers in a shop-made veneer press. The waxed platens resist glue, and the clamping cauls and battens transfer pressure to the glue-up. You can gently crown the battens or just glue a small section of veneer at the center of each batten.*

Labels (top to bottom, right side):
- Battens
- Caul
- Platen
- Veneer
- Substrate
- Veneer
- Platen
- Caul
- Battens

them thoroughly after the glue has cured. (There are two different sizes of biscuits in this project. If your biscuit joiner won't accommodate the small biscuits, substitute dowels or pocket hole joints instead.) Move to your router table, and cut the rabbets on the inside edges of the bottom stringer and foot subassemblies (see the drawings on page 108).

Your next step is to make a frame that nestles inside the upper perimeter of the lower cabinet. Cut the top stringers and supports (pieces 8 and 9), and join them at the corners, using a pocket hole jig, to create a rectangular frame. On the drill press, predrill and countersink elongated holes in the top supports for the screws that will hold the top in place. Bore countersunk holes across the bottom edge of the back top stringer; these screw holes will also be used to secure the top.

Assembling the Base

You're now ready to assemble the base. It's a good idea to have some help for this. Begin by notching the trim and gluing the vertical divider into its dado in the horizontal divider. (It's easier to do this now than it is after the base has been assembled.) Next, cut the biscuit slots into the sides and feet, as shown in the exploded view on page 109.

After the glue sets, dry fit the base together. When everything works, glue and clamp the leg subassemblies

to the sides, along with the bottom shelf and horizontal divider. Drop the top stringer and support subassembly in from the top. Make sure the assembly is square as you tighten the clamps. Drive screws through the top supports into the base sides.

After the glue dries, use a rabbeting bit to reveal the ½" x ½"-deep rabbet for the base back (piece 10), and then square the corners of the rabbet with a chisel. Next, use a pencil to mark the location of the horizontal divider's dado on the back edge of each cabinet side. Install the back with 1" panel nails, using your pencil marks to locate the centerline of the horizontal divider. The two glue blocks (pieces 11) are now snugged and glued into place, where the vertical divider meets the front top stringer.

Building the Base Top

The edge-glued solid-hardwood top (piece 12) increases the overall quality of the project. Have a local cabinet shop run the top through its wide belt sander before you trim it to size: They won't charge much, and you'll get very uniform results. Use your table saw to form the 45° chamfers on the bottom edge, along the front and both ends, and then sand the top. Install the top by driving screws up through the top supports and the top back stringer.

Adding Sliding Shelves

All five sliding shelves are built in a similar fashion; only the dimensions change. Move to the table saw, install a ⅜" dado head, and attach an auxiliary fence to the miter gauge. Cut dadoes on the sides and rabbets on the fronts and backs. Note that the ⅜" locking joint uses the same setup to mill both the dadoes and the rabbets on the shelf sides and fronts (pieces 13 through 17). All of these dimensions can be found in the drawings on page 109.

Reconfigure your dado head to form ½"-wide x ⅜"-deep cuts for the bottoms, and plow the grooves for the shelf bottoms (pieces 18 and 19) in the fronts, sides, and back. Assemble the shelves, gluing and clamping the corners while letting the bottoms float freely in their grooves to accommodate wood movement.

Trim the shelf faces (pieces 20 and 21) to size, double-checking these measurements with a dry fit in the assembled base cabinet. Following the layout on page 109, band saw the arc-shaped handle openings, and then drum sand the saw marks smooth.

Install the drawer slides (pieces 22) and the shelves according to the slide manufacturer's instructions. With the shelves installed, locate the faces so there is a ⅛" gap between the pairs of small ones, and screw all five in place from the back through predrilled, countersunk holes.

Making the Base Doors

The base doors are plywood panels (pieces 23) with hardwood trim (pieces 24 and 25) wrapped around the top and side edges. Miter cut, glue, and clamp these solid-wood strips in place. Sand the doors after the glue dries, and then veneer both the front and back faces with cherry veneer (pieces 26). It's essential to veneer the back faces to achieve balance and avoid warping. Use a shop-built veneer press like the one shown in Figure 2.

After the glue cures, lay the doors on their openings, and scribe the arcs onto their bottom edges. Band saw the curves, and then sand all the edges gently and set the doors aside.

Constructing the Upper Carcass

Refer to the Material List on page 112 for the dimensions of the upper cabinet parts. Now, remember those two large boards you glued up for the sides? Be sure to trim the correct edge of each to make the upper sides (pieces 27), so the grain pattern is carried through from the base. After the upper sides are trimmed, use a straightedge and a dovetail bit chucked in your router to plow four sliding dovetails across the inside face of each (see the drawings on page 112 for locations, and see Super-Easy Sliding Dovetails on page 114 for details). Note that these are stopped dovetails.

The three shelves that hold the glass in the upper cabinet are simple frame construction. Cut tenons on the ends of the six shelf ends (pieces 28), using your table saw's miter gauge and a dado head. Use a ¼" bit in your router table to create an open-saddle mortise on the end of each shelf rail (pieces 29), and square up the mortises (see the drawings on page 113).

Assemble the shelves with glue and clamps. Machine their long

dovetailed shape on the ends (see Super-Easy Sliding Dovetails), and cut them back to match the stopped dovetail slots in the sides. Use a bearing-guided rabbeting bit to create the lip for the glass inserts (pieces 30), squaring up the corners with a sharp chisel.

Cut the cabinet bottom (piece 31) to size from solid hardwood, and then form the dovetailed ends as you did on the shelves. Band saw the arc on the bottom edge of the lower stringer (piece 32) and front upper stringer (piece 33). Sand out the saw marks.

Dry fit the shelves and the cabinet bottom to the upper sides. Cut biscuit slots to attach the stringers to the cabinet sides (with the curved ones to the front). When you're satisfied with the fit, disassemble the upper cabinet, sand all parts thoroughly, and then reassemble it with glue and clamps. With a project of this size, have a buddy give you a hand during assembly and glue-up.

Forming the Upper Top and Back

The upper top (piece 34) is another edge-glued solid-hardwood board like the top of the base cabinet. Cut it to size, and form the 45° chamfer on the bottom lip of its front and side edges. To install it, predrill slightly oversize holes (to allow for wood movement), and countersink for screws driven down through the top into the sides and the upper stringers.

Follow the same procedure used earlier to create the rabbet for the upper back (piece 35). Then, chisel out the corners, and nail the back in place.

Machining the Upper Doors

The upper doors are really what sets this china cabinet apart. They simultaneously enclose and protect the treasures within while offering them for display. The door style continues the graceful arcs used throughout the project, and while they look difficult to build, they really aren't.

Cutting Curved Door Rails

Band saw the matching curved rails. Cut the tenons and back rabbets first, while you still have flat reference edges to work from.

Cut the tenons and rabbet for the glass before cutting the curved shape on the rails.

The curved door rails on this cabinet are an important visual design element. With these rails, the key to success is to complete as much machining as possible while they are still rectangular and then cut the curves on a band saw, as shown above. Remember, once they are curved, they become left and right upper and lower rails.

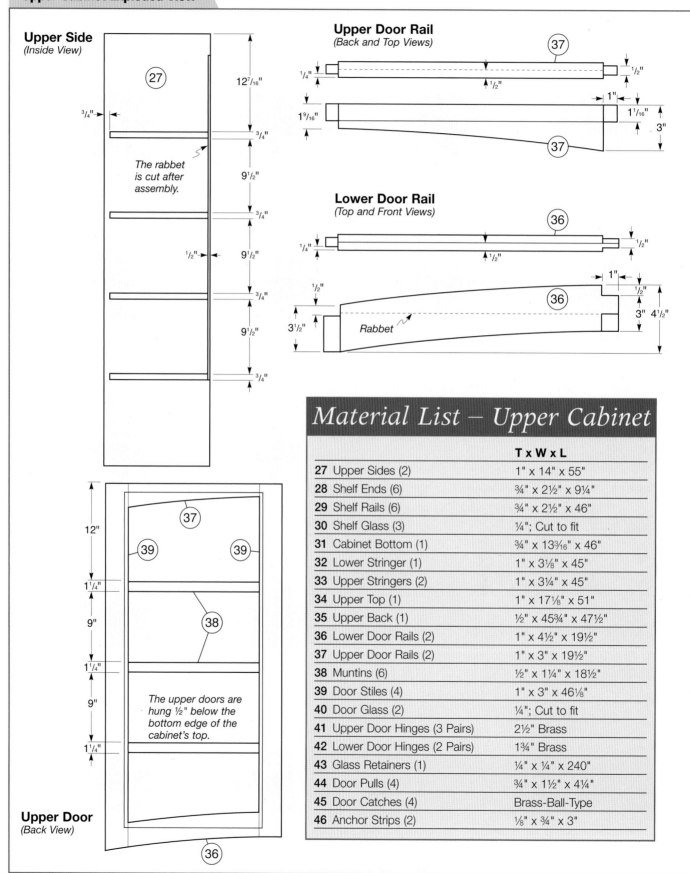

Upper Side
(Inside View)

27

12⁷/₁₆"

³/₄"

³/₄"

The rabbet is cut after assembly.

9¹/₂"

³/₄"

¹/₂"

9¹/₂"

³/₄"

9¹/₂"

³/₄"

Upper Door Rail
(Back and Top Views)

37

¹/₄"

¹/₂"

¹/₂"

1¹/₁₆"

1"

1"

3"

1⁹/₁₆"

37

Lower Door Rail
(Top and Front Views)

36

¹/₄"

¹/₂"

¹/₂"

1"

¹/₂"

3"

4¹/₂"

3¹/₂"

Rabbet

36

Upper Door
(Back View)

12"

37

39

39

1¹/₄"

9"

38

1¹/₄"

9"

The upper doors are hung ¹/₂" below the bottom edge of the cabinet's top.

1¹/₄"

36

Material List – Upper Cabinet

		T x W x L
27	Upper Sides (2)	1" x 14" x 55"
28	Shelf Ends (6)	¾" x 2½" x 9¼"
29	Shelf Rails (6)	¾" x 2½" x 46"
30	Shelf Glass (3)	¼"; Cut to fit
31	Cabinet Bottom (1)	¾" x 13³/₁₆" x 46"
32	Lower Stringer (1)	1" x 3⅛" x 45"
33	Upper Stringers (2)	1" x 3¼" x 45"
34	Upper Top (1)	1" x 17⅛" x 51"
35	Upper Back (1)	½" x 45¾" x 47½"
36	Lower Door Rails (2)	1" x 4½" x 19½"
37	Upper Door Rails (2)	1" x 3" x 19½"
38	Muntins (6)	½" x 1¼" x 18½"
39	Door Stiles (4)	1" x 3" x 46⅛"
40	Door Glass (2)	¼"; Cut to fit
41	Upper Door Hinges (3 Pairs)	2½" Brass
42	Lower Door Hinges (2 Pairs)	1¾" Brass
43	Glass Retainers (1)	¼" x ¼" x 240"
44	Door Pulls (4)	¾" x 1½" x 4¼"
45	Door Catches (4)	Brass-Ball-Type
46	Anchor Strips (2)	⅛" x ¾" x 3"

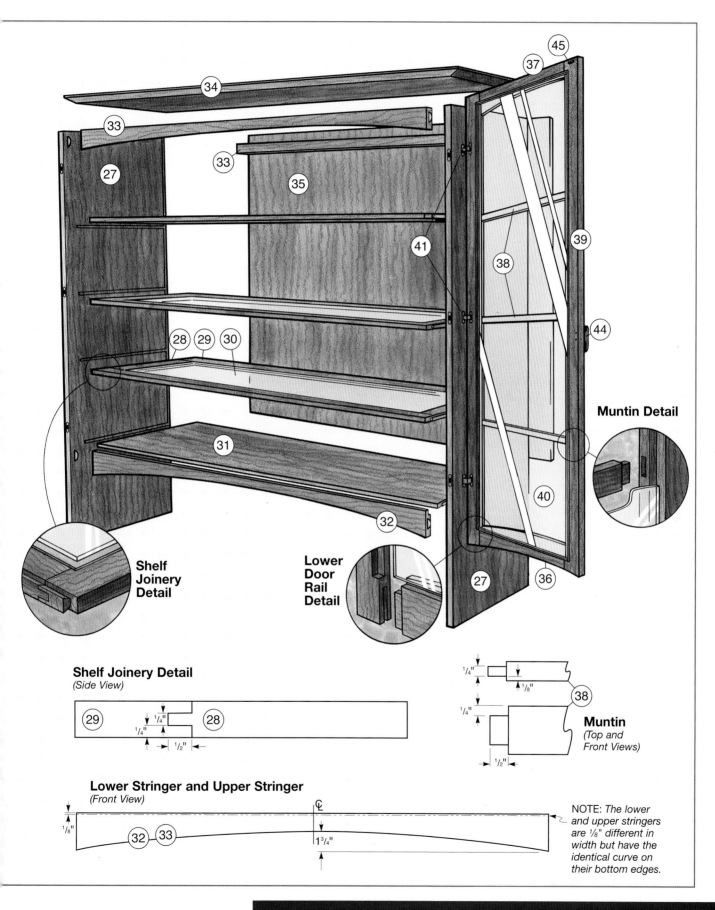

Shelf Joinery Detail

Muntin Detail

Lower Door Rail Detail

Shelf Joinery Detail
(Side View)

29   1/4"   1/4"   28
     1/2"

Lower Stringer and Upper Stringer
(Front View)

1/8"

32   33

₵

1³/₄"

NOTE: *The lower and upper stringers are ¹/₈" different in width but have the identical curve on their bottom edges.*

Muntin
(Top and Front Views)

1/4"   1/8"   38

1/4"

1/2"

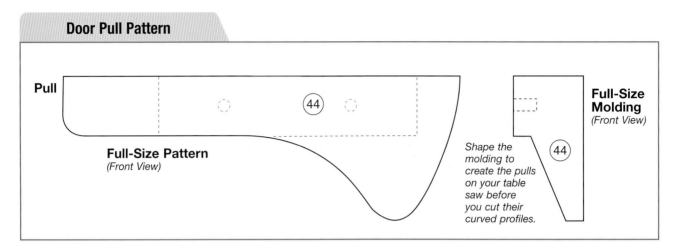

Pull

Full-Size Pattern
(Front View)

(44)

Full-Size Molding
(Front View)

(44)

Shape the molding to create the pulls on your table saw before you cut their curved profiles.

With the parts already cut to the rectangular dimensions given in the Material List, begin construction by setting up a dado head in your table saw. Use it and the miter gauge to create tenons on the ends of all four door rails (pieces 36 and 37) and the six small muntins (pieces 38). Dimensions for these are given in the drawings on pages 112–113. On the rails, you have to cut the large rabbets before you cut their curved aspects. Now, lay out the shape of the door rails, and using a band saw, create their graceful arcs (see Cutting Curved Door Rails on page 111). Sand these pieces smooth.

Again referring to the drawings, lay out the five mortises in each door stile (piece 39). If you do not have access to a dedicated mortising machine, use a Forstner bit in your drill press to remove most of the waste in these mortises, and finish up with a sharp chisel.

Glue and clamp the door parts, making sure the assemblies are absolutely flat and square. After the glue dries, sand each door.

Completing the rabbet in the back of each door stile for the door glass (piece 40) takes a little thought. Use a straightedge and a ½"-diameter straight bit for this operation. You'll need to stop the rabbet short and square your corners with a chisel.

Super-Easy Sliding Dovetails

Sliding dovetails are really just an upscale version of dadoes. The main advantage to the sliding dovetail is that it is a truly mechanical joint—its shape will not allow the joint to pull apart. Plow the dovetail as you would a dado, with a router and a straightedge. It may be apparent, but it's important to note that you can't stop your router as you plow the dovetail: You must cut it in one pass with the dovetail bit; its shape makes this essential. It is a good idea to remove some material first with a straight bit and follow behind with the dovetail cutter to keep from overloading and breaking the fragile bit. When you're done plowing the dovetail grooves, chuck the same bit into your router table and create the shoulders (tails) of the joint, one side at a time.

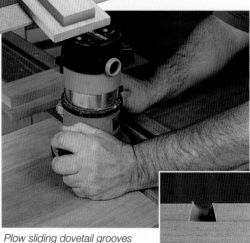

Plow sliding dovetail grooves with a router and clamped-on straightedge.

Create the matching tails on your router table after you've plowed the grooves, so you can easily test the fit.

Installing the Doors

To maintain the clean lines of this project, use Soss hinges (pieces 41 and 42), which are invisible when the doors are closed. Follow the manufacturer's instructions to create the two-level mortises for these hinges (see Installing Soss Hidden Hinges at right), and then dry fit the doors. Be aware that the hinges are *not* adjustable, so you need to place them correctly the first time.

Do a final sanding of all parts, and then apply three coats of clear satin finish, sanding between coats with 400-grit wet/dry paper. Don't forget to finish all four sides of the glass retainer strips for the upper doors (pieces 43). After the finish dries, install the glass. This must be safety glass—anything else presents a real physical danger to your family in the event of breakage. Also, never order the glass until you have your doors built. Miter the retainer strips to fit, and secure them with ½" pin nails. Predrill the strips to avoid splitting.

Forming Ebony Door Pulls

The door pulls (pieces 44) are made from solid ebony. This cabinet will last generations and deserves the best details. You'll also notice that when the cabinet is closed up, there is no hardware visible . . . just wood.

The pulls start out as a piece of molding (see the drawings on page 114 for the profile) and are then cut and sanded to their final shape. Crosscut them to length, and notch out their backs to raise the mounting area of the pulls. Use a band saw and disc sander to complete the shape (see Figure 3). Polish them to 600-grit, and apply a coat of penetrating oil for their finish. Wrap up by installing the brass door catches (pieces 45), as shown in the exploded view on page 113.

The last step is to cut a piece of ⅛"-thick, ¾" metal bar stock to create the anchor strips (pieces 46). Counterbore four holes, and use the anchors to secure the top and bottom units together. This is an important step to keep the tall upper cabinet from tipping during use.

With the final details completed, move the cabinet to your dining room and load it up with the good china. Let's just hope your painstaking work doesn't put the china to shame!

Figure 3: *For the solid-ebony pulls, first create a molding, as shown in the drawing on page 114. Complete the pulls' organic shape with a band saw and disc sander.*

Installing Soss Hidden Hinges

The unique construction of Soss hinges means you'll have to rout a two-step mortise.

Step 1

Step 2

Use a shop-made or commercially available jig to create the mortises for the Soss hinges. This china cabinet required two different sizes.

Tight-fitting and extremely strong, Soss hinges were the best solution for this design.

Finding hidden hinges sturdy enough to hang these large, heavy doors was a challenge. The answer turned out to be Soss hinges—which are elegant to look at and very strong. The larger model is on the upper cabinet doors. They are undeniably tricky to install but well worth the effort. This style of hinge fits into a two-level mortise that is best created with a router and a jig. As with any tricky operation, practice your cuts on scrap lumber before milling the project parts.

Greene and Greene–Inspired Dresser

This chest of drawers has an extraordinary number of pieces, and putting them together is like solving a Rubik's Cube—if you don't do it in the right order, it won't work out. There are a lot of projects that you can approach in a random fashion, making whatever part strikes your fancy, in any order. This is not one of those projects.

by Mike McGlynn

This chest is influenced by a Greene and Greene chest of drawers that I first viewed at the Gamble house in California. Among many other factors, I was especially drawn to the chest's staggered drawers and its small mirror.

Sheet Stock Galore

The Material List for this piece contains a lot more sheet stock than you would expect with a piece this size. The amount of solid wood is surprisingly small. I started selecting my material by picking out some nice 8/4 mahogany for the legs and some 4/4 stock. For the drawer fronts, I selected boards from which I could get the full width of the fronts and that were long enough that I could have the grain run across each pair of fronts. I also selected a piece of rough 4/4 from which I could get the 1" thickness needed for the breadboard ends. In addition, I made the entire top out of one board. I made the drawer pulls out of some choice 6/4 quarter-sawn mahogany that was lying around my shop.

I chose to make all of the interior dividers out of ¾" (two sheets, plus) shop-grade birch plywood; there is no reason to use anything fancy for these dividers, as they will never be seen. The back, side, and interior panels are made of ¼" MDF (medium-density fiberboard, two full sheets). I made the drawer bottoms out of maple-veneered ¼" MDF; note that it's only possible to get 11 of the 12 bottoms out of one sheet of ply, so I hope you have a little leftover lying around your shop. The last sheet stock pieces that I bought were two sheets (5' x 5') of Baltic birch plywood.

There are two other types of wood that I had to purchase before I could start on the cabinet. The plugs and splines on Greene and Greene pieces are almost always made of Gaboon ebony, but, unable to find any decent Gaboon, I chose instead to make these pieces out of African blackwood. I like the blackwood better than the ebony, as it has a subtle grain, yet is almost black, and polishes just like the ebony. Lastly, I bought two 4' x 8' sheets of paper-backed mahogany veneer to cover the side panels and back. I selected sheets with seam lines to help me create a balanced-looking panel.

The first thing I did after getting back from the lumberyard was to rough mill all of my solid-wood pieces. (I generally like to leave all pieces a couple of inches long and at least ¼" oversize in the other dimensions. This allows the wood to adjust to my shop conditions, and I end up with milled straight, flat pieces.) Then, I marked all of the drawer fronts with chalk so I could quickly tell which fronts went together and in what orientation.

There are four sections that make up this cabinet: the sides, the center section, the top and mirror, and the drawers. I started with the sides.

Start with the Sides

My first step with the sides was to create their veneered panels. I cut the MDF substrate oversize and their veneer pieces to match (see the Material List on page 118). I chose the best pieces of veneer for the face sides of the panels. The veneer can be applied in a number of ways; my choice was a vacuum bag, but most folks use a simple veneer press like the one shown on page 110.

While the panels cured, I milled the legs and rails to final dimensions. Again, I took care to keep my orientations marked with chalk.

There were a surprising number of plug holes, mortises, and slots that had to be cut in each of the legs. This was an excellent place to completely mess up the project, or at least the four nicely matched legs. So, I laid out each and every plug hole, mortise, panel slot, and back rabbet so there would be no chance of a mistake.

I use a multi-router to form my mortises and tenons, but I think you would do just fine here with a mortising machine or attachment to your drill press. Look to the elevation drawings on page 119 for construction details. The last step on the legs is to break (or round over) the appropriate edges with a 1/8" roundover bit.

Next, I milled all of the rails to size and cut their tenons. The bottom rails get the traditional Greene and Greene cloud lift. I laid them out, cut them on the band saw, and finished them with a file and hard sanding block. Finally, I rounded over the selected edges of the rails.

By this time, the panels were finished being veneered, so I cut them to size on the table saw. Now, I could measure their edge thickness to find the size of the panel slots. In my case, the panels came out to just about 5/16".

I cut the panel slots on the router table using a 1/4" down-spiral bit to plow a 1/2"-deep groove down the middle of each piece. To widen the slot, I moved the fence a tiny bit and made two passes —one on each side of the main slot. I did this until I got a nice slip fit.

Prior to staining and assembly, I went through a four-step process to prepare the parts for staining. First, I sanded all pieces with 120-grit sandpaper. Then, I detailed all of the edges and cloud lifts. Next, I went over everything with a damp rag to raise the grain, and finally, I sanded everything with 220-grit sandpaper on a slightly soft block.

Like most of the Greene and Greene pieces I've built, this chest has a water-based aniline dye stain on it. I have found that it is almost impossible to end up with a good stain job if the piece is assembled. For this reason, I try, as much as possible, to stain all the parts before they are assembled.

With that step completed, I buffed the surface of all the pieces with a fine Scotch-Brite pad. After buffing, I assembled both of the ends, using epoxy and padded bar clamps. It's essential to handle all the stained parts with rubber gloves, or moisture from your hands will damage the dye.

Getting to Your Center

The center section of this cabinet is very complicated (see the Material List and drawings on pages 120–121), but I was drawn to this design because of its asymmetrical drawers. Just my luck that they added such a degree of difficulty.

I started by milling the divider edging. As seen in the drawings, there is a subtle difference in width between the horizontal and vertical edges. The horizontal edges are 7/8" wide, and the vertical edges are 3/4" wide. With the divider sheet stock 3/4" thick, I chose to rabbet the horizontal edging 1/4" deep so it would nicely cap the edges. To prevent breaking off the 1/16" lips, I made the rabbet with several passes on the table saw (see Figure 1 on page 120). I then made the edging for the vertical dividers 13/16" wide so I could easily flush it up after gluing it on.

When slicing up the birch plywood, I would recommend trying to eliminate veneer chipout by carefully knife scoring the cut line and using a very sharp plywood blade. I cut the dividers so the grain went from side to side on the horizontals, and from top to bottom on the verticals. Then, I glued all the edging on using Titebond glue and bar clamps.

Because I chose to leave them a little long for the glue-up, all of the ends

of the edging needed to be trimmed, and the ones on the vertical dividers needed to be notched to fit over the horizontal edging's 1/16" lip. It's important to note that all of the vertical dividers don't get exactly the same size notch. The bottom divider is flush on the bottom because there isn't a 1/16" lip to clear, and the top divider gets a 1/2" x 2" notch for the top rails. All the others get the standard 1/16" notch on both edges.

Now, I was ready to sort out the vertical and horizontal dividers and mark them for assembly. Using a long square, I marked a line for each side of the vertical panels and the centerline on the horizontal dividers. I also carried the centerline of each panel around to the opposite side. I then drilled three attachment holes for each vertical edge.

Before going any further, you must make two bottom rails and install them in the bottom divider panel before the center section can be assembled. Each of these rails has its own details to take care of: rabbets, cloud lifts, etc. Once my rails were detailed, I glued them to the bottom divider.

Rounding over the vertical edges was my last step before assembling the center section. The horizontal edges are not rounded over until after the dividers have been joined.

I assembled the center section on a large, flat bench. This was very helpful, as it kept the back edges all lined up. It was also very useful—almost imperative—to have a right-angle cordless drill driver. I started at the top and worked my way down, clamping each vertical in place, drilling pilot holes, and then attaching

Material List – Sides

	T x W x L
1 Side Panels (4)	1/4" x 19 3/8" x 21 13/16"
2 Veneers (Paper-Backed) (8)	1/16" x 19 3/8" x 21 13/16"
3 Legs (4)	1 3/4" x 1 3/4" x 51 5/8"
4 Side Rails (6)	7/8" x 2 3/4" x 21"

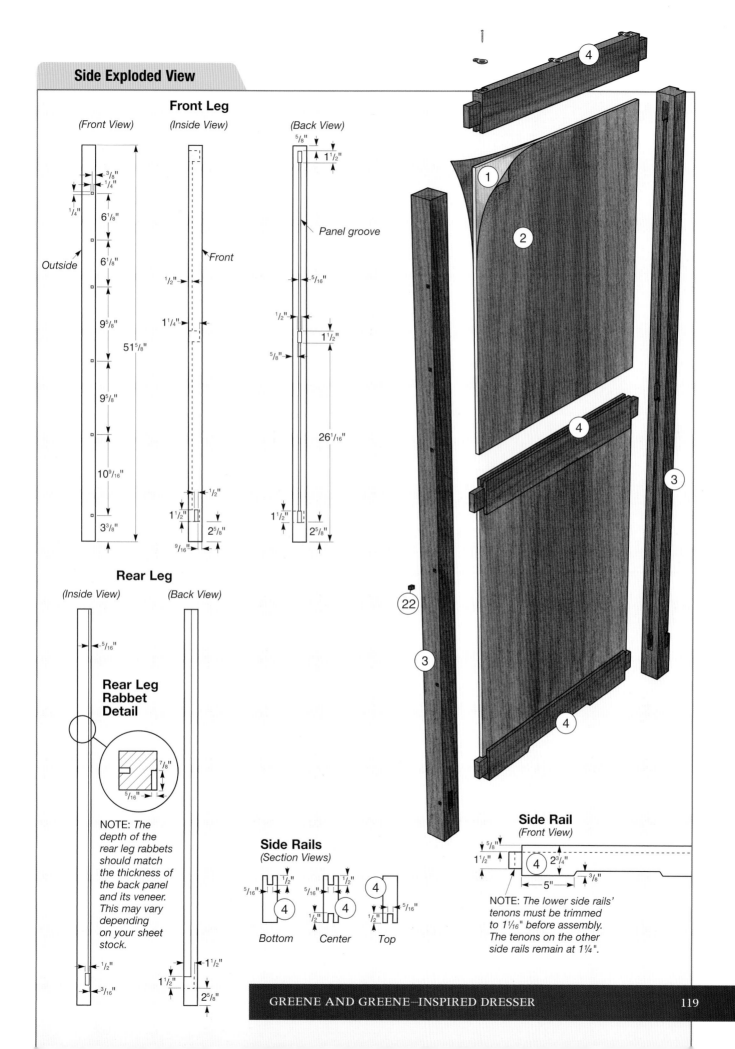

Front Leg

(Front View) *(Inside View)* *(Back View)*

Panel groove

Outside

Front

3/8"
1/4"
1/4"
6 1/8"
6 1/8"
9 5/8"
51 5/8"
9 5/8"
10 9/16"
3 3/8"

1/2"
1 1/4"
1 1/2"
2 5/8"
9/16"
1/2"

5/8"
1 1/2"
5/16"
1/2"
1 1/2"
5/8"
26 1/16"
1 1/2"
2 5/8"

Rear Leg

(Inside View) *(Back View)*

5/16"

Rear Leg Rabbet Detail

7/8"
5/16"

NOTE: *The depth of the rear leg rabbets should match the thickness of the back panel and its veneer. This may vary depending on your sheet stock.*

1/2"
3/16"

1 1/2"
1 1/2"
2 5/8"

Side Rails
(Section Views)

5/16" 1/2"
1/2"
4
Bottom

5/16" 1/2"
1/2"
4
Center

4
5/16"
1/2"
Top

Side Rail
(Front View)

5/8"
1 1/2"
4
2 3/4"
5"
3/8"

NOTE: *The lower side rails' tenons must be trimmed to 1 1/16" before assembly. The tenons on the other side rails remain at 1 1/4".*

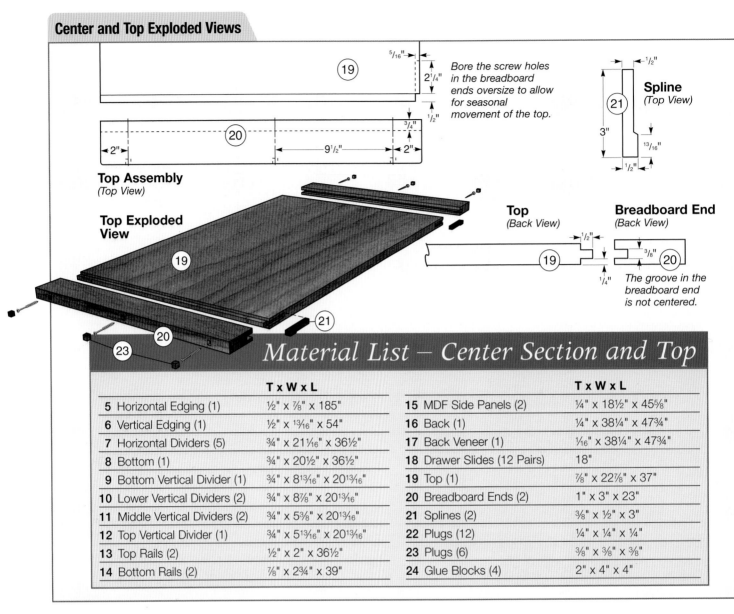

Center and Top Exploded Views

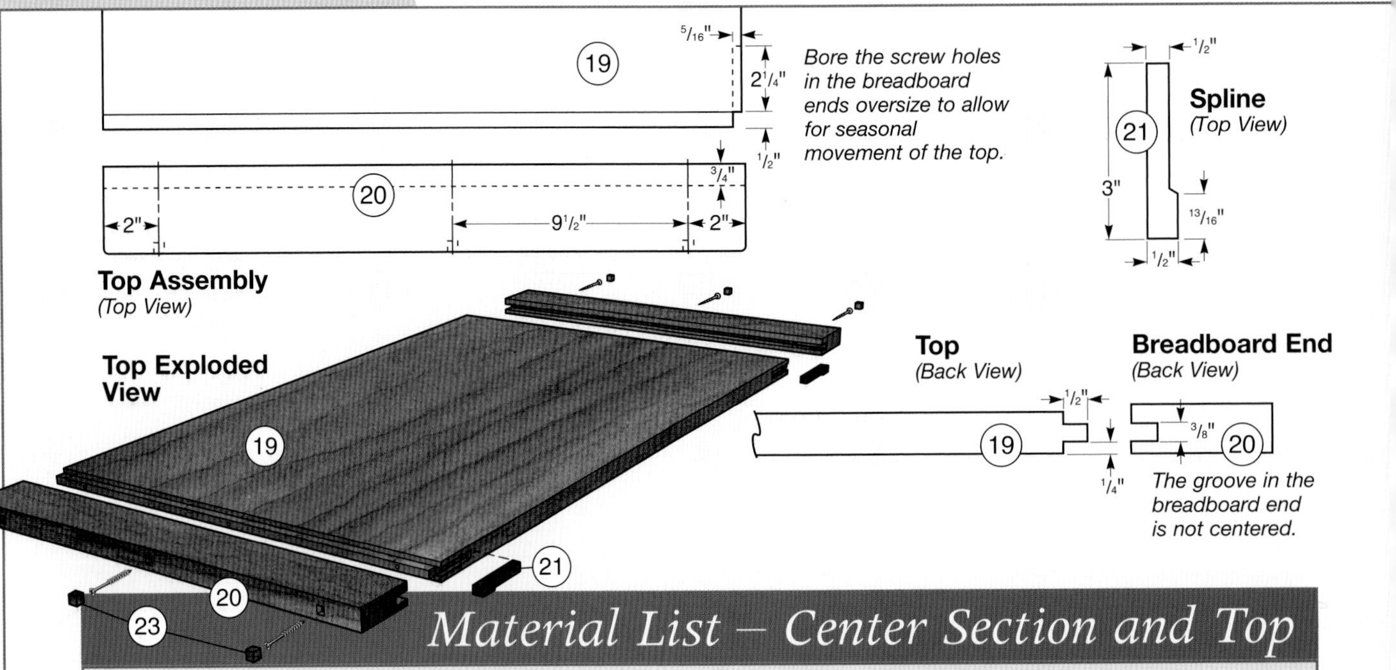
5/16"
2 1/4"
1/2"
3/4"
2"
9 1/2"
2"
Bore the screw holes in the breadboard ends oversize to allow for seasonal movement of the top.
1/2"
Spline
(Top View)
3"
13/16"
1/2"
Top Assembly
(Top View)
Top Exploded View
Top
(Back View)
1/2"
1/4"
Breadboard End
(Back View)
3/8"
The groove in the breadboard end is not centered.
19
20
21
23

Material List – Center Section and Top

	T x W x L		T x W x L
5 Horizontal Edging (1)	½" x ⅞" x 185"	**15** MDF Side Panels (2)	¼" x 18½" x 45⅝"
6 Vertical Edging (1)	½" x 13/16" x 54"	**16** Back (1)	¼" x 38¼" x 47¾"
7 Horizontal Dividers (5)	¾" x 21 1/16" x 36½"	**17** Back Veneer (1)	1/16" x 38¼" x 47¾"
8 Bottom (1)	¾" x 20½" x 36½"	**18** Drawer Slides (12 Pairs)	18"
9 Bottom Vertical Divider (1)	¾" x 8 13/16" x 20 13/16"	**19** Top (1)	⅞" x 22⅞" x 37"
10 Lower Vertical Dividers (2)	¾" x 8⅞" x 20 13/16"	**20** Breadboard Ends (2)	1" x 3" x 23"
11 Middle Vertical Dividers (2)	¾" x 5⅜" x 20 13/16"	**21** Splines (2)	⅜" x ½" x 3"
12 Top Vertical Divider (1)	¾" x 5 13/16" x 20 13/16"	**22** Plugs (12)	¼" x ¼" x ¼"
13 Top Rails (2)	½" x 2" x 36½"	**23** Plugs (6)	⅜" x ⅜" x ⅜"
14 Bottom Rails (2)	⅞" x 2¾" x 39"	**24** Glue Blocks (4)	2" x 4" x 4"

each vertical with glue and screws. I then used a ⅛" roundover bit to break the horizontal edges.

The two top rails are the last parts of the center section. They are simply glued and screwed to the vertical divider.

Figure 1: *When forming the groove in the horizontal edging, be sure to handle the delicate 1/16" lips of the edging carefully.*

With the dividers joined in a single unit, I attached the MDF side panels that hold everything in alignment and provide a surface for the outside drawer slides to attach to. I used spacer blocks at the outboard ends of the horizontal dividers to hold them exactly the right distance apart. Once again, I attached the panels with glue and screws.

The center section was now done and ready to be stained. My first step was to detail the intersections of the vertical and horizontal edges with 120-grit sandpaper. Then, I raised the grain and lightly sanded with 220-grit paper.

Staining this section was an exercise in being methodical and careful. It was simply not possible to stain the whole

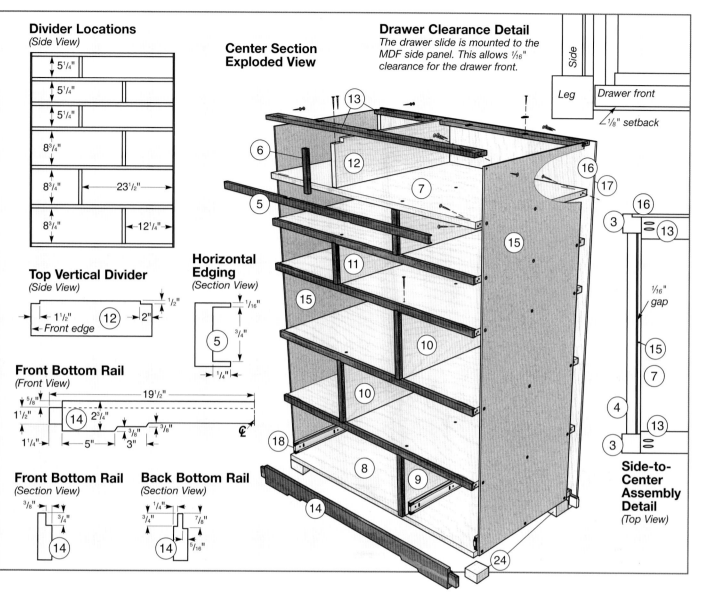

Divider Locations
(Side View)

5¼"
5¼"
5¼"
8¾"
8¾" ←23½"→
8¾" ←12¼"→

Center Section Exploded View

Drawer Clearance Detail
The drawer slide is mounted to the MDF side panel. This allows ¹⁄₁₆" clearance for the drawer front.

Side
Leg | Drawer front
⅛" setback

Top Vertical Divider
(Side View)

1½" (12) 2"
Front edge
½"

Horizontal Edging
(Section View)

¹⁄₁₆"
¾"
¼"
(5)

Front Bottom Rail
(Front View)

⁵⁄₈"
1½"
←————19½"————→
(14) 2¾"
⅜" ⅜"
1¼" ←5"→ 3"

Front Bottom Rail
(Section View)

⅜"
¾"
(14)

Back Bottom Rail
(Section View)

¼"
¾" ⅞"
(14) ⁵⁄₁₆"

Side-to-Center Assembly Detail
(Top View)

¹⁄₁₆" gap

---

thing at the same time without a disaster taking place. So, I stained one drawer bay at a time, wiped off the excess, and then moved on to the next section to avoid drying and blending problems. Once it was stained, I buffed it all as before.

With caution being the better part of valor, I assembled one side at a time to the center section. This was a fairly straightforward matter of gluing, clamping, and pocket screwing. (As I mentioned before, wear rubber gloves when handling the stained, but not finished, wood.) I assembled the unit by attaching the horizontal dividers to the ends with pocket holes—two per corner, one top and one bottom. After I had both sides attached, I made and attached

large corner blocks to join the rails and legs on the bottom of the cabinet.

To prevent the stain from being marred at this point, I sprayed the assembled cabinet with a sealer.

A Classic Breadboard Top
The top is a classic Greene and Greene top: breadboard ends and exposed splines at the joints. I began by milling my board to thickness and then used my table saw to cut the top to size. Staying at the table saw, I formed the tenons with a vertical and horizontal cut.

I milled the breadboard ends to size and cut the groove in them on the table saw. This groove is not down the middle of these pieces, but instead, it's offset due to

the ⅛" thickness difference between it and the top. These pieces are flush with the underside of the top and proud on the top. Cutting the spline slot was best done by chopping it by hand with a sharp chisel.

As with the plug holes in the legs, I used a square mortising chisel in the drill press to cut the plug holes in the breadboard ends. After cutting the plug holes, I used the drill press to drill the attachment holes. I then slipped the ends into place, marked the screw holes, and drilled the pilot holes in the tenons.

Rounding over and detailing the top and ends is a bit tricky if you're not careful. It's important to remember that the ends stand proud on the top and the front, and you must be very careful to keep the back and bottom edges square. Once again, I went through the prep steps and then stained the top and ends.

Once the stain was dry and buffed, I attached the ends to the top with 3" screws.

The Drawers and Pulls

As I mentioned earlier, I selected the wood for the drawer fronts carefully so that the grain ran continuously across all of the pairs. I milled the boards to thickness and width, and then cut them (see the Material List on page 123). I used my block plane to fine-tune the fit of each front so that I had an even, and parallel, gap all the way around. After fitting, I marked each front as to which opening it fit in. In a routine you're probably tired of by now, I rounded over the corners of the fronts and then went through the sanding and staining process.

I made the drawer boxes out of ½" Baltic birch plywood. I cut the parts to size and machined their joints. When I finished routing the rabbets, I sanded all the sides, fronts, and backs to 120 grit.

Using a brad nailer and Titebond, I assembled the drawer boxes. Before the glue had set, I laid each drawer box on my bench, measured it from corner to corner for squareness, and tweaked it if necessary.

While the boxes were drying, I cut the bottoms from the maple-veneered ¼" MDF. To prep for finishing, I sanded them to 120 grit. I attached the bottoms with glue and brad nails.

One of the defining characteristics of Greene and Greene casework pieces is the styling of the drawer and door pulls. There are as many different variations of pulls as pieces they designed—it's the sculptural quality of these pulls that ties them together. For this cabinet, I designed pulls that were based on an amalgam of several different designs, the primary one being the chest of drawers from the Gamble house that I referred to earlier. I'll tell you from the start that these pulls take an inordinate amount of time.

In search of pleasing aesthetics, I tried to choose straight-grained wood

for these pulls. I milled all of the pieces to their rectangular dimensions and cut them to length.

To lay out the curved steps, I made a very accurate tag-board template and used it to mark out the steps. I marked the steps on the side of each pull with a black fine-line ballpoint pen (it's easier to see). Using a 6 TPI x ¼" blade, I very carefully band sawed the steps. I was careful to cut just on the fat side of the line so I could clean up the saw marks without going past the layout line. Once the steps were sawed, I smoothed them to the line with a combination of a hard sanding block, files, and a block plane (see Figure 2).

I found a pleasing curve for the edge of the steps, and after experimenting a bit, I found that a pillar file, with its one smooth edge, was the best way to cut and smooth these curves.

Making the finger relief could probably all be done with a single, though somewhat elaborate, router jig. I found it just as easy to do this with a combination of a pass on the router table and some handwork. I started by making a pass on the router table with a coving bit. This left me with a straight relief that needed to be modified into a curved one to match the curve of the pull face. I marked a line about ⅜" back from and parallel to the pull face. A few good swipes with a sharp gouge and a little cleaning up with sandpaper finished the job.

The final shaping to be done on the pulls is the undercutting of the ends. I did this freehand by judiciously grinding the ends on the end roller of my stationary belt sander.

There was a surprising amount of very painstaking sanding and detailing to be done before the pulls were ready for stain. I made quite an effort to get all of the pulls to look exactly the same. When all the detailing was done, I went through the staining process.

Figure 2: *Forming the quarter-sawn mahogany drawer pulls is a time-consuming task.*

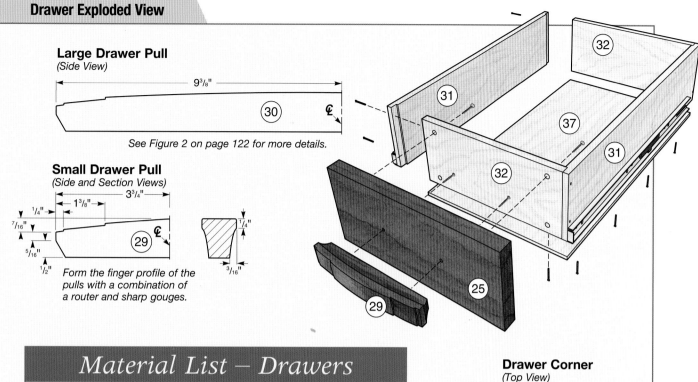

Drawer Exploded View

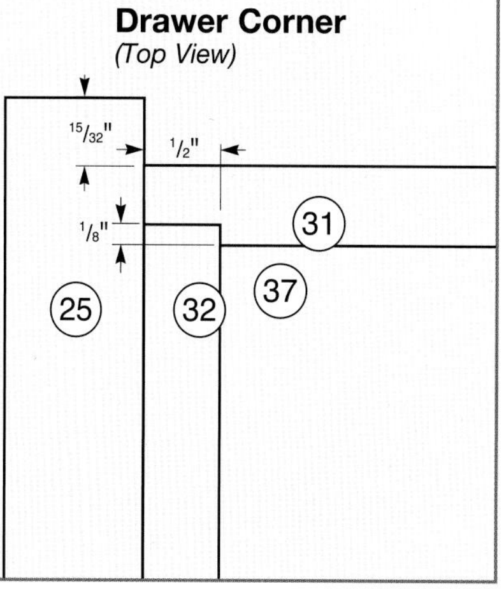

Large Drawer Pull
(Side View)

9³/₈"

30 ℄

See Figure 2 on page 122 for more details.

Small Drawer Pull
(Side and Section Views)

3³/₄"
1³/₈"
¹/₄"
⁷/₁₆"
⁵/₁₆"
¹/₂"
29 ℄
¹/₄"
³/₁₆"

Form the finger profile of the
pulls with a combination of
a router and sharp gouges.

Drawer Corner
(Top View)

¹⁵/₃₂" ¹/₂"
¹/₈"
31
25 32 37

	T x W x L
25 Upper Small Drawer Fronts (3)	⅞" x 5⅛" x 12³/₁₆"
26 Upper Large Drawer Fronts (3)	⅞" x 5⅛" x 23⅜"
27 Lower Small Drawer Fronts (3)	⅞" x 8⅝" x 12³/₁₆"
28 Lower Large Drawer Fronts (3)	⅞" x 8⅝" x 23⅜"
29 Small Drawer Pulls (6)	1⅛" x 1¼" x 7½"
30 Large Drawer Pulls (6)	1⅛" x 1¼" x 18¾"
31 Upper Drawer Sides (12)	½" x 4⅝" x 19½"
32 Upper Small Drawer Fronts, Backs (6)	½" x 4⅝" x 10½"
33 Upper Large Drawer Fronts, Backs (6)	½" x 4⅝" x 21¾"
34 Lower Drawer Sides (12)	½" x 8¹/₁₆" x 19½"
35 Lower Small Drawer Fronts, Backs (6)	½" x 8¹/₁₆" x 10½"
36 Lower Large Drawer Fronts, Backs (6)	½" x 8¹/₁₆" x 21¾"
37 Small Drawer Bottoms (6)	¼" x 11¼" x 19½"
38 Large Drawer Bottoms (6)	¼" x 22½" x 19½"

Material List – Drawers

If this cabinet was always going to be up against a wall, I probably could have made the back out of a piece of ¼" MDF. Alas, that was not the case, so I opted for a piece of mahogany-veneered ¼" MDF. I veneered the back in a vacuum bag the same as I did the side panels. I veneered only one side of the back, but since it was screwed down with about 20 screws, I knew warpage wouldn't be a problem. After cutting it to size, I sanded and stained the back in the usual method.

Mirror, Mirror

The mirror and its supports were the last things I needed to build before the cabinet could be finished and assembled (see the Material List and drawings on page 125). I started by milling all of the pieces to their rough, nonshaped sizes. With the pieces still in this rectilinear shape, I cut the miter joints on the top and sides. After cutting the miters, I used a thin wood batten to lay out the curves and steps on both the top and sides. I cut

the pieces to shape on the band saw and then smoothed them with sandpaper and files.

The corners of the mirror are joined with face-frame-size biscuit joints, but you can substitute dowels. Before gluing up the frame, I made sure to sand the inside edges, as this is much harder to do once the frame is assembled. I glued up the frame using Titebond, a bar clamp on the bottom, and 3M packing tape on the miter joints. When the glue had set, I used a rabbeting bit in a router to cut most of the mirror rabbet. I used a sharp paring chisel to finish off the rabbet.

Before moving on to staining the mirror frame, you'll have to follow the detailing steps I used on the other subassemblies, starting with rounding over all of the appropriate edges.

Moving to the mirror posts, I started by cutting the posts to length. Then, I laid out their curves and used a band saw to shape them.

After looking at most of the available mirror pivot hardware—and finding it lacking—I decided to make my own, which was fairly simple to do and also resulted in a clean design. I ended up using 1" x ¼" steel dowels and a ¹⁄₁₆" black nylon washer, which added up to a grand total of about $2. The spacers serve to make a ⅛" gap, so the assembled mirror has room to swing. With that done, I sanded and detailed all the parts and stained them.

The finishing process was quite straightforward. The first step was to go over everything with a good-quality tack rag to remove any residual dust. Then, for a finish, I sprayed on three coats of catalyzed synthetic lacquer, but you can use the finish

of your choice. I usually buff with a fine Scotch-Brite or sand with 220-grit sandpaper between coats, depending on how the surface feels.

Assembling a cabinet with this many drawers is rather time-consuming and needs to be done carefully. I started the assembly by attaching the mirror assembly to the top. First, I used clear silicone adhesive to glue a piece of ⅛" mirror into the mirror rabbet. While the silicone was drying, I marked and drilled attachment holes in the bottoms of the support posts. With the mirror assembly together, I carefully marked and drilled mounting holes in the top, and then I mounted the mirror to the top (see Figure 3). Then, I attached the top to the carcass with tabletop fasteners and screws.

Next, I installed the drawer slides. This was straightforward, but it required the use of a right-angle drill driver to install them, especially in those smaller compartments. I attached the drawer pulls to the drawer fronts before installing the fronts on the drawer boxes. After the pulls were attached, I attached the fronts to the drawer boxes. I used my usual method, which is to drill four ⅜" holes in the front of the drawer boxes and then attach the fronts with drawer front attachment screws that have an oversize head. This allows for some minute adjusting to get the fronts perfectly aligned.

Once all the drawers were in place and the fronts were attached and adjusted, I installed the back using 1" screws and finishing washers.

Ebony-Like Accents

The very last items to complete on the cabinet were the African blackwood plugs and splines (see Figure 4). I made all of the plugs in my usual way: Make a stick of the right dimension, dome the end with sandpaper, polish it on a buffer, cut it off on the band saw, and repeat. I also cut the splines on the band saw and then sanded them to shape and polished them. I installed the plugs and splines by applying a small drop of clear silicone and then tapping them in place. The silicone allows for a little movement and reduces the possibility of them falling out if the humidity changes. The cabinet was now complete.

I found this to be a very satisfying project, but in a different way from many other projects I have done. There isn't any part of this cabinet that was particularly hard to construct, but it had engineering questions galore. I love the process of thinking through how something is going to go together, and in what order. It was satisfying to work through the challenges presented by this cabinet and have it come together so well. I would like to think that the Greene brothers, especially Henry (the engineering half), would have found this an interesting project. I hope that you do and that it provides many years of service and pleasure.

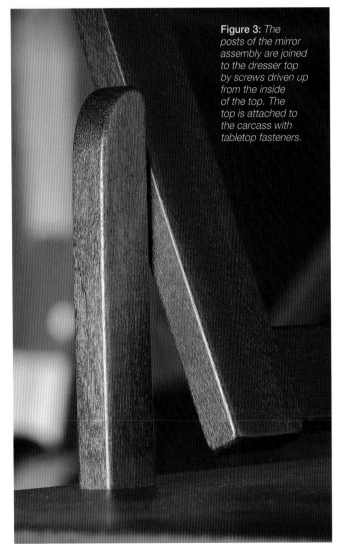

Figure 3: *The posts of the mirror assembly are joined to the dresser top by screws driven up from the inside of the top. The top is attached to the carcass with tabletop fasteners.*

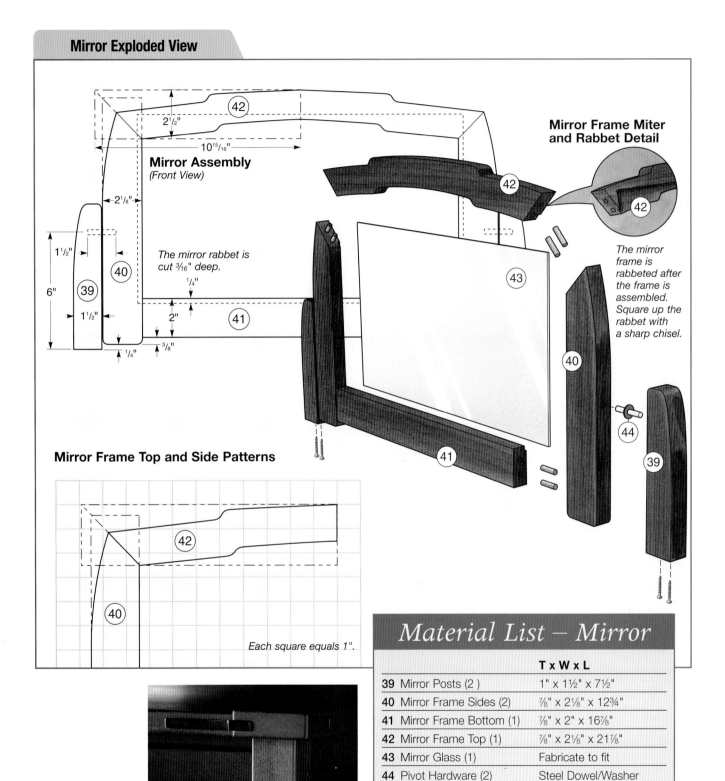

Mirror Exploded View

Mirror Assembly
(Front View)

42

2½"

10¹⁵⁄₁₆"

Mirror Frame Miter and Rabbet Detail

42

42

42

The mirror frame is rabbeted after the frame is assembled. Square up the rabbet with a sharp chisel.

2⅛"

1½"

6"

39

40

The mirror rabbet is cut ³⁄₁₆" deep.

¼"

43

2"

41

40

1½"

¼"

³⁄₈"

44

39

Mirror Frame Top and Side Patterns

42

40

Each square equals 1".

Material List – Mirror

		T x W x L
39	Mirror Posts (2)	1" x 1½" x 7½"
40	Mirror Frame Sides (2)	⅞" x 2⅛" x 12¾"
41	Mirror Frame Bottom (1)	⅞" x 2" x 16⅞"
42	Mirror Frame Top (1)	⅞" x 2⅛" x 21⅞"
43	Mirror Glass (1)	Fabricate to fit
44	Pivot Hardware (2)	Steel Dowel/Washer

Figure 4: *Details such as the African blackwood splines lend a sense of elegance to the dresser.*

Weekend Toy Box

Safe and sturdy, stylish and practical, this weekend project is easy to build. Butt joints covered by simple fluted moldings create a classic toy box that stores tons of fun and is attractive enough to keep in the living room. This project easily transforms into a keepsake chest and also doubles as extra seating.

by Mike McGlynn

As Easy As 1-2-3...4

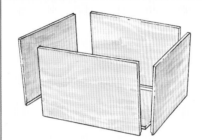

Step 1: *Cut the plywood panels to size, machine the four rabbets, and test the fit.*

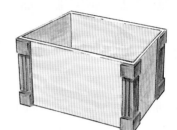

Step 2: *Add the edge banding, fluted molding, and plinth blocks.*

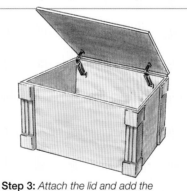

Step 3: *Attach the lid and add the hardware: two child-safe lid supports and a simple piano hinge hold it securely.*

Step 4: *Add the finish of your choice, a few strips of Velcro, and a nice cushion.*

Toys are a lot more than mere playthings. They represent everything from a child's dreams for the future to a parent's paradise lost. But even with such wonderful esoteric values, the reality is that most of the time, they're just a huge mess all over the house. That's particularly true nowadays, when most kids seem to own every toy that's ever appeared on TV.

The rules are a little different these days, too. Kids are often allowed to set up fun shops in the middle of the living room. On the other hand, you may have memories of your old toy box being relegated to a bedroom because it didn't "go" with mom's decor.

So, here is a toy box for today. It's designed to look great in the living room or basement, featuring basic construction with elegant results. Purchase the cushion or have it made, and you have a toy box that will easily convert to a blanket chest or perhaps an extra seat for the big game.

Whether you're an old hand at woodworking or a raw recruit, this project is manageable with just the barest array of tools. All you'll need are a table saw, a router, and a few basic hand tools. A circular saw might come in handy, but it isn't absolutely essential.

Keep two things in mind when choosing the wood for your toy box. First, look for a species that your lumberyard stocks in both ¾"-thick hardwood stock and ¾" veneered plywood. I found both in cherry for this box. Second, think about how your choice will match your room decor.

Cutting Major Components to Size

Dimensions for the top, sides, front, and back (pieces 1, 2, and 3) are given in the Material List on page 129. All five parts can be cut from a single sheet of veneered

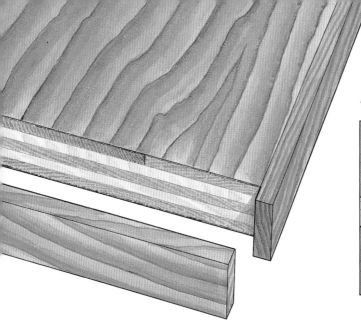

Plywood Cutting Guide
(NOTE: *You don't have to cut the bottom piece from your expensive plywood.*)

Top ①	Bottom ④	Side ②
Make this cut first.		
Front ③	Back ③	Side ②

plywood, as shown in the Plywood Cutting Guide, above. When laying out these cuts, pay special attention to grain direction, so the lines run horizontally around the box. You'll find some helpful pointers on handling large sheets in Splinter-Free Cuts on Large Sheet Stock on page 132. The bottom (piece 4) can be squeezed out of your nice plywood, but since it won't be seen, you're better off cutting it from any halfway respectable-looking sheet stock you have lying around.

Most hardwood-veneered sheets come with an A (or A2) side and a B side. The A side is a better-quality veneer, and it should be facing out on the finished project. Make sure the blade always enters the good side and exits the B side, to avoid splintering. So, if you're using a circular saw to cut a full sheet to size, the A side should be facing down. On the table saw, orient it so the A side faces up instead. Either way, use a sharp, fine-toothed blade.

Milling Rabbets for the Bottom
The bottom is secured to the sides, front, and back by setting it in matching rabbets. These can be cut on the table saw using a dado head (see Figure 1 on page 130) or with a router using a ½" straight bit. For the table saw method, just set the fence and blade according to the dimensions shown in the rabbet detail drawing on page 129, and then make the cuts. If you go with a router (either portable with a clamped-on guide

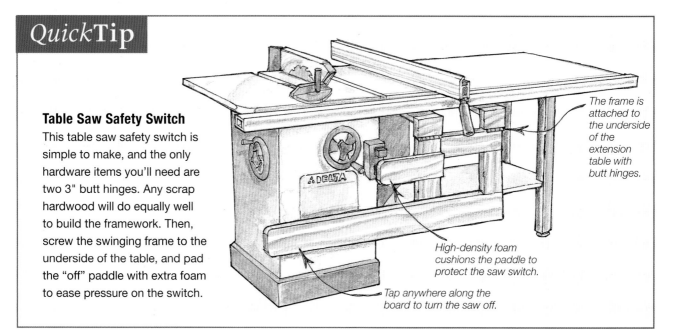

QuickTip

Table Saw Safety Switch
This table saw safety switch is simple to make, and the only hardware items you'll need are two 3" butt hinges. Any scrap hardwood will do equally well to build the framework. Then, screw the swinging frame to the underside of the table, and pad the "off" paddle with extra foam to ease pressure on the switch.

The frame is attached to the underside of the extension table with butt hinges.

High-density foam cushions the paddle to protect the saw switch.

Tap anywhere along the board to turn the saw off.

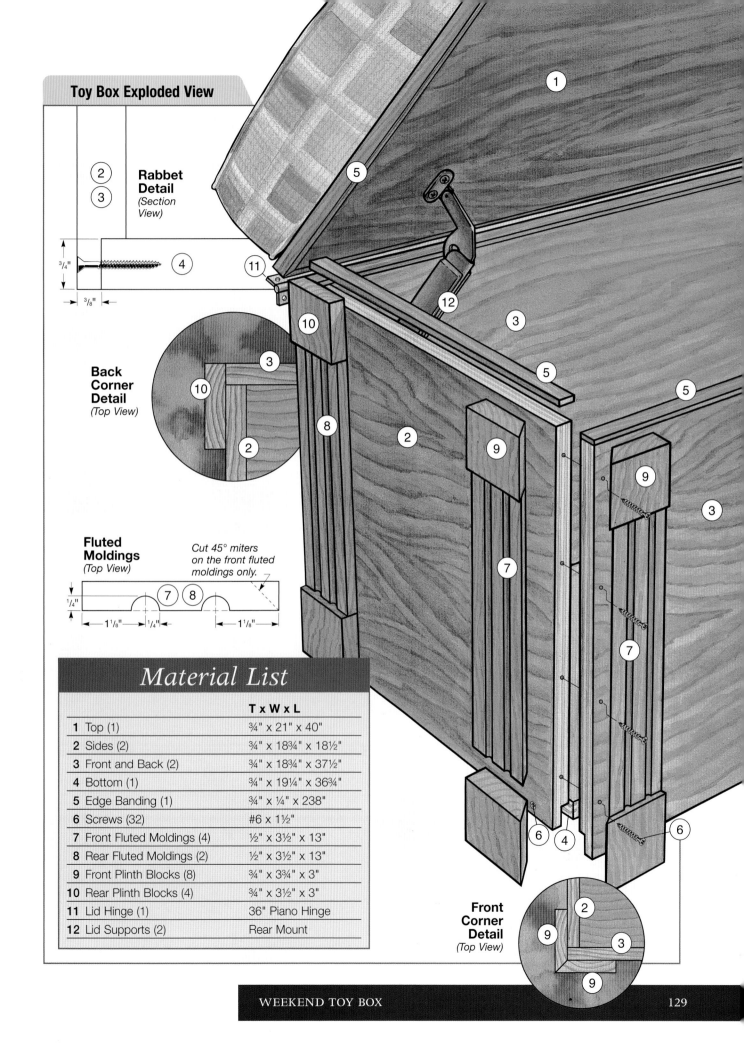

Toy Box Exploded View

Rabbet Detail
(Section View)

¾"

⅜"

Back Corner Detail
(Top View)

Fluted Moldings
(Top View)

Cut 45° miters on the front fluted moldings only.

¼"

1⅛"   ¼"   1⅛"

Material List

	T x W x L
1 Top (1)	¾" x 21" x 40"
2 Sides (2)	¾" x 18¾" x 18½"
3 Front and Back (2)	¾" x 18¾" x 37½"
4 Bottom (1)	¾" x 19¼" x 36¾"
5 Edge Banding (1)	¾" x ¼" x 238"
6 Screws (32)	#6 x 1½"
7 Front Fluted Moldings (4)	½" x 3½" x 13"
8 Rear Fluted Moldings (2)	½" x 3½" x 13"
9 Front Plinth Blocks (8)	¾" x 3¾" x 3"
10 Rear Plinth Blocks (4)	¾" x 3½" x 3"
11 Lid Hinge (1)	36" Piano Hinge
12 Lid Supports (2)	Rear Mount

Front Corner Detail
(Top View)

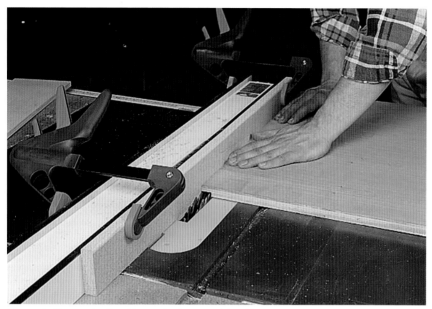

Figure 1: *Form a simple rabbet at the bottom of the sides, front, and back for the bottom piece. There's no need to stop the cuts, since molding will cover the corners.*

or table mounted), make each rabbet in two passes to lessen the strain on the router bit.

Disguising the Plywood Edges

Although veneered plywood is an excellent building material and does a wonderful job of replicating wide boards, it has one minor drawback: The edges of a cut sheet reveal the alternating layers within the board. There are a couple of ways to deal with this. One is to apply an iron-on veneer tape, but with the usage this toy box may see over the next several decades, strips of hardwood edge banding (piece 5) would be a much more durable edging.

Rip enough ¼"-thick stock to cover both the top edges of the carcass and the outer edges of the lid. This stock should be the exact width of the plywood thickness. Trim it to length (create mitered corners on the lid pieces), and apply it with glue and clamps. If you're short on clamps, you can use 1¼" hardened trim nails, predrilling the trim every 6" so it won't split

(chuck one of the nails in your drill to use instead of a drill bit). Set the nail heads after the glue dries, and then fill and sand them.

If the trim is minutely wider than the plywood, make sure the outsides

(appearance sides) are absolutely flush. You can belt sand the inside faces with 220-grit sandpaper after the glue dries. Go slow—you don't want to sand through the veneer.

Assembling the Box

The box carcass is held together with glue and screws driven through simple butt joints. Refer to the exploded view on page 129 to orient the parts properly. With the bottom in place, butt the joints together, and hold them temporarily with clamps (or an extra pair of hands if they're available). As you work, make sure the carcass is square and plumb. Measure diagonally across the top in both directions: When these measurements are identical, your assembly is square. Adjust clamping pressure to tweak the box for squareness.

Predrill for the screws (pieces 6), using a bit about half the thickness of the screws in the second piece and

Figure 2: *Rout the flutes in your stock before cutting it to length to ensure uniformity.*

the full thickness of the screws in the first piece. This will ensure that the screws pull the joints tight as they are driven home. Be sure to countersink for the heads so they'll lie flush with the wood. Apply glue to both joint surfaces, set the bottom in its rabbet, and drive the screws home.

Keep a damp cloth handy to wipe off any excess glue. If you miss some glue spots, wait until they become rubbery, and then clean them up with a sharp chisel, using the blade as a scraper.

Adding Fluted Corners

A simple molding application takes this project from a mundane cube to an elegant toy box. I used a fluted molding, created by milling a pair of large grooves (called flutes) in one face of ½"-thick pieces of stock (pieces 7 and 8). The best way to do this is with a table-mounted router, using an inexpensive ¼"-radius core-box bit to form ½" flutes (see Figure 2). Refer to the fluted moldings drawing on page 129 for the dimensions for both the front and rear moldings, and make the cuts in two passes.

*Quick*Tip

Create Your Own Expanding Mandrels

If you like to make napkin rings and other hollow turnings, here's a way to hold your work securely: Cut a number of plywood discs (depending on the length of the mandrel), thread them on a hex-headed machine bolt, and then turn them to the exact inside diameter required. Now, cut discs from an old inner tube, and reassemble the mandrel, as shown below. Tightening the nut squeezes the rubber discs so the mandrel expands and grips the turning. If the mandrel is longer than about 2", it will need end support. Create this by countersinking the exact center of the bolt head, and then mount a live center in the tailstock. You may find it best to draw a reference line on the plywood discs so they can be reassembled in the original order.

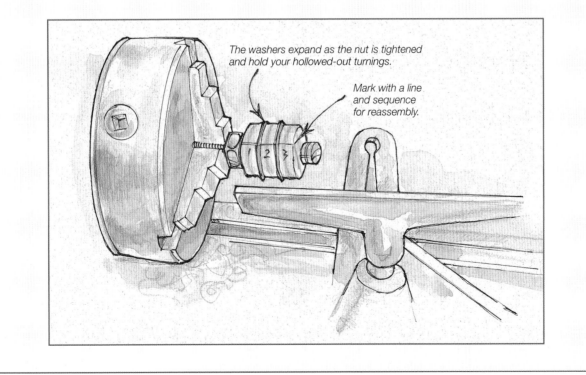

The washers expand as the nut is tightened and hold your hollowed-out turnings.

Mark with a line and sequence for reassembly.

Splinter-Free Cuts on Large Sheet Stock

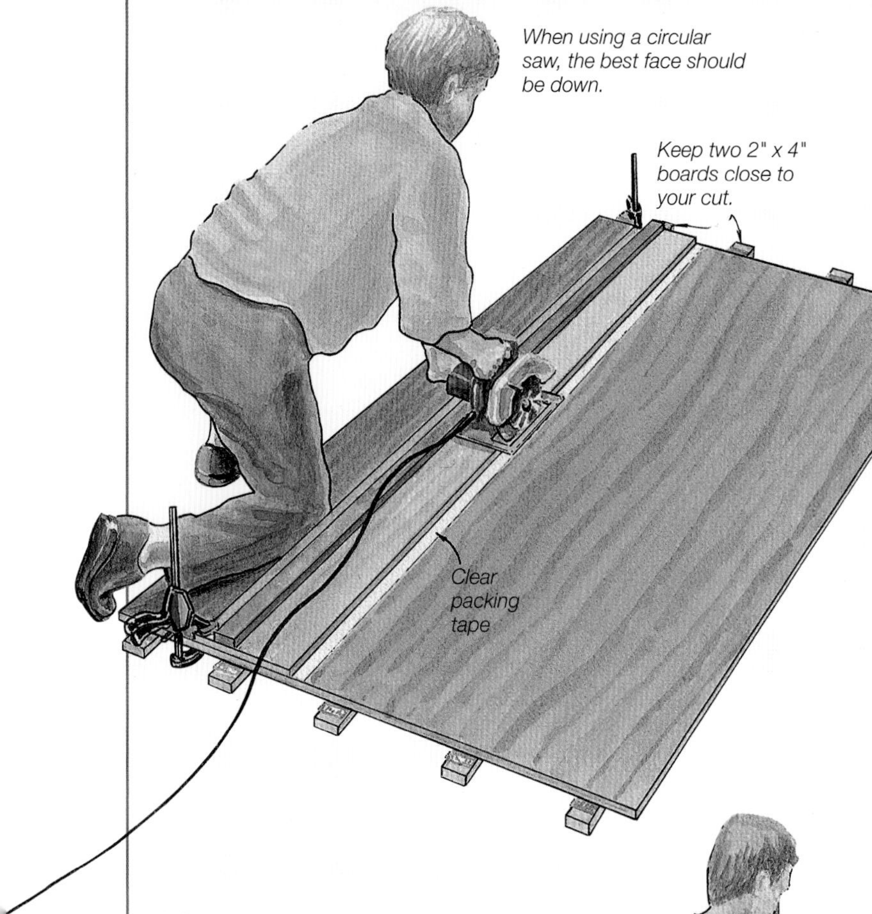

When using a circular saw, the best face should be down.

Keep two 2" x 4" boards close to your cut.

Clear packing tape

Using a Circular Saw

When cutting a full sheet of plywood into components, lay a few 9'-long 2" x 4" boards on the floor. Since the best face of the stock should face down (the exit side of a cut is more likely to splinter), glue thin carpet to one face of each 2" x 4" to protect the plywood's veneer. I also recommend applying 3M-brand clear packing tape along the path of the cut (both sides) to reduce splintering. To get a perfect cut every time, make a jig by gluing an 8"-wide length of ¼" ply to a straightedge. Trim through this piece with your saw against the straightedge. Until you get a new saw, that's where your blade will always cut. Just line up that trimmed edge with your pencil mark, and clamp the jig in place.

Using a Table Saw

In this case, the best face of your plywood must face up as you cut. Full sheets shouldn't really be handled alone on a table saw—you're just a bit too far from the shut-off to be safe. And if your stock is more than a couple of feet long, be sure to provide a solid outfeed support; roller stands or a large outfeed table are two good options. Take care when cutting thin sheet stock such as laminate, because it may slide under the fence and go out of alignment, causing binding on the blade. And speaking of blades, a blade with a reverse hook angle (a melamine blade) works much better than a crosscut version on veneered panels. Score through the veneer on cross-grain cuts, setting the blade at about ¹⁄₃₂" for the first cut. Then, turn the sheet over, and raise the blade to about one and a half times the thickness of the stock for your second cut.

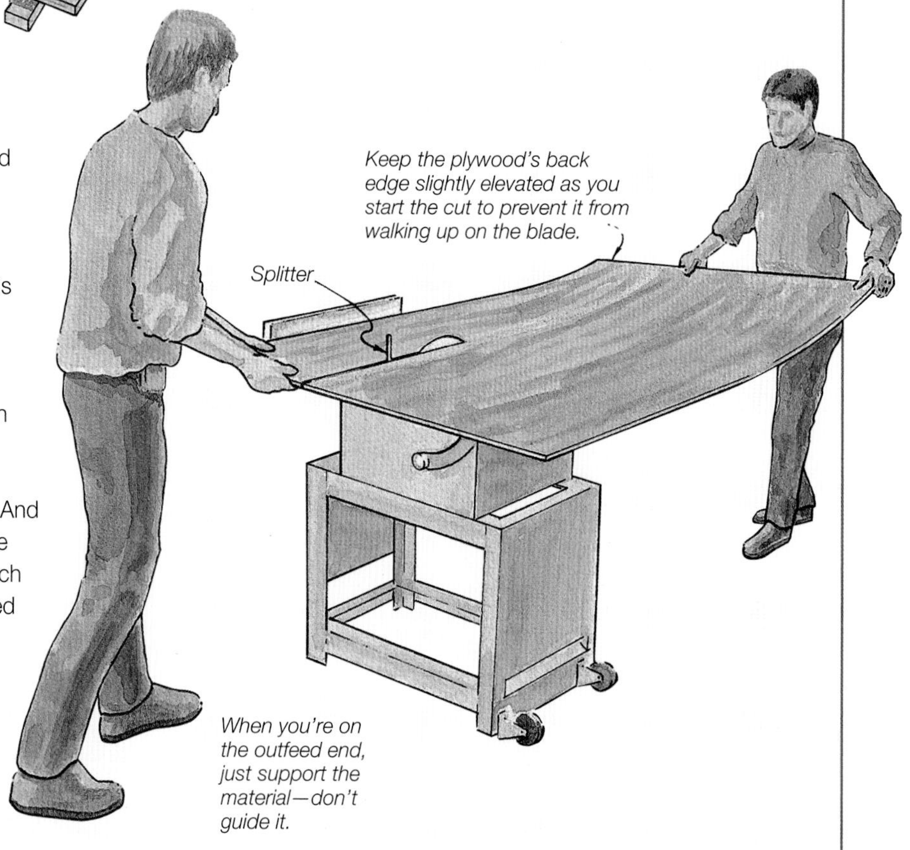

Keep the plywood's back edge slightly elevated as you start the cut to prevent it from walking up on the blade.

Splitter

When you're on the outfeed end, just support the material—don't guide it.

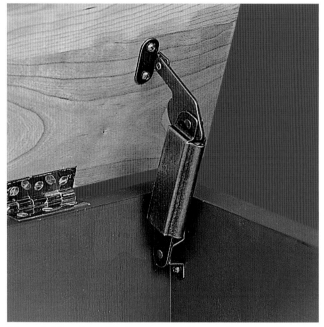

Figure 3: *Keep those little fingers safe with a quality support like the one used for this project, approved for use on toy boxes by the Consumer Product Safety Commission.*

Since this toy box will receive heavy usage over the generations, I suggest applying three or four coats of nontoxic clear finish over the stain, sanding all but the final coat with 400-grit wet/dry sandpaper.

Installing the Hardware

After the finish is dry, attach the lid with a continuous piano hinge (piece 11), predrilling for the screws. Piano hinges are durable and strong and will provide years of service for a reasonable price. You can rout a mortise for this in the bottom of the lid if you like, but it isn't necessary. To save little fingers from getting pinched (a real hazard with large doors or lids), install a pair of child-safe lid supports (pieces 12), which regulate the speed at which the lid closes (see Figure 3). Installation instructions are included with this hardware.

Now, all that's left to do is to convince all those boisterous kids that the scattered toys belong in their brand-new toy box when not in use. You're on your own for that job!

After the grooving is complete, use your table saw to create a 45° chamfer on one edge of each piece of the front molding. The rear moldings need not be chamfered. Now, use the same saw angle to chamfer one edge of each of the front plinth blocks (pieces 9). Again, since the back is flush, it's not necessary to chamfer the rear plinth blocks (pieces 10). Glue and clamp the blocks in place, using the exploded view for orientation. Now, trim the lengths of molding to fit snugly between the blocks, and glue and clamp them in place. Clean up any glue squeeze-out, and set the project aside to dry.

Applying a Finish

The most important step in any finish is the preparation that goes into it. Fill all the nail holes and any minute gaps that appear in the mitered joints, and let the filler dry thoroughly. Sand the entire project with 120-, then 180-, and finally 220-grit sandpaper. Chisel out any minor accumulations of glue in the corners, and you're ready to apply a finish. Many furniture builders like to wipe on a matching stain (in this case, medium cherry) to even out any tonal differences between the plywood veneers and the solid hardwoods. This is also a great way to achieve instant aging—that magnificent patina that cherry develops over the years due to exposure to light and air.

Flat-Screen TV Cabinet

Here's a sleek, modern cabinet with a tricky motorized lift for your flat-screen TV. It's a slick solution to the problem of making that dead-black screen go away when you're not watching it.

by Mike McGlynn

When I was invited to come up with a flat-screen TV media center, I had a bit of a struggle with the design. My usual leaning toward the Greene and Greene brothers' style wasn't helping much. Ultimately, I found the answer with clean, straight lines and exposed edges of built-up ApplePly sheet stock.

ApplePly is available in several thicknesses with maple faces and comes in standard 4' x 8' sheets. Although it is a very high-grade product, ApplePly has a couple of quirks that annoy the tar out of me, especially considering that it costs about $100 for a ½"-thick sheet. The first and most annoying problem is that the sheets are rarely flat—in fact, I've yet to see a flat sheet of ApplePly in 20 years of woodworking. Every sheet seems to have a "potato chip" quality to it. Years ago, I gave up trying to fight this annoyance and switched to gluing two sheets together using a vacuum bag system to get the thickness I needed. This results in a dead-flat panel.

The second little annoyance is that ApplePly isn't truly void free. A much better description would be "99% void free." This isn't that big of a deal; just keep in mind that those voids are going to require some edge filling in places.

Sheet Stock Construction

The upside of this cabinet being made entirely of sheet stock is that the layout and the prep are greatly simplified. When making sheet stock cabinets, I make a parts list and then lay out the parts on scale drawings of 4' x 8' sheets. While laying out the parts for this cabinet, I kept three things in mind:

1. All parts, with the exception of the middle divider, are 1" finished thickness and are thus actually two pieces of ½" material glued together—two sets of everything.
2. Related to #1: All the pieces need to be cut 1" oversize to allow for trimming after vacuum bagging.
3. Most sheets of ApplePly have a slight taper around the edge of the panel. You'll probably take care of this in the previously mentioned trim step, but keep it in mind.

Cutting veneered sheet stock, especially across the grain, is a pain in the neck. If you are not lucky enough to own a table saw with a scoring blade, you'll need to use an extremely sharp blade. Score the cut line on the bottom side with a knife, and tape the bottom cut line with masking tape. Or you can cut close to the line with a circular saw and then trim to the line with a router and straightedge.

Vacuum Bag Gluing

Once I had all my panels cut up, it was time for an adventure in Vacuum Bagging Land. I have done a lot of this work over the years, so I have some hard-earned information that I can pass on. My first tip is to use Titebond Cold Press for Veneer glue. I like it because it has a fairly long open time—very good when working

with large panels. In addition, it dries quickly and doesn't bleed through when working with veneer. My second piece of advice is to have a dead-flat platen on which to do the bagging. I have a 4' x 8' bench that is absolutely flat. I put the bag on top of this bench and use a ¾" melamine platen inside the bag. I scored the melamine with a shallow 2" x 2" gridwork of saw kerfs to allow for air evacuation. After I glue the panels and put them together, I tape them tightly with blue 3M masking tape. This prevents a sliding mess as the panels go into the bag. Practically everything you read about vacuum bagging will tell you not to use masking tape, as it supposedly will get so firmly stuck that it won't come off without

Material List

		T x W x L				T x W x L
1	Top (1)	1" x 22¼" x 95"		11	Base – Long (1)	1" x 4" x 95"
2	Interior Top (1)	1" x 20¾" x 93"		12	Bases – Short (2)	1" x 4" x 22¼"
3	Bottom (1)	1" x 22¼" x 95"		13	Side Shelves (8)	1" x 19⅞" x 20¾"
4	Interior Bottom (1)	1" x 20¾" x 93"		14	Middle Shelves (8)	1" x 9⅝" x 24⅞"
5	Middle Back (1)	½" x 52" x 38"		15	Outer Doors (2)	1" x 21⅞" x 38"
6	Outer Backs (2)	½" x 21" x 38"		16	Inner Doors (2)	1" x 25¹⁵⁄₁₆" x 38"
7	Sides (2)	1" x 21¼" x 38"		17	Support Blocks (2)	⅞" x 1½" x 5¹³⁄₁₆"
8	Front-to-Back Dividers (2)	1" x 20¾" x 36"		18	Hinges (4 Sets)	European and Soss
9	False Back (1)	½" x 51½" x 36"		19	Door Catches (4)	Häfele
10	Partial Divider (1)	1" x 9¹¹⁄₁₆" x 36"		20	TV Lift (1)	(See Figure 3, page 138)

damaging the panel. This is not so. Even after 24 hours in a vacuum bag, the blue tape comes off with no problem at all.

Before putting the taped-together panels in the bag, I lay a piece of breather fabric over the top and lightly tape it down at the corners. Breather fabric is thin polyester batting that allows the air to evacuate quickly and evenly. Sometimes it ends up getting glued to the panel, but you can rip it right off. My last suggestion for vacuum bagging is to get a reservoir tank, if possible. I have a 50-gallon tank salvaged from an old air compressor that I use for my reservoir tank. It is hooked up in-line between the pump and the bag. With a reservoir tank, the pump only cycles about every 30 minutes or so; without it, the pump will probably cycle once a minute.

Working with the Panels

Once the panels come out of the vacuum bag, you can begin to cut them into the proper size parts (see the Material List, above). This is not quite as easy as it might seem. Despite taping the panels together, there is always a bit of shifting

Figure 1: *Use a sharp block plane, followed by careful sanding, to clean up saw marks on the exposed plywood edges.*

in the bag, which leaves the panel edges uneven. It's a pretty elementary thing, but to create a square panel, you have to start out with at least one straight edge. On my sliding-top saw, this is easy to accomplish. Alternately, you could use a long straightedge and then trim the panel with a router.

The top, which has a hole for the TV lift, is made by what I call the "saw it apart and then glue it back together" method. After straightening one long edge on the top panel, I ripped it into three pieces, as shown in the drawings on page 137. To minimize the effect of the saw cuts, I used the thinnest thin-kerf saw blade that I have. Sliding these strips together, I marked a centerline across all three, and then cut out the lift opening (retaining the drop to make the lid). Next, I used biscuits and glue to reassemble the top. When it dried, I trimmed the top to size the same way as the rest of the panels. Then, I repeated this step for the interior top—except I tossed the drop this time.

Smoothing the Edges

If you have never used exposed-edge plywood before, one of the unexpected things you will encounter is how long and painstaking it is to finish all those exposed edges. From my experience, no matter how careful you are, there will still be saw marks to remove. The logical choice for this job would seem to be sandpaper, but this just isn't so—unless you want

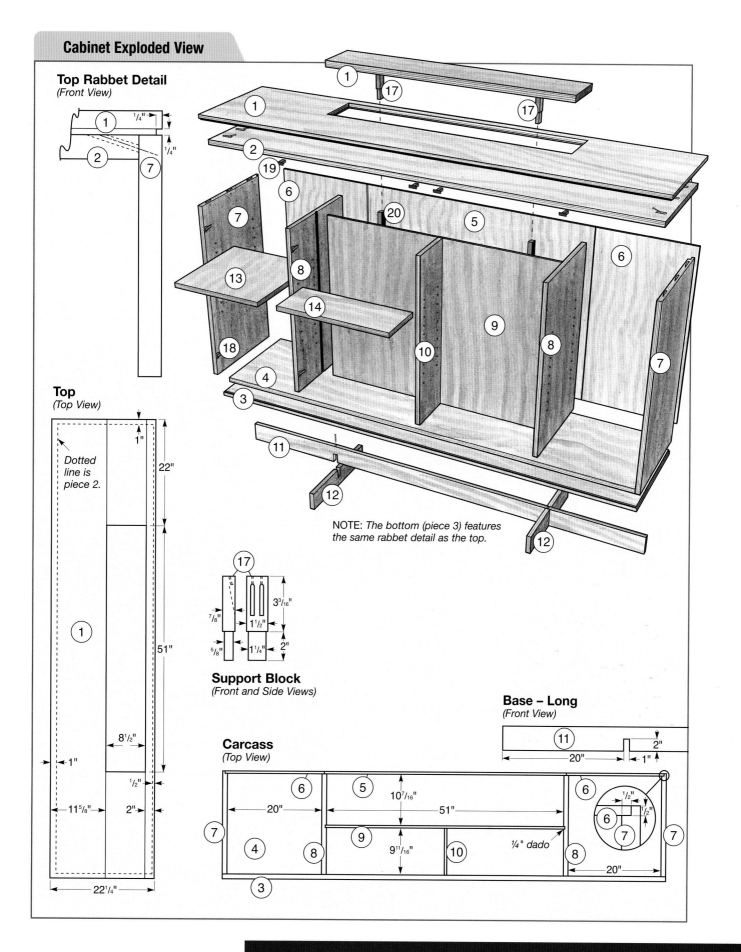

Top Rabbet Detail
(Front View)

¼"
¼"

Top
(Top View)

Dotted line is piece 2.

1"
22"
51"
8½"
½"
1"
11⅝"
2"
22¼"

Support Block
(Front and Side Views)

3³⁄₁₆"
⅞"
1½"
⅝"
1¼"
2"

NOTE: *The bottom (piece 3) features the same rabbet detail as the top.*

Carcass
(Top View)

20"
51"
10⁷⁄₁₆"
9¹¹⁄₁₆"
¼" dado

Base – Long
(Front View)

2"
20"
1"
½"
½"
20"

a good shoulder workout. What I found works the fastest is to take a very thin cut with a very sharp low-angle block plane, followed by sanding with a hard block and 220-grit sandpaper (see Figure 1 on page 136). As with any plywood edge, it's important not to chip out the corners. I prevent chipping by stopping just short of the corner and then planing from the other direction. The glues in plywood dull plane blades quickly, and an even slightly dull blade makes a rough cut, so I hone the cutting edge frequently as I go along.

The ¼" x ¼" rabbet on the top and bottom panels is a subtle detail that nicely breaks up the faces of the cabinet. I made quick work of these rabbets using a router and a rabbeting bit. Just as with planing the edges, I was careful not to chip out the corners while routing. When I finished routing the reveal, I used a hard block and 220-grit sandpaper to detail the rabbets.

I also had to rout rabbets and dadoes in four other panels. I started by routing the ¼"-deep x ½"-wide dadoes in the two front-to-back dividers for the false back. This was easily accomplished on a router table with a fence. I then routed rabbets in the two side panels, to accept the back.

For me, sanding a furniture project is a two-step affair. I do all the sanding I can before I assemble the pieces, and then I do a detail/touch-up sanding on the assembled piece before finishing. This is especially true on a project that has a lot of flat panels. I sanded all the panels with a random orbit sander, starting with 120-grit sandpaper and finishing with 220.

Center-Out Assembly

Assembling this cabinet was a matter of starting at the center and working outward. I began by attaching the short partial divider to the false back with screws and glue. I then attached that assembly to the longer front-to-back dividers using glue and screws. Before attaching the interior bottom panel and interior top panel, I laid out and cut a series of pocket holes on the ends of the hidden face of each piece. I then attached these panels to the center assembly with glue and screws. I made sure to lay everything out and drill pilot holes for all the screws. I laid out biscuit joints on the ends of the bottom panel and top panel and their corresponding side panels. Using pocket screws, biscuit joints, and glue, I attached the side panels.

The foot on this cabinet consists of three pieces that are joined together

Figure 2: *The short and long members of the base are connected with half-lap joints. First, cut the slots to width on the table saw, and then nibble away the waste in between.*

Figure 3: *I used a motor-driven, forklift-style lift to raise and lower the television in the cabinet. A remote control activates the lift mechanism and lowers the TV (and its lid) into a compartment at the back of the unit.*

Figure 4: *I turned to a combination of Soss and Euro hinges to hang the thick doors.*

with a half-lap joint (see Figure 2). I attached the three pieces with a single long screw driven into each joint. Once assembled, I fastened the foot to the bottom with multiple screws and glue. I love it when something is hidden like this: I can screw parts together to my heart's content—and none of the screws show.

I attached the top to the assembled center section using screws through the interior top. The bottom and foot subassembly was attached to the center section with screws.

Tricking Out the Lift

I chose a forklift-style motorized TV lift for this project (see Figure 3), available from *www.rockler.com*. It's a pricey item, perhaps as much as your flat-screen TV, but it is an extremely slick solution to an otherwise difficult engineering problem. The directions for this lift showed the top cover being hinged and the lift pushing it open as it raised. I found this to be a completely ludicrous idea. For starters, the cover would either flop back out of the way or ride against the lift as it rose. I found both options unacceptable. With a little Rube Goldberg–style engineering, I was able to figure out a way to have the cover rise with the lift. My solution was to take the caps off the top of the rectangular steel tubes that support the back of the TV and make wood plugs to fit in them. I could then attach the cover to the plugs with pocket screws.

To make sure the TV would be completely visible when the lift was up, I blocked up the base of the lift about 3". Once the lift was in place, I was able to fine-tune the height of my top mounting blocks until the cover sat perfectly flush with the cabinet top when closed.

Installing the Hinges

This cabinet has two different types of hinges on it: Soss hinges for the outside doors and Euro-style hinges for the inside doors (see Figure 4). I would have preferred to use Euro hinges throughout, but you can't get Euro hinges that will completely overlay a 1" edge. This is regrettable, as Euro hinges are so much easier to install and adjust. My desire to have full overlay doors without seeing the hinges pretty much limited me to Soss hinges. Installing the Euro hinges on the center doors was a simple matter of drilling the appropriate holes and mounting the hinges. Installing the Soss hinges was quite another matter. You can buy templates for routing Soss hinges, but I prefer to use my own shop-built jig. In any case, be extremely careful as you rout out the mortises for these hinges. You basically have one shot to do it right, so practice on some scrap wood!

After installing the hinges, I hung the doors and did whatever adjusting and trimming was necessary to have them all line up properly.

There are an amazing number of shelf support holes in this cabinet. It is much easier to drill them with the back off and before, rather than after, finishing. I used a shelf pin drilling template, clamped it in place with a couple of spring clamps, and methodically drilled all the holes with a brad-point bit (see Figure 5). A simple masking tape stop controlled the hole depths.

The next thing to do was to fit the back. I chose to make the back in three pieces, so that if I needed access to only one section, I wouldn't have to remove the whole back. After fitting the three pieces, I drilled them all for attachment screws. I have found that it is almost always better to attach cabinet backs with screws rather than nails. You just never know when you will have to take the back off a cabinet for some reason. When the back is attached with screws, removal is a piece of cake; with nails, it is a major pain in the neck.

The shelves were the last thing to do before finishing. Because they are 1" thick and have an exposed edge, these were probably the easiest shelves I have ever made.

Applying the Finish

The cabinet is now complete except for finishing. Before finishing, I disassembled the entire cabinet. I made sure to mark all the hinges and their corresponding pockets to ease reassembly. I then went over the entire cabinet methodically and touched up any scuffs or sharp edges with 220-grit sandpaper. Sprayed synthetic, catalyzed lacquer (three coats) was my choice of finish.

When I was done finishing, I reassembled the cabinet. For door catches, I used item #245.50.301

Figure 5: *There's no way around it—shelf pin holes are tedious to drill. A drilling jig at least ensures that they'll all be evenly spaced when you're done.*

from Häfele. These are touch-latch catches that use a ball system instead of magnets. I have always hated the way that magnetic touch latches barely have the strength to hold a fly; on the other hand, you could probably pull a truck with these ball-system catches without them opening. They are really great in an application like this, where there is potential for a large door to warp a little bit and get out of alignment.

Good Old 20/20 Hindsight

I have a great love of Arts and Crafts–style furniture, especially the designs of Charles and Henry Greene. But I'm also a huge fan of modernist architecture and design. I have a really great appreciation for a clean, modern piece that is simple and aesthetically pleasing. In some ways, this is more difficult to pull off than the more traditional designs. I'm relatively pleased with how this project turned out—I like the simplicity of the lines. However, I don't think the exposed edges were worth the trouble. I think the project would have been just as successful if it had been made from MDF (medium-density fiberboard) veneered sheet stock with veneered edges.

Ruhlmann Cabinet

Early in the twentieth century, a group of far-thinking designers began to mantle the world in new ideas expressed in beautiful new shapes. In the realm of furniture making, the high priest of this Art Deco movement was Jacques-Emile Ruhlmann. Here's an impressive Ruhlmann-style cabinet you can build.

by Mike McGlynn

Ruhlmann. The name is enough to strike fear into the heart of even the most experienced woodworker. Jacques-Emile Ruhlmann designed some of the most complex and finely crafted furniture of the early twentieth century. He is considered the high priest of the Art Deco furniture movement, and the craftsmen he employed were the finest of their day.

I have long admired his designs and contemplated making a Ruhlmann-style piece for years. A recent room remodel at my home provided an ideal chance, in the form of a new entertainment center. I pulled out all the stops for this piece.

Design Considerations and Construction Methods

After studying Ruhlmann's work, much of which has survived in wonderful condition, I chose Maccassar ebony for the veneer and Avonite, a humane, man-made ivory substitute.

My next challenge was to figure out the construction methods and their sequence. Veneering is one of those tasks that give even accomplished woodworkers pause. Here are a few general suggestions and pitfalls to avoid: First, have the most stable core possible. In today's world, this means MDF (medium-density fiberboard) and, where you must use solid wood, something like poplar or soft maple.

Second, whenever possible, avoid veneering over joints, especially if the core is solid wood. I've seen it result in cracks too often. Third, vacuum bagging is by far the best way to lay up large, flat panels. And finally, the best way to veneer edges and curved parts is with the iron-on method. Coat both the veneer and core with Titebond II, let it dry, and apply the veneer with a hot iron. More on that later.

With those points in mind, you're ready to start your veneer work. Unfortunately, the first step is one of the most nerve-racking: cutting and taping up the veneer panels. There is no way I can overemphasize the importance of planning your veneer

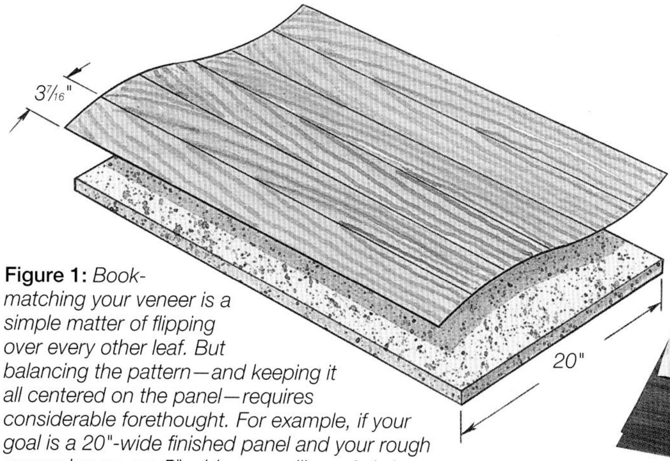

Figure 1: *Book-matching your veneer is a simple matter of flipping over every other leaf. But balancing the pattern—and keeping it all centered on the panel—requires considerable forethought. For example, if your goal is a 20"-wide finished panel and your rough veneer leaves are 5" wide, you will need six leaves approximately 3⁷⁄₁₆" wide (allowing for about ¼" trim on each edge of the veneered panel).*

3⁷⁄₁₆"

20"

Figure 2: *Create straight veneer edges using a sliding carriage that clamps all of the leaves together at the same time, with fully supported edges. This jig creates clean, dead-straight edges. After the first edge is established (right), small blocks (above) are screwed in to adjust the width of the veneer.*

layout in advance. My veneer arrived as 19 consecutive leaves approximately 11' long and 5¼" wide (see the Material List on page 145). My first step was to label the leaves on all four ends, including the leaf number, to keep track of them during layup (see Figure 1 on page 141). Then, I made a list of the veneer panel sizes I needed to lay up. To determine this, I increased the panel dimensions by ½" in width and 1" in length over the stock it needed to cover. I also determined the balanced book-matched pattern of my veneer leaves by laying them out side by side.

Taping Up Veneer Panels

Once you've edged your veneer (see Figure 2), you're ready to tape. As far as I'm concerned, when it comes to flat panels, throw your traditional veneer tape as far as you can. Now, pick it up and throw it again! I tried some on the pediment top, and it took forever to sand off. So I decided to try an experiment using clear packing tape instead. With some scrap veneer, I taped up a small piece and vacuum bagged it with epoxy. When I took the piece out of the bag, the tape peeled off perfectly clean, with no problem. I found it works best if you put a piece of packing tape across the joint every 3" to 4" and then lay another piece the full length of the seam.

With the veneer all laid up, you're ready to prepare the core stock. Cut your panels ½" larger than the veneered panels so the veneer edges won't get crushed in the bag. My choice of glue also runs counter to commonly held

wisdom: I use epoxy because the panels end up dead-flat, and the epoxy allows plenty of open time, which is important when working alone. Roll the glue on with a short nap roller, applying a single coat on both the core panel face and the veneer back, and then place the taped-up veneer on the core stock. For the core stock, I used white-birch-veneered MDF. Conventional wisdom says that ending up with two layers of veneer on one side and one on the other makes for an unbalanced panel. I have discovered that, with the use of epoxy glue, this is not a problem.

The last step before placing the panel in the bag is to put a ¼" melamine caul in place with some masking tape to make a sandwich that is easy to move. Vacuum bagging is a topic all its own; suffice it to say that you should leave the panels in the bag for about 10 hours.

The veneers for the sides and pediment are fairly easy to lay up, but the front is much more complicated. The reason for this is that after taping up the veneer, but before laying it up, the parts that make up the face frame veneer must be trimmed off. I did this with a clamped straightedge and a sharp knife. I cut the vertical pieces, or stiles, off first because seams with the grain are harder to see than cross-grain ones. Then, I cut the top and bottom rail portions off. Once you've carefully marked these pieces' orientations and relationships to each other, set them aside until you are ready to veneer the face frame. After the veneered panels have dried, they should be sanded before being cut to size. It's easier to sand when you don't have to worry about burning through a sharp edge. Sand the panels to 120 grit, making sure to remove any epoxy bleed-through.

Contemplating the Face Frames

Building and veneering the face frames (front and back) is like a puzzle. To prevent significant problems, you need to machine and assemble them in exactly the right order. The first step is to cut the birch-veneered MDF strips that make up the face frames. I made the stiles an extra ¾" wide for mitering purposes, but I cut the rails to exact width. All were left 1" long. Next, you'll need to veneer the appropriate edges of the face frame, including the inside edges of the stiles and the inside (or exposed) edges of the top and bottom rails. Use the iron-on method for this process. (Oops! When you tape up this veneer, you'll have to go find the old-fashioned paper tape you already threw away.) After veneering, trim the edges with a flush-trimming bit and finish up with 80-grit sticky-back sandpaper on a hard block. Then, trim the parts to length.

With any popular artistic movement, there are those designers or craftsmen whose names immediately evoke the genre. Think of Frank Lloyd Wright and the Prairie School, or Gustav Stickley and the Arts and Crafts movement. But no name is more thoroughly identified with a school of thought than Jacques-Emile Ruhlmann and the Art Deco movement. Ruhlmann (1879–1933) was nothing less than the high priest and foremost practitioner of Art Deco. From 1919 until his death, Ruhlmann's name and Art Deco were virtually synonymous.

There is no doubt that Ruhlmann was a brilliant, original designer and that he pushed his highly talented craftsmen to staggering levels of fit and finish, but he also had one other small detail working in his favor: At the age of 27, after the death of his father, Ruhlmann took over his family's business, Société Ruhlmann, a highly successful commercial painting and wallpapering firm. The success of Société Ruhlmann allowed him to run his interior design firm, Ruhlmann et Laurent, essentially as a money-losing business. In his notebooks, Ruhlmann freely admits to losing money on virtually everything his firm turned out. Making an elaborate piece of furniture is much easier if you don't have to worry about making a profit. That's not to say his pieces weren't expensive. There was, for example, a so-called slipper bed that sold for 19,000 francs in the mid-1920s—

sufficient funds at the time to buy a nice house in Paris. By the way, the bed took 1,200 hours to build.

Ruhlmann employed the very finest craftsmen—more than 60 woodworkers, finishers, and specialists, who were paid 30% to 50% more than comparable workers of the day. I have had the privilege of viewing a number of Ruhlmann's pieces in person, and I can say, without hesitation, that the woodworking his shop turned out is the finest I've ever seen. The veneer and inlay work is simply mind-boggling, with striking details such as a $\frac{1}{32}$" band of ivory inlay at the corner of each facet of an eight-sided, curved, torpedo-shaped leg veneered in amboina burl. Ruhlmann noted that a highly skilled craftsman needed 40 hours to make one of these legs.

The materials used in a Ruhlmann piece were the richest available. Many were veneered in either Maccassar ebony or amboina burl veneer. Often, writing or interior surfaces were covered in shagreen (sharkskin) or doeskin. Several of his cabinets feature elaborate metal lock plates created by either Foucault or Janniot—well-known metal sculptors of the day. And, in addition to furniture pieces, Ruhlmann designed a wide variety of lighting fixtures, fabrics, rugs, and other decorative items.

Ready to Invest in a Ruhlmann?

Stunning design, spectacular execution, and limited volume combine to make Ruhlmann pieces among the most sought-after and expensive antiques on the market. Once while in New York, I spotted a Ruhlmann sideboard cabinet in an antiques gallery. It was 7' long x 3' high x 20" deep. It was veneered in Maccassar ebony with a stylized horse-and-chariot inlay done in ivory on the front. The price: a cool $2.5 million. Recently, I returned to the gallery, and the piece had been sold.

Ruhlmann was one of those rare individuals who had an endless amount of God-given talent and the financial means to bring his ideas to life. And it is a richer, more beautiful world because he did so.

—*Mike McGlynn*

Jacques-Emile Ruhlmann
1879–1933

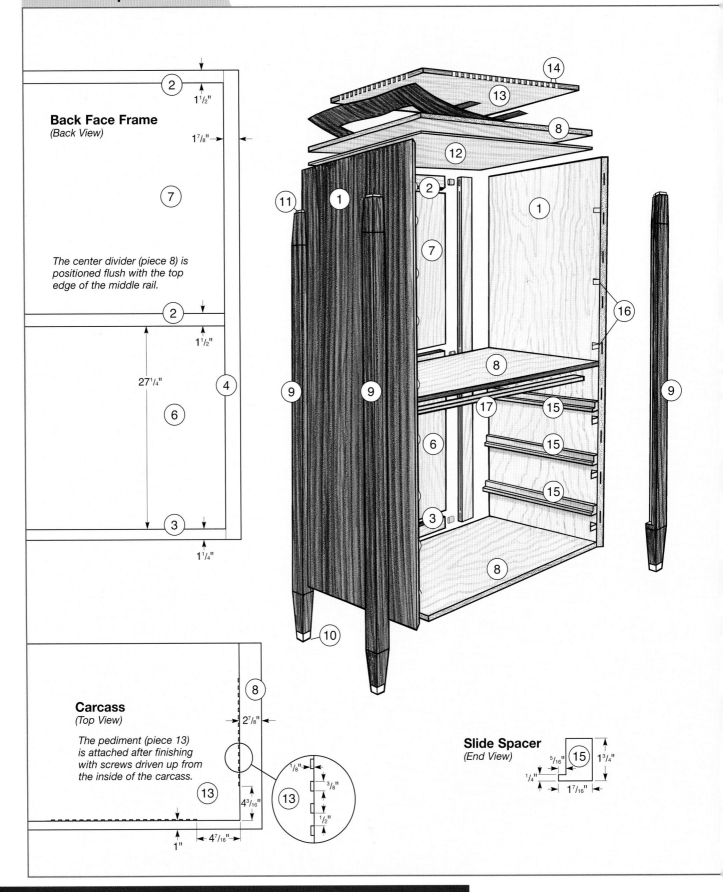

Back Face Frame
(Back View)

2

1½"

1⁷⁄₈"

7

The center divider (piece 8) is positioned flush with the top edge of the middle rail.

2

1½"

27¼"

4

6

3

1¼"

14

13

8

12

11

1

2

7

9

9

16

8

17

15

15

6

15

3

8

9

10

Carcass
(Top View)

8

2⁷⁄₈"

The pediment (piece 13) is attached after finishing with screws driven up from the inside of the carcass.

13

13

1⁄8"

3⁄8"

4³⁄₁₆"

1⁄2"

1"

4⁷⁄₁₆"

Slide Spacer
(End View)

15

1³⁄₄"

5⁄16"

1⁄4"

1⁷⁄₁₆"

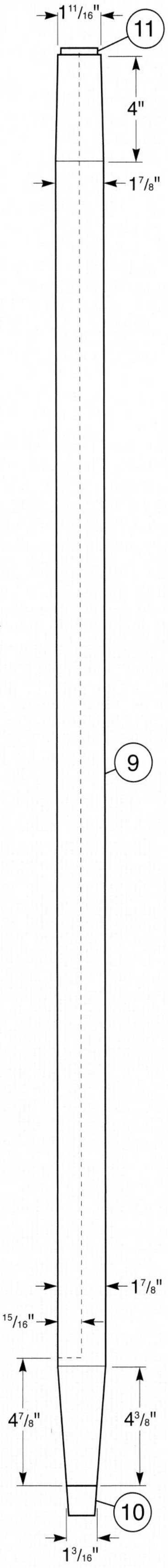

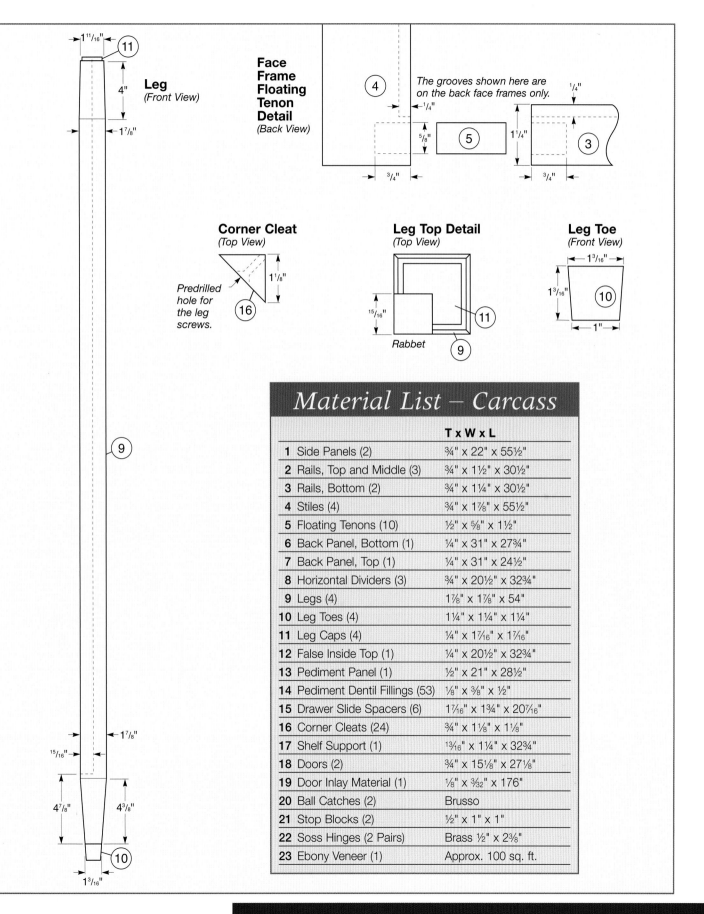

1 11/16"
11
4"
1 7/8"
9
1 7/8"
15/16"
4 7/8"
4 3/8"
10
1 3/16"

Leg
(Front View)

Face Frame Floating Tenon Detail
(Back View)

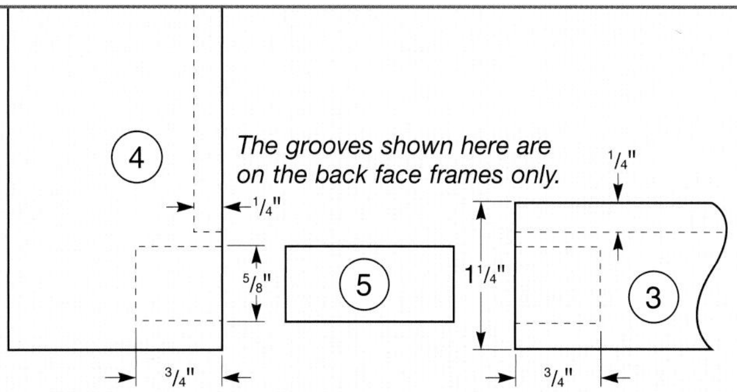

4
The grooves shown here are on the back face frames only.
1/4"
1/4"
5/8"
5
1 1/4"
3
3/4"
3/4"

Corner Cleat
(Top View)

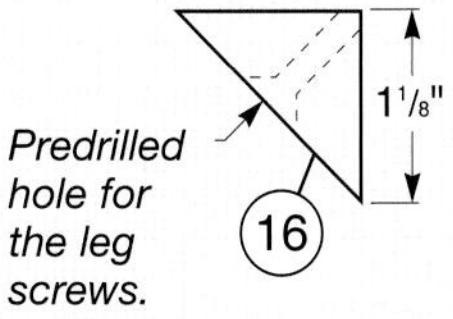

1 1/8"
Predrilled hole for the leg screws.
16

Leg Top Detail
(Top View)

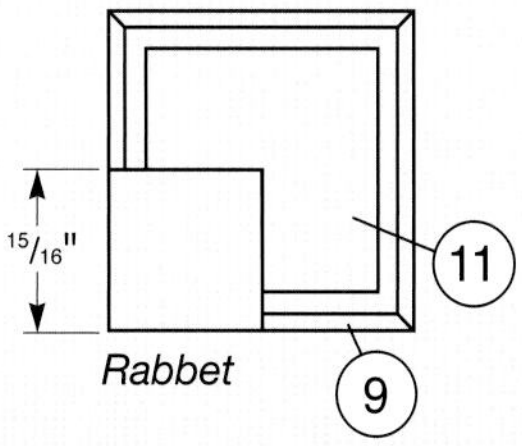

15/16"
11
Rabbet
9

Leg Toe
(Front View)

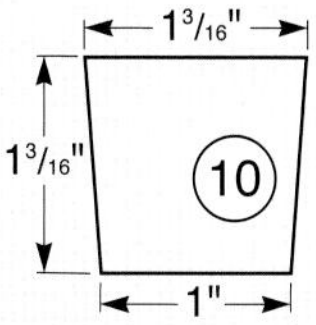

1 3/16"
1 3/16"
10
1"

Material List – Carcass

		T x W x L
1	Side Panels (2)	¾" x 22" x 55½"
2	Rails, Top and Middle (3)	¾" x 1½" x 30½"
3	Rails, Bottom (2)	¾" x 1¼" x 30½"
4	Stiles (4)	¾" x 1⅞" x 55½"
5	Floating Tenons (10)	½" x ⅝" x 1½"
6	Back Panel, Bottom (1)	¼" x 31" x 27¾"
7	Back Panel, Top (1)	¼" x 31" x 24½"
8	Horizontal Dividers (3)	¾" x 20½" x 32¾"
9	Legs (4)	1⅞" x 1⅞" x 54"
10	Leg Toes (4)	1¼" x 1¼" x 1¼"
11	Leg Caps (4)	¼" x 1 7/16" x 1 7/16"
12	False Inside Top (1)	¼" x 20½" x 32¾"
13	Pediment Panel (1)	½" x 21" x 28½"
14	Pediment Dentil Fillings (53)	⅛" x ⅜" x ½"
15	Drawer Slide Spacers (6)	1 7/16" x 1¾" x 20 7/16"
16	Corner Cleats (24)	¾" x 1⅛" x 1⅛"
17	Shelf Support (1)	13/16" x 1¼" x 32¾"
18	Doors (2)	¾" x 15⅛" x 27⅛"
19	Door Inlay Material (1)	⅛" x 3/32" x 176"
20	Ball Catches (2)	Brusso
21	Stop Blocks (2)	½" x 1" x 1"
22	Soss Hinges (2 Pairs)	Brass ½" x 2⅜"
23	Ebony Veneer (1)	Approx. 100 sq. ft.

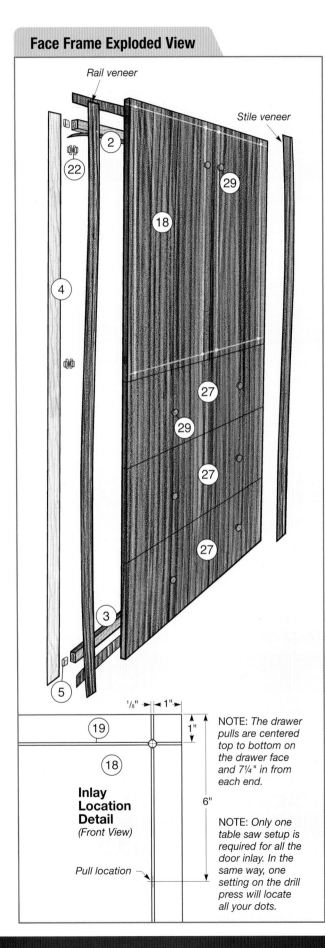

Rail veneer

Stile veneer

2

22

29

18

4

27

29

27

27

3

5

¹/₈" — 1"

**Inlay
Location
Detail**
(Front View)

19

18

1"

6"

Pull location

NOTE: *The drawer pulls are centered top to bottom on the drawer face and 7¼" in from each end.*

NOTE: *Only one table saw setup is required for all the door inlay. In the same way, one setting on the drill press will locate all your dots.*

Join the face frame members (there is both a front and a back face frame) with floating tenons made from yellow poplar or another affordable secondary wood. After marking their positions, I used my multi-router to cut the mortises in both the stiles and rails. For the back subassembly, the mortises need to accommodate the panel grooves. Plowing those grooves is the next step after cutting the mortises. Use ¼" white-birch-veneered MDF for the back panels. The grooves for these panels should be cut ¼" deep, using a router table and a down-spiral bit to prevent veneer chipping. Remember, only the back face frame has panels.

Before putting together the back subassembly, you'll need to take care of two more steps. First, the back panels have to be cut so their grain will be balanced and lined up vertically in the cabinet. Second, the edges of the face frame members and panels need to be cut to exact length and then sanded up to 120 grit. Assembling the face frames is routine. I used epoxy and meticulously cleaned up the squeeze-out with lacquer thinner.

While the face frames are drying, the side panels can be cut to length. These cuts are very important, because they are, in the case of the top edges, veneered over. The best way to make these cuts is on a table saw with a scoring blade. If that isn't available, be sure to apply tape and use a fine-toothed blade to prevent chip-out.

Once the face frames are dry, they and the sides have to be mitered. To ensure accuracy, install a temporary rail in the front face frame (to keep the stiles from flexing). I did this in the drawer area where the pocket screw holes are less noticeable.

Putting the Pieces Together

Assemble the carcass using biscuit joints, glue, and nails. It's critical that the biscuit joiner be indexed off the inside faces because the sides are slightly thicker than the face frames (due to being veneered). This will allow you to flush off the veneer on the side's miter and then overlay it with the face frame veneer. I applied Titebond glue to the biscuits and joints, assembled the pieces, and clamped them by nailing a few finishing nails through the face frames into the sides. These nail holes will be covered by veneer. Once the glue cures, flush up the side veneer to the face frame using a hard block and 80-grit sandpaper, and then putty the holes.

Before cutting the horizontal dividers, it's important to check their exact size, as these pieces need to be piston tight. All these dividers are made from birch-veneered MDF, but before you can properly size the center divider, it must have its front edge veneered. In a move that I'm sure will make purists scream (but I think Ruhlmann would have approved), attach the three dividers with a series of pocket holes and screws. Use four pocket holes per side and five on the front and back. Don't install pocket holes on the center divider's exposed front edge. You can't see the pockets on the bottom and center dividers. You'll cover the top ones with a false panel. Screw the dividers in place, keeping the top and bottom flush with the sides and the center divider exactly positioned.

Tricky Face Frame Veneering

Return to the iron-on method to secure the veneer to the face frames. On the front, I used the veneer I had cut from the large taped-up panel and then set aside. This achieves the seamless veneer pattern that is so Ruhlmannesque. The first step to veneering the face frames is to make sure the inside (veneered) edges of the stile veneer are perfectly straight. The stile veneers need to be glued in place very accurately, with their inside edges lined up exactly with the inside edges of the face frame and placed exactly vertical, so all the grain lines up.

Veneering the rails is probably the hardest part of the entire project. It is critically important that the centerline of the veneer strip is the centerline of the cabinet. The problem I experienced with this process is that the veneer strip expands and contracts as you apply the heat of the iron. And once you apply the veneer with the iron, it will not move. A note from personal experience: It is better to have a slight gap at a joint that needs to be filled than to have a bubble that you can't iron down. The veneer on the back face frame is not as critical and need not match quite as well.

Figure 3: *If veneering the face frames is the most difficult part of this project, cutting the veneered front panel into doors and drawer fronts surely is the most nerve-racking.*

Most of the top is covered by the pediment, so simply veneer around the edge to 1" under the pediment line. I strayed from my own advice here and covered a joint—two pieces of MDF screwed together (not likely to ever move). I applied a couple of veneer pads in the middle of the top so that when I drove screws up through them, the pediment wouldn't cup.

At this point, sand the face frame veneer and top carefully to 120 grit. Do not use a power sander for this operation, or you will almost certainly burn through, which, at this point, would be disastrous.

There is one last step that needs to be taken before the carcass is essentially complete. As you can see from the drawings on pages 144–145, I attached the legs by means of screws driven through angled interior corner blocks. The holes in those blocks were made on the drill press before installation so that they would be accurate. Finally, glue the blocks in place, and set the carcass aside for the time being.

Forming Doors and Drawers

If veneering the face frames is the most difficult part of this project, cutting the front panel up into the doors and drawer fronts surely is the most nerve-racking (see the Material Lists on pages 145 and 148). There is no room for error here. Proceeding with extreme caution, lay out, on bits of masking tape, your side cut lines (see Figure 3). As with the rail veneer, the center seam must be exactly in the middle of the panel. To get the panel width, it is necessary to subtract the edge gap and the width of the veneer edging from the face frame opening. I carefully cut the panel to width using my scoring saw. The next step is to lay out the horizontal cut lines. It is again necessary to account for the gap between the doors and drawer fronts and the veneer edging thickness. I had meticulously planned this from the very beginning, so I had a large enough panel to trim 1/8" off each end and then cut out three drawer fronts and the door panel exactly. The last step is to cut the door panel in half to make the two doors.

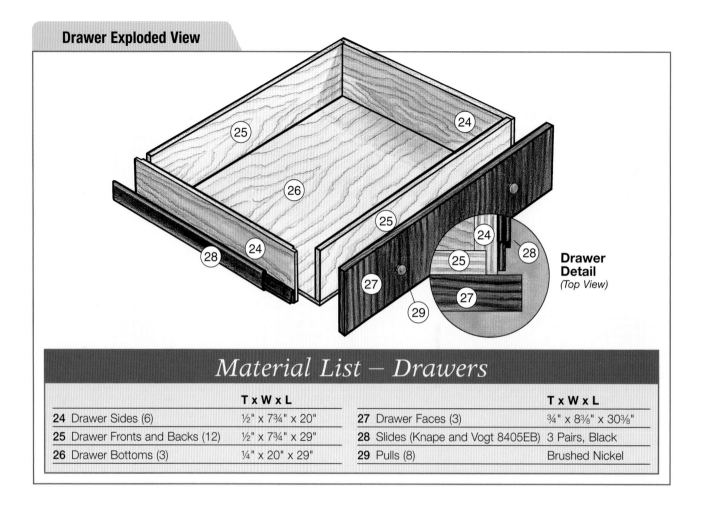

Drawer Exploded View

Drawer Detail *(Top View)*

Material List — Drawers

		T x W x L			T x W x L
24	Drawer Sides (6)	½" x 7¾" x 20"	27	Drawer Faces (3)	¾" x 8⅜" x 30⅜"
25	Drawer Fronts and Backs (12)	½" x 7¾" x 29"	28	Slides (Knape and Vogt 8405EB)	3 Pairs, Black
26	Drawer Bottoms (3)	¼" x 20" x 29"	29	Pulls (8)	Brushed Nickel

Edging the doors and fronts is fairly easy with one small caveat: Edge all the doors and fronts in the same order. Do all the sides edges first, then the top and bottom edges, etc. When you're done, sand the whole thing to 120 grit, and set the pieces aside for a bit.

Inlay: A Ruhlmann Hallmark

Inlay—one of Ruhlmann's hallmarks—must be precise. Cut your inlay grooves with a narrow-kerf saw blade with flat-topped teeth. If you don't use a blade with flat-topped teeth, there will be gaps under the inlay as it exits the door edges. I made the inlay grooves ³⁄₃₂" deep and designed things so that I could use a single fence setting to form all the grooves at once, thus ensuring that they would line up when the doors were installed. Using a wide belt stationary sander at a friend's shop, I was able to reduce strips of Avonite

(*www.avonite.com*) until they tapped perfectly into the saw kerf. Then, I carefully ripped strips that would be about ¹⁄₁₆" proud when installed. After doing a bit of experimenting, I chose

Roo glue to secure the inlay strips. This adhesive is made to be used with melamine, but it tested well with the Avonite, providing a tenacious grip. Knock off the bottom corners of the

Figure 4: *Ironing on preglued veneer ensures perfect placement. Use this method on the leg caps (shown here), the long aspect of the legs, and the cabinet's face frame members. The large panels are vacuum bagged.*

inlay strip with sandpaper to help slip it into the groove a bit more easily. The lines of inlay must be in place before the dot holes are drilled, to provide support for the drill point at the line intersections. But getting the crosspieces to butt perfectly is not essential, as the dots will hide the intersections.

When installing the inlay, I used a 4" block of wood to help tap it in with a hammer. This prevented the inlay from cracking (it's rather fragile). After the glue dries, smooth the inlay flush with a scraper and sandpaper. Using a drill press with a fence and stop is the best way to drill the dot holes. Because all the lines are exactly equal distance from the edge, you should be able to drill all of the holes with one setup. I used an 8 mm brad-point bit and moved to a tapered $\frac{5}{16}$" plug cutter to cut the plugs from a piece of $\frac{1}{2}$" Avonite. I found that it is crucial to keep blowing away the chips as the plugs are being made. Otherwise, the plugs end up undersize and break off while you are still drilling. Glue the plugs in place with cyanoacrylate glue, and flush them up with sandpaper. With everything in place, give the doors a once-over with 120-grit sandpaper, and set them aside.

Creating Legs That Can Handle a Little Stress

The legs of this cabinet take the most stress of any single part, so I decided to make the core from strong and stable poplar. First, I rough milled them about $\frac{3}{8}$" oversize and let them sit for several days to adjust to equilibrium. Next, I straightened and squared them on the jointer, and then I milled them to size. One of the elements that really makes this cabinet Ruhlmannesque is the tapering of the feet and tops of the legs. I shaped them with a sharp hand plane.

Veneering the legs is similar to veneering the door edges. Decide on a sequence, and do all four legs the same way. I chose to do the two side faces first and then the front and back faces. Apply one face of veneer at a time using the iron-on method (see Figure 4). After applying each face, flush up the edges with a hard block and 80-grit sandpaper. The iron-on method works particularly well here, as it is very easy to work the veneer over the tapers without the use of complex cauls. It should go without saying that it is of utmost importance to keep track of your veneer arrangement, because the leg veneers are book-matched. This is a subtle point, but when added to all the other subtle points, it sets the cabinet apart.

Another very subtle but important point is the veneer pattern on the top of the legs. After the Avonite caps are set in place, there will be little of the veneer showing, but it's still great to see the veneer parallel the exterior faces of the legs.

The caps are made by mitering, at 45°, two matched strips of veneer and then mirror-matching them. After you've taped up the mirror-match, cut squares from along the seam line that are large enough to cover the leg top, as shown in Figure 5. When gluing the caps on, it is important to have the grain pointing the right way, with the long grain on the outside edges.

White toes on the legs are another Ruhlmann trademark. I glued up a block of Avonite and milled it to slightly larger dimensions than the bottom of the leg. Using the miter gauge jig shown in Figure 6, in combination with a disc sander on the table saw, I tapered the Avonite blocks to match the leg taper. I intentionally made the toes just a hair larger than the leg bottoms so I could flush them up after they were glued on. Glue the toes in place with black cyanoacrylate glue. Once again,

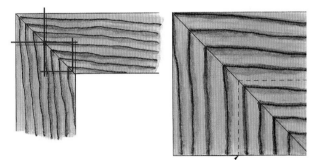

Rabbet where the leg joins the cabinet.

Figure 5: *Subtle but important details: Although only a small portion of this veneer is seen past the Avonite leg caps (pieces 11), tape up mirror-matched veneer for the tops of the legs, and then cut out two squares per seam line.*

Figure 6: *I installed a disc sander in my table saw, in combination with a miter gauge jig, to taper the Avonite toes, which must match the leg tapers. Here's the setup being tested with scrap lumber.*

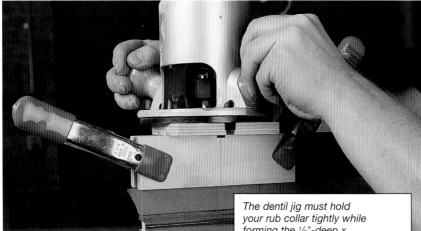

Figure 7: *I made this precise jig to form the dentil-inlay openings. Indexed off centerlines, the jig surrounds the sides and the edge of the pediment to prevent blowout. Once it's lined up with marks on the blue tape, the jig is clamped in place for each rout.*

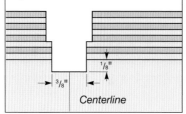

The dentil jig must hold your rub collar tightly while forming the 1/8"-deep x 3/8"-wide dadoes.

1/8"

3/8"

Centerline

flush up the toes with a hard block of 80- and then 120-grit sandpaper.

Rabbeting the legs to fit the cabinet corners is a two-step process. First, make two stopped cuts on the table saw to remove most of the rabbet. At the bottom end, the rabbet is carefully marked and then finished with a combination of a handsaw and chisels. It's imperative that these rabbets be exactly square and at exactly the same distance from the bottom. This is because the entire carcass rests on

them, and any variation will make the cabinet sit unevenly. Sand the legs up to 120 grit, but take care not to round over the edges that meet the cabinet, as this needs to be a tight joint. The last step on the legs is to install their Avonite caps. To make these, mill them to size, and then notch them to match the rabbet. Using a filler strip to simulate the carcass, glue the caps in place with clear cyanoacrylate.

Top It Off with a Dentil Pediment

Another typical Ruhlmann design, especially on his cabinets, is a dentil-inlaid cap or pediment. After cutting the veneered pediment blank to size and edging it with the iron-on method, make the dentil jig shown in Figure 7. There are several keys to this jig: It is indexed off the inlay centerline, it surrounds both the sides and the edge of the pediment to prevent veneer blowout, and it fits the router guide tightly for a no-slop cut. Before you begin, mark all of the centerlines on a piece of tape so they will be more visible. Then, carefully rout all of the recesses, making sure your jig is properly aligned and clamped for each cut. Mill the inlay material from Avonite so it has a nice press fit and stands a little proud of the edge. Glue the dentil in with a clear cyanoacrylate. When you are finished flushing up the dentil, give the entire pediment a sanding to 120, and set it aside.

Use a spacer the thickness of your door reveal to properly position the jig for the face frame mortises.

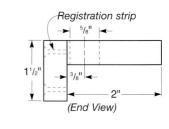

Registration strip

5/8"

1 1/2"

3/8"

2"

(End View)

Soss Hinge Jig
(Top View)

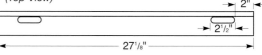

2"

2 1/2"

27 1/8"

Figure 8: *Soss hinges work great, but they're a pain to install. They must be installed perfectly; there's no adjustment to them. This door-length jig was designed to rout both the door and face frame mortises to be perfectly aligned. A dual set of screw holes on the registration strip lets you align the jig on the front face of the door and face frame, while keeping the hinge mortise holes in the same relative position. Soss hinges are bilevel, so you have to mortise the center portion after the wing portion.*

Drawers and Other Details

As this is a face frame cabinet, and I used ball-bearing slides, the slides need spacers to move them out flush with the face frame opening. As you can see in the drawings, these spacers have a lip on the bottom, which I incorporated so the slides will have something to rest on during installation.

In a break from the Ruhlmann originals, I made these drawers out of ½" Appleply plywood, with rabbeted, glued, and nailed corners—a very simple, strong drawer that will never shrink or swell, as many "traditional" drawers seem to do.

There is one last piece to make before starting the finishing process. As mentioned earlier, to cover the pocket holes in the top, a false inside top will need to be made out of ¼" birch-veneered MDF. Sand this piece to 120 grit, and set it aside.

The last step is to form the mortises for the Soss hinges on the doors and stiles. The drawings in Figure 8 provide the details of the jig I used to complete this step. Remember, there's no margin for error with these hinges! Once the mortises are formed, go over every surface, including the inside, with 220-grit sandpaper. Make careful note of all edges, easing those slightly that need it but leaving others, such as the leg rabbet edges, crisp and sharp. Take the time to go over every surface with a powerful light and to look for any scratches that you may have missed.

Now, it's time for finishing. To obtain the best results, I finished this cabinet in several stages: the carcass box, the legs, the doors and drawer fronts,

the false top, the pediment, and the drawer boxes. I sprayed everything with two coats of vinyl sealer and two coats of 25° sheen catalyzed synthetic lacquer. Be sure to sand between each coat with 220-grit sandpaper.

Once the individual pieces are finished, assembling the carcass is quite simple. Start by clamping each leg in place and drilling a pilot hole, guided by the predrilled angle blocks. Then, screw the legs in place with 2½" #8 screws. Attach the pediment with several 1" screws from the inside, two of which go through the veneer pads I mentioned earlier. After the pediment is installed, the false top can be added with a few small brads.

Because I use this cabinet for a TV, I decided to install a shelf support under the center divider. Set this piece 1½" back from the front edge, and attach it from the bottom. Then, wrap up by installing the drawers, doors, and their brushed-nickel pulls. Two small stop blocks attached to the top rail and a couple of Brusso ball catches hold the doors flush.

To paraphrase Johnny Cash, I've built harder cabinets, but I can't really remember when. In reality, building this cabinet will be a challenging and rewarding experience that will greatly enrich your woodworking experience and vocabulary. I admit that the level of precision and the cost might make most home woodworkers think this project is out of their reach, but I disagree. The one major thing that this project reinforces is that the keys to fine and complex work are to take plenty of time and to think things through thoroughly.

It's All in the Details

How does this cabinet reflect the style of Jacques-Emile Ruhlmann? In the harmony of its details— simple and elegant in themselves, yet beautiful and rich when viewed together. Dark, straight-grained veneer, laid up in a fluid book-matched pattern, contrasted by off-white inlay ... simple shapes combined into a pleasing complex design ... all join together to evoke Ruhlmann.

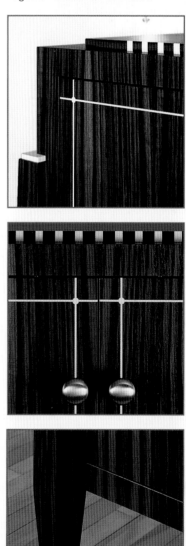

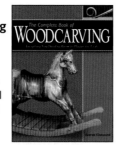